S0-CEY-546

Computer Concepts

FIFTH EDITION – ILLUSTRATED

BRIEF

Computer Concepts
FIFTH EDITION – ILLUSTRATED

BRIEF

June Jamrich Parsons / Dan Oja

THOMSON
COURSE TECHNOLOGY

Australia • Canada • Mexico • Singapore • Spain • United Kingdom • United States

THOMSON

COURSE TECHNOLOGY

Computer Concepts, Fifth Edition—Illustrated Brief
is published by Course Technology.

Adapting Author:
Rachel Biheller Bunin

Developmental Editor:
Pamela Conrad

Executive Editor:
Nicole Jones Pinard

Product Manager:
Christina Kling Garrett

Production Editor:
Debbie Masi

Associate Product Manager:
Emilie Perreault

Editorial Assistant:
Abbey Reider

Interior Designer:
Betsy Young

Photo and Video Researcher:
Abby Reip

Composition:
GEX Publishing Services

COPYRIGHT © 2004 Course Technology, a division of Thomson Learning, Inc. Thomson Learning™ is a trademark used herein under license.

Printed in the United States of America

1 2 3 4 5 6 7 8 9 BM 08 07 06 05 04

For more information, contact Course Technology, 25 Thomson Place, Boston, Massachusetts, 02210.

Or find us on the World Wide Web at: www.course.com

ALL RIGHTS RESERVED. No part of this work covered by the copyright hereon may be reproduced or used in any form or by any means—graphic, electronic, or mechanical, including photocopying, recording, taping, Web distribution, or information storage and retrieval systems—without the written permission of the publisher.

For permission to use material from this text or product, submit a request online at **www.thomsonrights.com**

Any additional questions about permissions can be submitted by e-mail to **thomsonrights@thomson.com**

Course Technology, the Course Technology logo and **Custom Edition®** are registered trademarks used under license. The Illustrated Series and Illustrated Projects are trademarks of Course Technology. All other names used herein are for identification purposes only and are trademarks of their respective owners.

Course Technology reserves the right to revise this publication and make changes from time to time in its content without notice.

ISBN 0-619-18817-0

Brief Contents

Contents

◈ = Info Web

Preface

Welcome to *Computer Concepts, Fifth Edition—Illustrated Brief*. We have incorporated several new features for the Fifth Edition including a new feature Computers in Context and a new Web site. The **Computers in Context** feature provides current information on how computers are used in various fields such as medicine and sports. A new **Web site** provides a wealth of online resources including pre-assessment tools, games, InfoWebs, and Student Edition Labs to reinforce concepts presented in this edition. To take advantage of this exclusive password protected site, visit **www.course.com/illustrated/concepts5** using the pincode included in the back of your book.

About the Illustrated Approach

What makes the information in this book so easy to access and digest? It's quite simple. As shown in this sample lesson, each concept is presented on two facing pages, with the main points discussed on the left page and large, dramatic illustrations presented on the right. Students can learn all they need to know about a particular topic without having to turn the page! This unique design makes information extremely accessible and easy to absorb, and makes a great reference for after the course is over. The modular structure of the book also allows for great flexibility; you can cover the units in any order you choose, and you can skip lessons if you like.

Icons in the margins indicate that an InfoWeb is featured for that lesson

A single concept is presented in a two-page "information display" to help students absorb information quickly and easily

Easy-to-follow introductions to every lesson focus on a single concept to help students get the information quickly

Details provide additional key information on the main concept

---

UNIT B

Comparing storage media and devices

When trying to determine the best storage media for a job, it is useful to apply four criteria: versatility, durability, speed, and capacity. Versatility is the ability of a device and its media to work in more than one way. After storing data using this storage technology, can that data be changed? Durability determines the ability of the device or media to last. How long will it work? How long will the data be accessible? Speed is the time it takes to retrieve or access the data, a factor that is very important in determining how efficiently you work. Finally, capacity is the amount of data each technology can store.

DETAILS

- Versatility. Some storage devices can access data from only one type of medium. More versatile devices can access data from several different media. A floppy disk drive, for example, can access only floppy disks, but a DVD drive can access data DVDs, DVD movies, audio CDs, data CDs, and CD-Rs.

- Durability. Most storage technologies are susceptible to damage from mishandling or other environmental factors, such as heat and moisture. Some technologies are less susceptible than others. Optical and solid state technologies tend to be less susceptible than magnetic technologies to damage that could cause data loss.

- Speed. Not surprisingly, fast storage devices are preferred over slower ones. **Access time** is the average time it takes a computer to locate data on the storage medium and read it. Access time for a personal computer storage device, such as a disk drive, is measured in **milliseconds** (thousandths of a second). Lower numbers indicate faster access times. For example, a drive with a 6 ms access time is faster than a drive with an access time of 11 ms. Random-access devices have the fastest access times.

  Random access (also called "direct access") is the ability of a device to "jump" directly to the

requested data. Floppy disk, hard disk, solid state, CD, and DVD drives are random-access devices. A tape drive, on the other hand, must use slower **sequential access**, which reads through the data from the beginning of the tape. The advantage of random access becomes clear when you consider how much faster and easier it is to locate a song on a CD (random access) than on a cassette tape (sequential access).

  Data transfer rate is the amount of data that a storage device can move from the storage medium to the computer per second. Higher numbers indicate faster transfer rates. For example, a CD-ROM drive with a 600 KBps (kilobytes per second) data transfer rate is faster than one with a 300 KBps transfer rate.

- Capacity. **Storage capacity** is the maximum amount of data that can be stored on a storage medium, measured in kilobytes (KB), megabytes (MB), gigabytes (GB), or terabytes (TB). The amount of data that a disk stores—its capacity—depends on its density. **Disk density** refers to the closeness of the data on the disk surface. The higher the disk density, the more data it can store. Higher capacity is almost always preferred. Table B-1 compares the capacity of various storage devices and media.

FYI

Storage media is divided into tracks and then into sectors to create electronic "addressable bins" in which to store data.

Adding storage devices to a computer

Computer users frequently want to upgrade their hard drives to gain capacity or to add CD or DVD drives to make their systems more versatile. The system unit case for a desktop computer contains several storage device "parking spaces" called **drive bays**. See Figure B-6. If you have an empty bay that is the right type and size, you can add a storage device. Bays come in two widths–5 ¼"

and 3½". CD and DVD drives require 5¼" bays; a floppy disk drive fits in a 3½" bay. Some drive bays provide access from the outside of the system unit, a necessity for a storage device with removable media, such as floppy disks, CDs, tapes, and DVDs. Internal drive bays are located inside the system unit and are designed for hard disk drives, which don't use removable storage media.

40 COMPUTER CONCEPTS

News to Use boxes relate the lesson material to real-world situations to provide students with additional practical information

Tables provide quick
reference information

TABLE B-1: Capacities of storage media

DEVICE	CAPACITY	COMMENTS
Floppy disk	1.44 MB	Low capacity means that the disk can hold small files but not large files; not suitable for graphics-intensive files
SuperDisk	120 MB or 240 MB	SuperDisks are manufactured by Imation; Zip disks are manufactured by Iomega; each holds much more than a floppy; each requires its own proprietary drive; a full system backup requires multiple disks
Zip disk	100 MB, 250 MB, and 750 MB	
Fixed hard disk	80 GB (average)	High storage capacity, fast and convenient, economical storage-cost/megabyte, is susceptible to damage or theft of your computer
External hard drive	80 GB	Fast, but transfer rate depends on computer system; drive can be removed and locked in a secure location
Removable hard disk	2.2 GB (average)	Fast, limited capacity, but disks can be removed and locked in a secure location
CD	700 MB	Limited capacity, can't be reused, long shelf life
CD-RW	700 MB	Limited capacity, reusable
Writable DVD	4.7 GB	Good capacity, standards still in development
Tape	30 GB (average)	Good capacity, reasonable media cost, convenient—you can let backups run overnight, but slow—it can take 15-20 minutes to back up 1 GB of data

FIGURE B-6: Drive bays

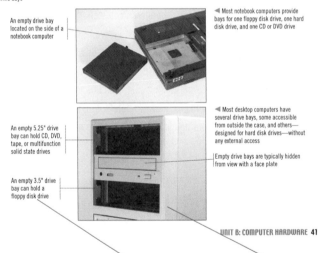

An empty drive bay located on the side of a notebook computer

◄ Most notebook computers provide bays for one floppy disk drive, one hard disk drive, and one CD or DVD drive

An empty 5.25" drive bay can hold CD, DVD, tape, or multifunction solid state drives

◄ Most desktop computers have several drive bays, some accessible from outside the case, and others—designed for hard disk drives—without any external access

Empty drive bays are typically hidden from view with a face plate

An empty 3.5" drive bay can hold a floppy disk drive

UNIT B: COMPUTER HARDWARE 41

The callouts point out key elements on each illustration

Large photos and screenshots illustrate the lesson concepts

Unit Features

Each unit contains the following features, providing a flexible teaching and learning package.

- **InfoWebs** The computer industry changes rapidly. Students can get up-to-date information by exploring the concept on the InfoWebLinks Web site, when indicated by an InfoWeb icon.

- **Tech Talk** Each unit ends with a Tech Talk lesson. These lessons go into greater depth on a technical topic related to the unit. Instructors have the option of assigning this lesson or skipping it, depending on the expertise of the students and the course goals.

- **Computers in Context** Each unit includes a **new** Computers in Context two-page spread, which highlights how computers and computer technologies are used in various disciplines, such as medicine, law enforcement, and sports.

- **Issue** It is important to keep abreast of issues that relate to technology. Each unit contains an interesting Issue article, followed by Expand the Ideas questions to encourage students to form and express their own opinions about the Issue.

- **Key Terms** Students can use this handy list to review bold terms that represent key concepts from the unit. Definitions are provided in the glossary.

- **Unit Review** After completing the Unit Review, students will have synthesized the unit content in their own words.

- **Fill in the Best Answer** Students can complete this exercise to determine how well they have learned the unit content.

- **Independent Challenges** These exercises enable students to explore and develop critical thinking skills. Challenges with an E-Quest icon point students to the Web to complete the exercise.

- **Visual Workshop** Based on a screenshot or illustration, Visual Workshops encourage independent thinking to explore a concept further.

The Instructor Resources CD is Course Technology's way of putting the resources and information needed to teach and learn effectively into your hands. With an integrated array of teaching and learning tools that offer you and your students a broad range of technology-based instructional options, we believe this CD represents the highest quality and most cutting edge resources available to instructors today. Many of these resources are available at **www.course.com**.

- **Figure Files**—Includes every image from the book, which you can use to create transparencies or a PowerPoint presentation.

- Solutions to Exercises—Solutions to Exercises contains every file students are asked to create or modify in the End-of-Unit material and Extra Independent Challenges.

- **Test Bank & Test Engine**—ExamView is a powerful testing software package that allows you to create and administer printed, computer (LAN-based), and Internet exams. ExamView includes hundreds of questions that correspond to the topics covered in this text, enabling students to generate detailed study guides that include page references for further review. The computer-based and Internet testing components allow students to take exams at their computers, and also saves you time by grading each exam automatically.

- **Instructor's Manual**—Available as an electronic file, the Instructor's Manual is quality-assurance tested and includes a Lecture Note for every lesson, Teaching Tips, Quick Quizzes and Classroom Activities.

- Syllabus—Prepare and customize your course easily using this sample outline.

- **PowerPoint Presentations**—Each unit has a corresponding PowerPoint presentation that you can use in lecture, distribute to your students, or customize to suit your course.

- Additional Activities for Students—Materials provided here are Extra Independent Challenge exercises and a first-time buyer's guide.

Bring concepts and lessons to life with **Student Edition Labs** and **SAM Computer Concepts**. For more information on Student Edition Labs visit **www.course.com/illustrated/concepts5**. And, for SAM Computer Concepts information visit **www.course.com/sam**.

Online Offerings We offer a full range of content for use with MyCourse 2.0, BlackBoard and WebCT to simplify the use of Computer Concepts in distance education settings, or to supplement your traditional class. Visit **www.course.com** for more information.

Before You Begin

 When you see an InfoWeb icon (shown to the left), you can access the latest information and explore the concepts in the book further by going to the InfoWebLinks Web site. To access this site, you'll need a Web browser and an Internet connection. If you can send e-mail and access the Web with your computer, you probably have such a connection. To access the Web site, simply type www.course.com/illustrated/concepts5 in the Address bar or Location bar of your Web browser.

If you are using your own computer, or if your computer lab allows you to make such changes, you can set the InfoWebLinks Web site as your browser home page by following these steps:

In Microsoft Internet Explorer:

1. Open the site at www.course.com/illustrated/concepts5

2. Click Tools on the menu bar, then click Internet Options

3. Click the Use Current button, then click OK

In Netscape:

1. Open the site at www.course.com/illustrated/concepts5

2. Click Edit on the menu bar, then click Preferences

3. Click Use Current Page, then click OK

If changing your home page is not an option, you can instead make the site easily accessible by adding it to your list of Favorites or Bookmarks (again, if you are using your own computer or your computer lab allows it).

To create this Web Page as a Favorite in Internet Explorer:

1. Open the site at www.course.com/illustrated/concepts5

2. Click Favorites on the menu bar, then click Add to Favorites

3. Click OK

To add this Web page as a Bookmark in Netscape:

1. Open the site at www.course.com/illustrated/concepts5

2. Click the Bookmarks button under the Location text box, then click Add Bookmark

See your instructor or technical support person for help in connecting to the Internet or using your Web browser.

About the Technology

Author Acknowledgements

My thanks to Dan Oja and June Parsons for entrusting me and the Illustrated team to once again, adapt their pioneering New Perspectives Computer Concepts book into the Illustrated format. Special thanks to Nicole Pinard for having the vision to let me create the first Illustrated Concepts book and then continue with the project through all the editions. I am grateful for the chance to work as the adapting author and see the book into this Fifth Edition. Working with Pam Conrad, the Development Editor has been a wonderful adventure. Pam is an invaluable asset to the team; as a personal friend and colleague she contributes strength, vision, and intelligence to the project. I am eternally grateful for her contributions and partnership.

Christina Kling Garrett was a wonderful Project Manager, keeping all the components on track and providing good humor and guidance throughout. Thanks to Debbie Masi, our excellent production editor, for always staying calm even while working with crazy schedules to deliver perfect pages on time. Thanks to GEX for all their work and those timely .pdf files. Thanks also to Abby Reip for the photograph and permissions research. Thanks to our manuscript reviewers Anthony Barbis, University of Missouri; Diane Larson, Indiana University Northwest; Dr. Cherie Stevens, South Florida Community College; Brenda Kennedy, Eastern Oklahoma State College; and Deborah Layton, Eastern Oklahoma State College for their insights and comments. On behalf of the entire Illustrated team, we hope you find this book a valuable resource for your students.

- Rachel Biheller Bunin, Adapting Author

We offer heartfelt thanks to all of the members of the Illustrated team for contributing their vision, talent, and skills to make this book a reality. Special thanks to Rachel Biheller Bunin for her fast and efficient work as the adapting author; Pamela Conrad for her insights as the developmental editor; Debbie Masi for her solid work as the production editor; and Christina Kling Garrett for tracking all the bits and pieces of this project. Whether you are a student or instructor, we thank you for using our book and hope that you find it to be a valuable guide to computers and software.

- June Parsons, Dan Oja, and MediaTechnics for the New Perspectives Series

Credits

Unit A:

Figure A-1: Courtesy of Acer Inc.; Courtesy of Microsoft Corporation; Courtesy of Apple Computer, Inc.

Figure A-5: Courtesy of palmOne, Inc.

Figure A-6: Courtesy of Fujitsu Ltd. and Microsoft Corporation

Figure A-7: Courtesy of Microsoft Corporation

Figure A-8: Courtesy of IBM Corporation

Figure A-9: b. Courtesy of AlienWare
    c. Courtesy of Apple Computer, Inc.
    d. Courtesy of IBM Corporation
    e. Courtesy of Sony Electronics, Inc.
    f. Courtesy of Apple Computer, Inc
    g. Courtesy of Dell, Inc.
    h. Courtesy of Acer Inc. and Microsoft Corporation

Figure A-11: Courtesy of NASA

Figure A-14: Courtesy of Apple Computer, Inc.

Figure A-18: NP Figure 1-15

Figure A-19: Courtesy of Linksys

Figure A-23: Reproduced with permission of Yahoo! Inc. © 2003 by Yahoo! Inc. YAHOO! and the YAHOO! logo are trademarks of Yahoo! inc.

Figure A-30: Courtesy of SensAble Technologies, Inc.

Figure A-31: © John Kelly/Getty Images

Figure A-32: Courtesy of The Digital Divide Network www.digitaldividenetwork.org

Unit B:

Figure B-1: b. Courtesy of TDK Corporation
    e. Courtesy of SanDisk Corporation

Figure B-4 Courtesy of IBM Research

Figure B-5 Courtesy of Intel Corporation

Figure B-13: a. Courtesy of Sony Electronics, Inc.
    b. Courtesy of Kingston Technology
    c. Courtesy of SanDisk Corporation
    d. Courtesy of SanDisk Corporation
    e. Courtesy of Kingston Technology

Figure B-14: a. Courtesy of Logitech, Inc.
    b. Courtesy of Microsoft Corporation
    c. Courtesy of Research In Motion
    e. Courtesy of Think Outside, Inc. and Palm, Inc.

Figure B-16: a. Courtesy of IBM Corporation
    c. Courtesy of Kensington Technology Group
    d. Courtesy of XGAMING, INC.

Figure B-17: a. Courtesy of Sony Electronics, Inc.
    b. Courtesy of Sony Electronics, Inc.
    c. Courtesy of ViewSonic® Corporation

Figure B-19: a. Courtesy of ATI Technologies, Inc.

Figure B-20: a. Courtesy of EPSON America, Inc.

Figure B-27: b. Courtesy of EPSON America, Inc.
    d. Courtesy of Olympus
    e. Courtesy of Wacom Technology Technology Corp.

Figure B-32: © Bettmann/CORBIS

Figure B-33: Courtesy of NASA

Figure B-34: © Gabe Palmer/CORBIS

Unit C:

Figure C-22: Courtesy of David S. Bunin

Figure C-26: a. Courtesy of Microsoft Corporation
    b. Courtesy of Symantec Corporation
    c. Courtesy of Adobe Systems, Inc.

Figure C-33: AP/Wide World Photos

Unit D:

Figure D-5: d. Courtesy of Intel Corporation

Figure D-32: NASA and The Hubble Heritage Team (STScI/AURA)

Figure D-33: Courtesy of Kinston Technology

UNIT A

Computer and Internet Basics

OBJECTIVES

Unit A provides an overview of computer and Internet technologies. The unit begins by defining the basic characteristics of a computer system and then provides a quick overview of data, information, and files. You will be introduced to application software, operating systems, and platform compatibility. You will get a basic overview of the Internet, the Web, and e-mail. The Tech Talk discusses the boot process, the sequence of events that happens when you turn on your computer. You will also have an opportunity to look at computers in the context of sports and the Issue looks at the effects of ever-present computing.

Defining computers

Whether you realize it or not, you already know a lot about computers. You've picked up information from commercials and magazine articles, from books and movies, from conversations and correspondence, and perhaps even from using your own computer and trying to figure it out. This lesson provides an overview designed to help you start organizing what you know about computers, provide you with a basic understanding of how computers work, and get you up to speed with basic computer vocabulary.

DETAILS

- The word "computer" has been part of the English language since 1646, but if you look in a dictionary printed before 1940, you might be surprised to find "computer" defined as a person who performs calculations! Prior to 1940, machines that were designed to perform calculations were referred to as calculators and tabulators, not computers. The modern definition and use of the term "computer" emerged in the 1940s, when the first electronic computing devices were developed.

- Most people can formulate a mental picture of a computer, but computers do so many things and come in such a variety of shapes and sizes that it might seem difficult to distill their common characteristics into an all-purpose definition. At its core, a **computer** is a device that accepts input, processes data, stores data, and produces output, all according to a series of stored instructions.

- A **computer system** includes hardware, peripheral devices, and software. Figure A-1 shows two examples of a basic computer system. **Hardware** includes the electronic and mechanical devices that process data. The term "hardware" refers to the computer as well as components called peripheral devices. **Peripheral devices** expand the computer's input, output, and storage capabilities.

- An **input device**, such as a keyboard or mouse, gathers input and transforms it into a series of electronic signals for the computer. An **output device**, such as a monitor or printer, displays, prints, or transmits the results of processing from the computer memory.

- A computer requires instructions called **software**, which is a **computer program** that tells the computer how to perform particular tasks.

- A **computer network** consists of two or more computers and other devices that are connected for the purpose of sharing data and programs. A **LAN (local area network)** is simply a computer network that is located within a limited geographical area, such as a school computer lab or a small business.

FYI

The term "personal computer" is sometimes abbreviated as "PC." However, "PC" is usually used for a specific type of personal computer that runs Windows software.

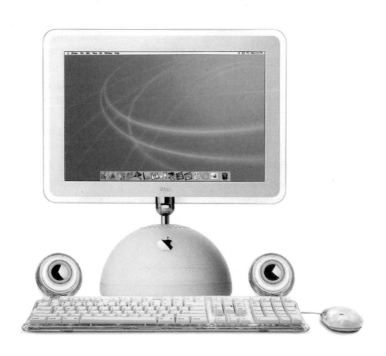

Exploring computer functions

To really understand computers, you need to understand the functions they perform. Figure A-2 illustrates the basic computer functions—accept input, process data, store data, and produce output—and shows the components that work together to accomplish each function.

DETAILS

- Accept input. A computer accepts input. Computer **input** is whatever is put into a computer system. Input can be supplied by a person, by the environment, or by another computer. Examples of the kinds of input that a computer can accept include the words and symbols in a document, numbers for a calculation, pictures, temperatures from a thermostat, music or voice audio signals from a microphone, and instructions from a computer program.

- Process data. A computer processes data. In the context of computing, **data** refers to the symbols that represent facts, objects, and ideas. Computers manipulate data in many ways, and we call this manipulation **processing**. Some of the ways that a computer can process data include performing calculations, sorting lists of words or numbers, modifying documents and pictures, and drawing graphs. The instructions that tell a computer how to carry out the processing tasks are referred to as a computer program, or simply a "program." These programs are the software. In a computer, most processing takes place in a **processor** (also known as a microprocessor) called the **central processing unit (CPU)**, which is sometimes described as the "brain" of the computer.

- Store data. A computer stores data so that it will be available for processing. Most computers have more than one location for storing data, depending on how the data is being used. **Memory** is an area of a computer that temporarily holds data waiting to be processed, stored, or output. **Storage** is the area of a computer that holds data on a permanent basis when it is not immediately needed for processing. For example, while you are working on it, a document is in memory; it is not in storage until you save it. After you save the document, it is still in memory until you close the document, exit the program, or turn off the computer. Documents in memory are lost when you turn off the power. Stored documents are not lost when the power is turned off.

- Produce output. **Output** consists of the processing results produced by a computer. Some examples of computer output include reports, documents, music, graphs, and pictures. An output device displays, prints, or transmits the results of processing. Figure A-2 helps you visualize the input, processing, storage, and output activities of a computer.

FIGURE A-2: Basic computer functions

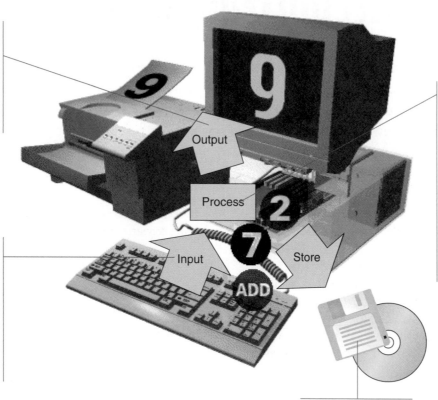

A computer produces output.
You use an output device, such as a printer or display screen, to see the results of processing, that is, the computer output

A computer processes data.
The CPU retrieves the numbers and the instruction, and then processes the numbers by performing addition; the result, 9, is temporarily held in memory; from memory, the result can be output, usually to a monitor, printer, or storage medium

A computer accepts input.
You use an input device, such as a keyboard, to input numbers, such as 2 and 7, along with the instruction ADD; the instruction and the numbers are temporarily held in memory

A computer stores data.
You can permanently store data on disks and CDs

Understanding the importance of stored programs

Early computers were really no more than calculating devices designed to carry out a specific mathematical task. To use one of these devices for another task, it was necessary to rewire or reset its circuits—a task best left to an engineer. In a modern computer, the idea of a **stored program** means that instructions for a computing task can be loaded into a computer's memory. These instructions can easily be replaced by different instructions when it is time for the computer to perform a different task. The stored program concept allows you to use your computer for one task, such as word processing, and then easily switch to a different type of computing task, such as editing a photo or sending an e-mail message. It is the single most important characteristic that distinguishes a computer from other simpler and less versatile devices.

Categorizing computers

Computers are versatile machines, but some types of computers are better suited to certain tasks than others. Computers are categorized according to criteria such as usage, cost, size, and capability to help consumers associate computers with appropriate tasks. To reflect today's computer technology, the following categories are appropriate: personal computers, handheld computers, workstations, videogame consoles, mainframes, supercomputers, and servers.

DETAILS

● A **personal computer**, also called a **microcomputer**, is designed to meet the computing needs of an individual. It typically provides access to a wide variety of computing applications, such as word processing, photo editing, e-mail, and Internet access. Personal computers include **desktop computers**, as illustrated in Figure A-3, and **notebook computers** (sometimes called "laptop computers"), as illustrated in Figure A-4. A desktop has separate components, while laptops have a keyboard, monitor, and system in one compact unit. Laptops can be more expensive than comparable desktops.

● A **handheld computer**, such as a Palm, an iPAQ, or a PocketPC, features a small keyboard or touch-sensitive screen and is designed to fit into a pocket, run on batteries, and be used while you are holding it. See Figure A-5. A **PDA (Personal Digital Assistant)** is typically used as an electronic appointment book, address book, calculator, and notepad. Inexpensive add-ons make it possible to send and receive e-mail, use maps and global positioning to get directions, maintain an expense account, and make voice calls using cellular service. With its slow processing speed and small screen, a handheld computer is not powerful enough to handle many of the tasks that can be accomplished using desktop or notebook personal computers.

● A **tablet computer** is a portable computing device featuring a touch-sensitive screen that can be used as a writing or drawing pad. A "pure" tablet configuration, like the one in Figure A-6, lacks a keyboard (although one can be attached) and resembles a high-tech clipboard. A "convertible" tablet computer is constructed like a notebook computer, but the screen folds face up over the keyboard to provide a horizontal writing surface.

● Computers that are advertised as **workstations** are usually powerful desktop computers designed for specialized tasks such as design tasks. A workstation can tackle tasks that require a lot of processing speed, such as medical imaging and computer-aided design. Some workstations contain more than one processor, and most have circuitry specially designed for creating and displaying three-dimensional and animated graphics.

"Workstation" can also mean an ordinary personal computer that is connected to a local area network.

● A **videogame console** (see Figure A-7), such as the Nintendo® GameCube™, the Sony PlayStation®, or the Microsoft XBox®, is a computer. In the past, a videogame console was not considered a computer because of its history as a dedicated game device that connects to a TV set and provides only a pair of joysticks for input. Today's videogame consoles, however, contain processors that are equivalent to any found in a fast personal computer, and they are equipped to produce graphics that rival those on sophisticated workstations. Add-ons make it possible to use a videogame console to watch DVD movies, send and receive e-mail, and participate in online activities, such as multiplayer games.

● A **mainframe computer** is a large and expensive computer capable of simultaneously processing data for hundreds or thousands of users. Mainframes are generally used by businesses, universities, or governments to provide centralized storage, processing, and management of large amounts of data where reliability, data security, and centralized control are necessary. Its main processing circuitry is housed in a closet-sized cabinet. See Figure A-8.

● A computer is a **supercomputer** if, at the time of construction, it is one of the fastest computers in the world. Because of their speed and complexity, supercomputers can tackle tasks that would not be practical for other computers. Typical uses for supercomputers include breaking codes and modeling worldwide weather systems. A supercomputer CPU is constructed from thousands of processors.

● In the computer industry, the term "server" has several meanings. It can refer to computer hardware, to a specific type of software, or to a combination of hardware and software. In any case, the purpose of a **server** is to "serve" the computers on a network (such as the Internet or a LAN) by supplying them with data. Just about any personal computer, workstation, mainframe, or supercomputer can be configured to perform the work of a server.

FIGURE A-3: A desktop personal computer

▲ A desktop computer fits on a desk and runs on power from an electrical wall outlet; the main unit can be housed in either a vertical case (like the one shown) or a horizontal case

FIGURE A-5: A handheld computer

▲ Many handheld computers feature a small keyboard, while others accept handwriting input

FIGURE A-7: A videogame console

▲ A videogame console includes circuitry similiar to a personal computer's, but its input and output devices are optimized for gaming

FIGURE A-4: A notebook personal computer

▲ A notebook computer is small and lightweight, giving it the advantage of portability; it can run on power supplied by an electrical outlet, or it can run on battery power

FIGURE A-6: A tablet computer

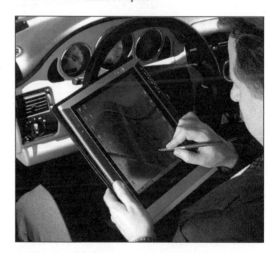

▲ A tablet computer is similiar in size to a notebook computer, but features a touch-sensitive screen that can be used for input instead of a keyboard

FIGURE A-8: A mainframe computer

▲ This IBM S/390 zSeries 900 mainframe computer weighs about 1,400 lbs and is about 6.5 feet tall

Examining personal computer systems

The term "computer system" usually refers to a computer and all of the input, output, and storage devices that are connected to it. Despite cosmetic differences among personal computers, see Figure A-9, a personal computer system usually includes standard equipment or devices. Devices may vary in color, size, and design for different personal computers. Figure A-10 illustrates a typical desktop personal computer system. Refer to Figure A-10 as you read through the list of devices below.

DETAILS

- **System unit**. The system unit is the case that holds the power supply, storage devices, and the circuit boards, including the main circuit board (also called the "motherboard"), which contains the processor. The system unit for most notebook computers also holds a built-in keyboard and speakers.

- **Display device**. Most desktop computers use a separate **monitor** as a display (output) device, whereas notebook computers use a flat panel display screen that is attached to the system unit.

- **Keyboard**. Most computers are equipped with a keyboard as the primary input device.

- **Mouse**. A mouse is a common input device designed to manipulate on-screen graphical objects and controls.

- **Storage devices**. Computers have many types of storage devices that are used to store data when the power is turned off. For example: A **floppy disk drive** is a storage device that reads data from and writes data to floppy disks. A **hard disk drive** can store billions of characters of data. It is usually mounted inside the computer's system unit. A small external light indicates when the drive is in use. A **CD-ROM drive** is a storage device that uses laser technology to read data that is permanently stored on data or audio CDs. A **DVD drive** can read data from data CDs, audio CDs, data DVDs, or DVD movie discs. CD-ROM and DVD drives typically cannot be used to write data onto discs. "ROM" stands for "read-only memory" and means that the drive can read data from discs, but cannot be used to store new data on them. Many computers, especially desktop models, include a **CD-writer** or **DVD-writer** that can be used to create and copy CDs and DVDs. There are a wide variety of CD-writers and DVD-writers including CD-R, CD-RW, DVD-R, and DVD+RW.

- **Speakers** and **sound card**. Desktop computers have a rudimentary built-in speaker that's mostly limited to playing beeps. A small circuit board, called a sound card, is required for high-quality music, narration, and sound effects. A desktop computer's sound card sends signals to external speakers. A notebook's sound card sends signals to speakers that are built into the notebook system unit. The sound card is an input and an output device, while speakers are output devices.

- **Modem**. Many personal computer systems include a built-in modem that can be used to establish an Internet connection using a standard telephone line. A modem is both an input and an output device.

- **Printer**. A computer printer is an output device that produces computer-generated text or graphical images on paper.

What's a peripheral device?

The word "peripheral" dates back to the days of mainframes when the CPU was housed in a giant box, and all input, output, and storage devices were housed separately. Today, the term "peripheral device" designates equipment that might be added to a computer system to enhance its functionality. A printer is a popular peripheral device, as is a digital camera, zip drive, scanner, joystick, or graphics tablet. Though a hard disk drive seems to be an integral part of a computer—after all, it's built right into the system unit—by the strictest technical definition, a hard disk drive is classified as a peripheral device. The same goes for other storage devices and the keyboard, monitor, sound card, speakers, and modem.

FIGURE A-9: Typical personal computer systems

FIGURE A-10: Components of a typical computer system

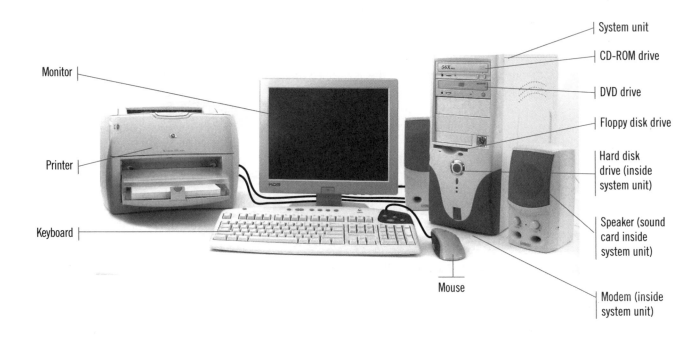

- System unit
- CD-ROM drive
- DVD drive
- Floppy disk drive
- Hard disk drive (inside system unit)
- Speaker (sound card inside system unit)
- Modem (inside system unit)
- Monitor
- Printer
- Keyboard
- Mouse

Exploring data, information, and files

In everyday conversation, people use the terms "data" and "information" interchangeably. Nevertheless, some computer professionals make a distinction between the two terms. They define **data** as the symbols that represent people, events, things, and ideas. Data becomes **information** when it is presented in a format that people can understand and use. As a rule of thumb, remember that data is used by computers; information is used by people. See Figure A-11.

DETAILS

● Have you ever gotten a computer file you couldn't read? It could be because the data has not been converted to information. Computers process and store data using the binary number system and several other codes designed expressly for electronic data. The **binary number system** has only two digits: 0 and 1. The binary number system can represent number data using only 0s and 1s.

● Computers use these codes to store data in a digital format as a series of 1s and 0s. Each 0 or 1 is a **bit**, and 8 bits are called a **byte**. The bits and bytes that are processed and stored by a computer are data. The output results of processing data—the words, numbers, sounds, and graphics—are information.

● A computer stores data in files. A **computer file**, usually referred to simply as a **file**, is a named collection of data that exists on a storage medium, such as a hard disk, a floppy disk, or a CD. Although all files contain data, some files are classified as "data files," whereas other files are classified as "executable files."

● A **data file** contains data. For example, it might contain the text for a document, the numbers for a calculation, the specifications for a graph, the frames of a video, or the notes of a musical passage.

● An **executable file** contains the programs or gives the instructions that tell a computer how to perform a specific task. For example, the word processing program that tells your computer how to display and print text is stored as an executable file.

You can think of data files as passive because the data does not instruct the computer to do anything. Executable files, on the other hand, are active because the instructions stored in the file cause the computer to carry out some action.

● Every file has a name, the **filename**, which often provides a clue to its contents. A file also has a **filename extension** usually referred to simply as an "extension" that further describes a file's contents. For example, in Pbrush.exe, "Pbrush" is the filename and "exe" is the extension. As you can see, the filename is separated from the extension by a period called a "dot." To tell someone the name of this file, you would say, "P brush dot e-x-e."

Executable files typically have .exe extensions. Data files have a variety of extensions, such as .jpg, .bmp or .tif for a graphic, .mid for synthesized music, .wav for recorded music, or .htm for a Web page. Each software program assigns a specific filename extension to the data files it creates. As a user, you do not decide the extension; rather, it is automatically included when files are created and saved, for example .xls for files created with Excel or .doc for files created with Word. Depending on your computer settings, you may or may not see the filename extension assigned to a file. Figure A-12 shows a list of files, including the filename extensions.

FIGURE A-11: The difference between data and information

The computer reads the data in the file and produces the output image as information that the viewer can understand

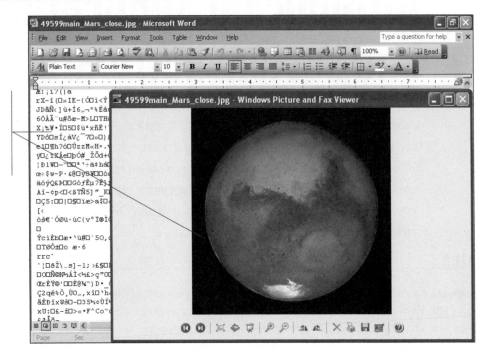

FIGURE A-12: Filenames and filename extensions

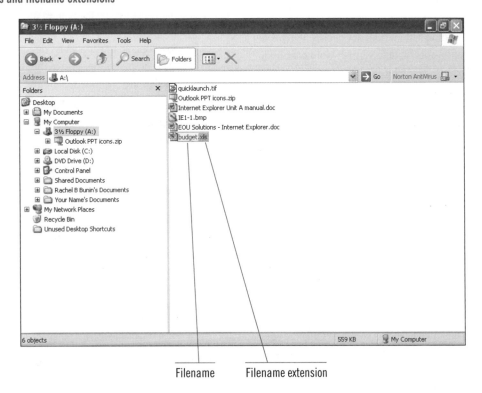

Filename   Filename extension

Introducing application and system software

A computer's application software and operating system make a computer run. As a computer user, you are probably most familiar with application software. In fact, you probably use many different types of application software that are installed on your computer. As a computer user, your computing experience is driven by the operating system. There is usually only one operating system on your computer; the operating system is not another type of application software. You can run many applications at one time, but only one operating system at one time.

DETAILS

- **Application software** is a set of computer programs that helps a person carry out a task. Word processing software, for example, helps people create, edit, and print documents. Personal finance software helps people keep track of their money and investments. Video editing software helps people create and edit home movies and even some professional, commercially-released films.

- An operating system is essentially the master controller for all of the activities that take place within a computer. An **operating system** is classified as **system software**, not application software, because its primary purpose is to help the computer system monitor itself in order to function efficiently. Unlike application software, an operating system does not directly help people perform application-specific tasks, such as word processing. Most of the time people interact with the operating system without realizing it. However, people do interact with the operating system for certain operational and storage tasks, such as starting programs and locating data files.

- Popular personal computer operating systems include Microsoft Windows and Mac OS. Microsoft Windows Mobile and Palm OS control most handheld computers. Linux and UNIX are popular operating systems for servers. Microsoft Windows (usually referred to simply as "Windows") is probably the most widely used operating system for personal computers. As shown in Figure A-13, the Windows operating system displays menus and simulated on-screen controls designed to be manipulated by a mouse.

- Windows software is not the same as the Windows operating system. The term "Windows software" refers to any application software that is designed to run on computers that use Microsoft Windows as their operating system. For example, a program called Microsoft Word for Windows is a word processing program; it is an application program that is referred to as "Windows software."

- An operating system affects compatibility. Computers that operate in essentially the same way are said to be "compatible." Two of the most important factors that influence compatibility and define a computer's platform are the processor and the operating system. A **platform** consists of the underlying hardware and software of the computer system. Today, two of the most popular personal computer platforms are PCs and Macs.

  PCs are based on the design for one of the first personal computer "superstars"—the IBM PC. A huge selection of personal computer brands and models based on the original PC design and manufactured by companies such as IBM, Hewlett-Packard, Toshiba, Dell, and Gateway are on the shelves today. The Windows operating system was designed specifically for these personal computers. Because of this, the PC platform is sometimes called the "Windows platform." Most of the examples in this book pertain to PCs because they are so popular.

  Macs are based on a proprietary design for a personal computer called the Macintosh, manufactured almost exclusively by Apple Computer, Inc. The stylish iMac is one of Apple's most popular computers, and like other computers in the Mac platform, it uses Mac OS as its operating system. See Figure A-14.

- The PC and Mac platforms are not compatible because their processors and operating systems differ. Consequently, application software designed for Macs does not typically work with PCs. When shopping for new software, it is important to read the package to make sure that it is designed to work with your computer platform.

  Different versions of some operating systems have been created to operate with more than one processor. For example, one version of the Linux operating system exists for the PC platform and another version exists for the Mac platform.

FIGURE A-13: The Windows interface

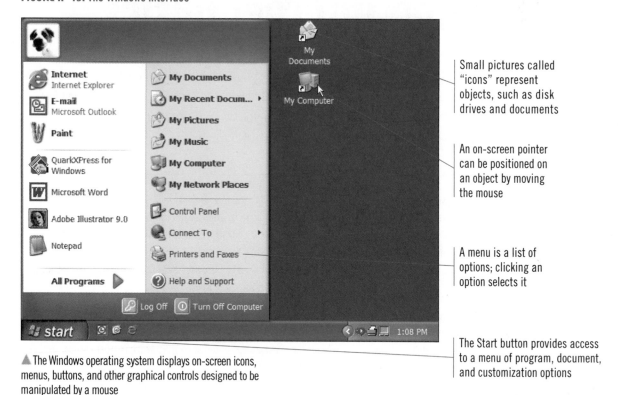

Small pictures called "icons" represent objects, such as disk drives and documents

An on-screen pointer can be positioned on an object by moving the mouse

A menu is a list of options; clicking an option selects it

The Start button provides access to a menu of program, document, and customization options

▲ The Windows operating system displays on-screen icons, menus, buttons, and other graphical controls designed to be manipulated by a mouse

FIGURE A-14: The Mac OS

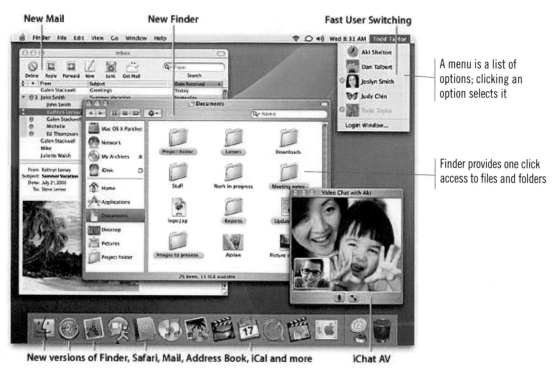

New Mail

New Finder

Fast User Switching

A menu is a list of options; clicking an option selects it

Finder provides one click access to files and folders

New versions of Finder, Safari, Mail, Address Book, iCal and more

iChat AV

▲ The Mac OS displays on-screen icons, menus, buttons, and other grapical controls designed to be manipulated by a mouse

Defining Internet basics

Sometimes referred to as "cyberspace," the **Internet** is a collection of local, regional, national, and international computer networks that are linked together to exchange data and distribute processing tasks. If you're looking for information, if you want to communicate with someone, or if you want to buy something, the Internet offers abundant resources.

DETAILS

- The **Internet backbone** defines the main routes of the Internet. See Figure A-15. Analogous to interstate highways, the Internet backbone is constructed and maintained by major telecommunications companies. These telecommunications links can move huge amounts of data at incredible speeds.

- In addition to the backbone, the Internet encompasses an intricate collection of regional and local communications links. These links can include local telephone systems, cable television lines, cellular telephone systems, and personal satellite dishes that transport data to and from millions of computers and other electronic devices.

- Communication among all of the different devices on the Internet is made possible by **TCP/IP (Transmission Control Protocol/Internet Protocol)**, which is a standard set of rules for electronically addressing and transmitting data.

- Most of the information that is accessible on the Internet is stored on servers. These servers use special **server software** to locate and distribute data requested by Internet users.

- Every device that's connected to the Internet is assigned a unique number, called an **IP address** that pinpoints its location in cyberspace. To prepare data for transport, a computer divides the data into small chunks called **packets**. Each packet is labeled with the IP address of its destination and then transmitted. When a packet reaches an intersection in the Internet's communications links, a device called a **router** examines the packet's address. The router checks the address in a routing table and then sends the packet along the appropriate link towards its destination. As packets arrive at their destinations, they are reassembled into a replica of the original file.

- A **Web site** can provide information, collect information through forms, or provide access to other resources, such as search engines and e-mail.

- The Internet revolutionized business by directly linking consumers with retailers, manufacturers, and distributors through electronic commerce, or **e-commerce**.

- Electronic mail, known as **e-mail**, allows one person to send an electronic message to another person or to a group of people. A variation of e-mail called a **mailing list server**, or "listserv," maintains a public list of people who are interested in a particular topic. Messages sent to the list server are automatically distributed to everyone on the mailing list.

- **Usenet** is a worldwide bulletin board system that contains thousands of discussion forums on every imaginable topic called **newsgroups**. Newsgroup members post messages based on their interests to the bulletin board; these messages can be read and responded to by other group members.

- The Internet allows real-time communication. For example, a **chat group** consists of several people who connect to the Internet and communicate in real time by typing comments to each other. A private version of a chat room, called **instant messaging**, allows people to send typed messages back and forth. **Internet telephony** allows telephone-style conversations to travel over the Internet. Internet telephony requires special software at both ends of the conversation and, instead of a telephone, it uses a microphone connected to a computer.

- The Internet carries radio shows and teleconferences that can be broadcast worldwide. Internet radio is popular because broadcasts aren't limited to a small local region.

- Internet servers store a variety of files including documents, music, software, videos, animations, and photos. The process of transferring one of these files from a remote computer, such as a server, to a local computer, such as your personal computer, is called **downloading**. Sending a file from a local computer to a remote computer is called **uploading**. See Figure A-16.

- P2P file sharing. A technology known as **peer-to-peer (P2P)** file sharing makes it possible to access files stored on another Internet user's hard disk—with permission, of course. This technology is the basis for popular music and file exchange Web sites, such as Morpheus, WinMX, and Kazaa.

FIGURE A-15: The Internet backbone

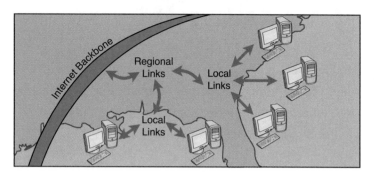

◀ Personal computers are connected to regional and local communications links, which in turn connect to the Internet backbone; data transport works seemlessly between any two platforms—between PCs and Macs, and even between personal computers and mainframes

FIGURE A-16: Web sites provide files

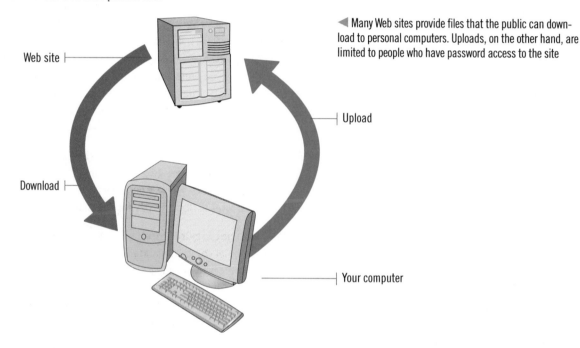

◀ Many Web sites provide files that the public can download to personal computers. Uploads, on the other hand, are limited to people who have password access to the site

What is a blog?

The term **blog**, derived from the phrase "WeB LOG," refers to a personal journal posted on the Web for access by the general public. Blogs can focus on a single topic or cover a variety of issues. A typical blog includes commentary by the author as well as links to additional information. Blogs have become a popular way of disseminating information over the Internet. Blog directories, such as the one shown in Figure A-17, provide links to blogs on all sorts of topics.

FIGURE A-17: Blogs

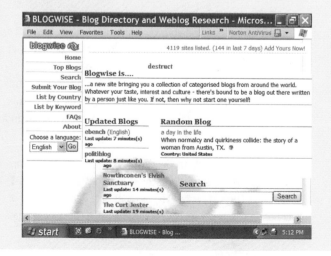

Connecting to the Internet

To take advantage of the Internet, you'll have to establish a communications link between your computer and the Internet. Possibilities include using your existing telephone line, a cable television line, a personal satellite link, wireless or cell phone service, or special high-speed telephone services. Being on the Internet is often referred to as being **online**.

DETAILS

- A **dial-up connection** requires a device called a **voice band modem**, or "modem," which converts your computer's digital signals into a type of signal that can travel over telephone lines. Figure A-18 shows various types of computer modems.

  To establish a dial-up connection, your computer's modem dials a special access number, which is answered by an Internet modem. Once the connection is established, your computer is "on the Internet." When you complete an Internet session, you must "hang up" your modem. You can choose to disconnect automatically or manually; either way the connection is discontinued until the next time you dial in.

  Theoretically, the top speed of a dial-up connection is 56 K, meaning that 56,000 bits of data are transmitted per second. Actual speed is usually reduced by distance, interference, and other technical problems, however, so the speed of most 56 K dial-up connections is more like 45 K. This speed is useable for e-mail, e-commerce, and chat. It is not, however, really optimal for applications that require large amounts of data to be transferred quickly over the Internet.

- **Cable modem service** is offered to a cable company's customers for an additional monthly charge and usually requires two pieces of equipment: a network card and a cable modem. A **network card** is a device that's designed to connect a personal computer to a local area network. A **cable modem** (see Figure A-19) is a device that changes a computer's signals into a form that can travel over cable TV links.

  Cable modem access is referred to as an **always-on connection**, because your computer is, in effect, always connected to the Internet, unlike a dial-up connection that is established only when the dialing sequence is completed. A cable modem receives data at about 1.5 million bits per second (1.5 Mbps) more than 25 times faster than a dial-up connection. This speed is suitable for most Internet activities, including real-time video and teleconferencing.

- Many telephone and independent telecommunications companies offer high-speed, always-on connections. **ISDN (Integrated Services Digital Network)** provides data transfer speeds of either 64 K (bits per second, or bps) or 128 K (bps). Given data

transfer speeds that are only marginally better than a 56 K dial-up connection and substantial monthly fees, ISDN ranks low on the list of high-speed Internet options for most consumers. **DSL (Digital Subscriber Line)** is a generic name for a family of high-speed Internet links, including ADSL, SDSL, and DSL lite. Each type of DSL provides different maximum speeds from twice as fast to approximately 125 times faster than a 56 K dial-up connection. Both ISDN and DSL connections require proximity to a telephone switching station, which can be a problem for speed-hungry consumers who don't live near one.

- Another Internet connection option is **DSS (Digital Satellite Service)**, which today offers two-way Internet access at an average speed of about 500 K. Consumers are required to rent or purchase a satellite dish and pay for its installation.

- An **ISP (Internet Service Provider)** is a company that maintains Internet computers and telecommunications equipment in order to provide Internet access to businesses, organizations, and individuals. Some parts of the Internet (such as military computers) are off limits to the general public. Other parts of the Internet limit access to paid members.

- User IDs and passwords are designed to provide access to authorized users and to prevent unauthorized access. A **user ID** is a series of characters, letters, and possibly numbers that becomes a person's unique identifier, similar to a social security number. A **password** is a different series of characters that verifies the user ID, sort of like a PIN (personal identification number) verifies your identity at an ATM machine.

- Typically, your ISP provides you with a user ID and password that you use to connect to the Internet. You will accumulate additional user IDs and passwords from other sources for specific Internet activities, such as reading New York Times articles or participating in an online auction. The process of entering a user ID and password is usually referred to as "logging in" or "logging on." See Figure A-20. The rules for creating a user ID are not consistent throughout the Internet, so it is important to read all of the instructions carefully before finalizing your ID.

FIGURE A-18: Computer modems

▲ To determine whether a computer has a modem, look for a place to plug in a standard phone cable

▲ A modem card slides into a notebook computer's PC card slot

FIGURE A-19: Cable modem

▲ A cable modem can be a standalone device set up close to a computer, or it can be integrated with other electronic components in a "set-top box" on top of a television

▲ An external modem (top left) connects to the computer with a cable; an internal modem (top right) is installed inside the computer's system unit; a PC card modem (bottom center) is typically used in a notebook computer

FIGURE A-20: Entering a password

▲ Typically, when you log in and enter your password, a series of asterisks appears on the screen to prevent someone looking over your shoulder from discovering your password; don't share your password with anyone, or write it down where it could be found; your password should be a sequence of characters and numbers that is easy for you to remember, but would be difficult for someone else to guess

What services does an Internet Service Provider provide?

To access the Internet, you do not typically connect your computer directly to the backbone. Instead, you connect it to an ISP that in turn connects to the backbone. An ISP is a point of access to the Internet. An ISP typically provides a connection to the Internet and an e-mail account. Some ISPs offer proprietary services that are available only to subscribers. These services might include content channels with articles on health, hobbies, investing, and sports; activities specially designed for kids and teens; anti-spam and security software; a variety of voice and text messaging services; and free (and virus-free) software. ISP customers arrange for service, in this case for Internet access, for which they pay a monthly fee. In addition to a monthly fee, an ISP might also charge an installation fee. The ISP that you select should provide service in the places that you typically use your computer. If your work takes you on the road a lot, you'll want to consider a national ISP that provides local access numbers in the cities that you visit.

Understanding World Wide Web basics

In the 1960s, long before personal computers or the Internet existed, a Harvard student named Ted Nelson wrote a term paper in which he described a set of documents, called **hypertext**, that would be stored on a computer. He envisioned that while reading a document in hypertext, a person could use a set of "links" to view related documents. A revolutionary idea for its time, today hypertext is the foundation for a part of the Internet that's often called "the Web" by the millions of people who use it every day.

DETAILS

● One of the Internet's most captivating attractions, the **Web** (short for "World Wide Web") is a collection of files that are interconnected through the use of hypertext. Many of these files produce documents called **Web pages**. Other files contain photos, videos, animations, and sounds that can be incorporated into specific Web pages. Most Web pages contain **links** (sometimes called "hyperlinks") to related documents and media files. See Figure A-21.

● A series of Web pages can be grouped into a **Web site**—a sort of virtual "place" in cyberspace. Every day, thousands of people shop at online department stores featuring clothing, shoes, and jewelry; visit research Web sites to look up information; and go to news Web sites, not only to read about the latest news, sports, and weather, but also to discuss current issues with other readers. The Web encompasses these and many other types of sites.

● Web sites are hosted by corporations, government agencies, colleges, and private organizations all over the world. The computers and software that store and distribute Web pages are called **Web servers**.

● Every Web page has a unique address called a **URL (uniform resource locator)**. For example, the URL for the Cable News Network Web site is http://www.cnn.com. Most URLs begin with http://. **HTTP (Hypertext Transfer Protocol)** is the communications standard that's instrumental in transporting Web documents over the Internet. When typing a URL, the http:// can usually be omitted, so www.cnn.com works just as well as http://www.cnn.com.

● Most Web sites have a main page that acts as a doorway to the rest of the pages at the site. This main page is sometimes referred to as a **home page**. The URL for a Web site's main page is typically short and to the point, like www.cnn.com.

● The site might then be divided into topic areas that are reflected in the URL. For example, the CNN site might include a weather center www.cnn.com/weather/ and an entertainment desk www.cnn.com/showbiz/. A series of Web pages will then be grouped under the appropriate topic. For example, you might find a page about hurricanes at the URL www.cnn.com/weather/hurricanes.html or a page about El Niño at www.cnn.com/weather/elnino.htm. The filename of a specific Web page always appears last in the URL—hurricanes.html and elnino.htm are the names of two Web pages. Web page filenames usually have an .htm or .html extension, indicating that the page was created with **HTML** (Hypertext Markup Language), a standard format for Web documents. Figure A-22 identifies the parts of a URL.

● A URL never contains a space, even after a punctuation mark. An underline character is sometimes used to give the appearance of a space between words, as in the URL www.detroit.com/restaurants/best_restaurants.html. Be sure to use the correct type of slash—always a forward slash (/)—and duplicate the URL's capitalization exactly. The servers that run some Web sites are case sensitive, which means that an uppercase letter is not the same as a lowercase letter. On these servers, typing www.cmu.edu/Overview.html (with an uppercase "O") will not locate the page that's stored as www.cmu.edu/overview.html (with a lowercase "o").

FIGURE A-21: A Web page

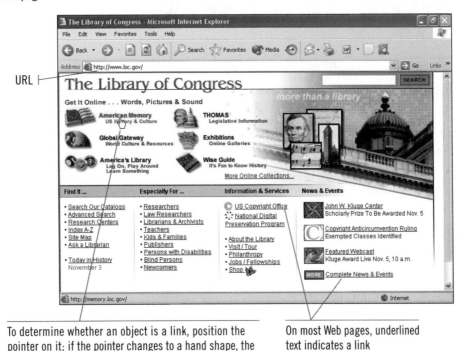

URL

To determine whether an object is a link, position the pointer on it; if the pointer changes to a hand shape, the object is a link; to activate a link, simply click it

On most Web pages, underlined text indicates a link

FIGURE A-22: A URL

http://www.cnn.com/showbiz/movies.htm

| Web protocol standard | Web server name | Folder name | Document name and filename extension |

◀ The URL for a Web page indicates the computer on which it is stored, its location on the Web server, a folder name, its filename, and its filename extension

Using search engines

The term **"search engine"** popularly refers to a Web site that provides a variety of tools to help you find information on the Web. A **keyword** is any word or phrase that you type to describe the information that you're trying to find. Based on your input, the search engine provides a list of pages. Depending on the search engine that you use, you may be able to find information by entering a description, filling out a form, or clicking a series of links to review a list of topics and subtopics (Topic Directory). To use a topic directory, simply click a general topic. When a list of subtopics appears, click the one that's most relevant to the information you are trying to locate. If your selection results in another list of subtopics, continue to select the most relevant one until the search engine presents a list of Web pages. You can then link to these pages just as though you had used a keyword query. See Figure A-23. Without search engines, using the Internet would be like trying to find a book in the Library of Congress by wandering around the stacks. To discover exactly how to use a particular search engine effectively, refer to its Help pages.

FIGURE A-23: Search engines

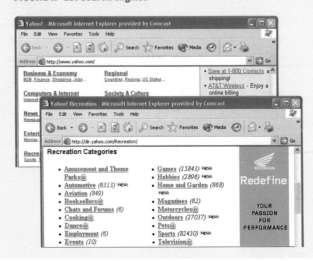

Using browsers

A Web browser, usually referred to simply as a **browser**, is a software program that runs on your computer and helps you view and navigate Web pages. See Figure A-25. A browser provides a window in which it displays a Web page. The borders of the window contain a set of menus and controls to help you navigate from one Web page to another. Today's most popular browsers are Microsoft Internet Explorer® (IE) and Netscape Navigator® (Navigator).

DETAILS

- Whether it's called a "URL box," an "Address box," or a "Location box," most browsers provide a space for entering URLs.

- If you want to view the Web page www.dogs.com/boxer.html, you enter the URL into the Address box provided by your browser. When you press [Enter] on the keyboard, the browser contacts the Web server at www.dogs.com and requests the boxer.html page. The server sends your computer the data stored in boxer.html. This data includes two things: the information that you want to view and embedded codes, called **HTML tags**, that tell your browser how to display the information. The tags specify details such as the color of the background, the text color and size, and the placement of graphics. Figure A-26 shows that a browser assembles a document on your computer screen according to the specifications contained in the HTML tags.

- Web browsers offer a remarkably similar set of features and capabilities. HTML tags make it possible for Web pages to appear similar from one browser to the next.

- The browser's Back button lets you retrace your steps to view pages that you've seen previously. Most browsers also have a Forward button, which shows you the page that you were viewing before you clicked the Back button.

- Your browser lets you select a **home page**, which is the Web page that appears every time you start your browser. Whenever you click the Home button, your browser displays your home page. This home page is different than the home page of a Web site.

- Typically, a browser provides access to a print option from a button or a menu, allowing you to print the contents of a Web page. You should always preview before printing because a Web page on the screen may print out as several printed pages.

- To help you revisit sites from previous sessions, your browser provides a **History list**. You can display this list by clicking a button or menu option provided by your browser. To revisit any site in the History list, click its URL. Many browsers allow you to specify how long a URL will remain in the History list.

- If you find a great Web site and you want to revisit it sometime in the future, you can add the URL to a list, typically called **Favorites** or **Bookmarks** so you can simply click its URL to display it.

- Sometimes a Web page takes a very long time to appear on your screen. If you don't want to wait for a page, click the Stop button.

- If you're looking for information on a Web page, use the Find option on your browser's Edit menu to locate a word or phrase.

Copying a Web page

Most browsers let you save a copy of a Web page and place it at the storage location of your choice. Most allow you to save a copy of a graphic or sound that you find on a Web page. Most browsers also provide a Copy command that allows you to copy a section of text from a Web page, which you can then paste into one of your own documents. To copy a passage of text from a Web page, highlight the text (see Figure A-24), click the Edit menu, then select Copy. Next, switch to your own document and use the Paste option. To keep track of the source for each insertion, you can also use the Copy command to copy the Web page's URL from the Address box, and then paste the URL into your document.

FIGURE A-24:

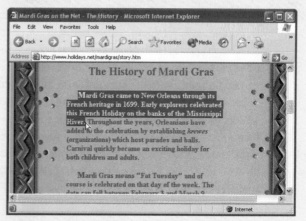

FIGURE A-25: Internet Explorer browser

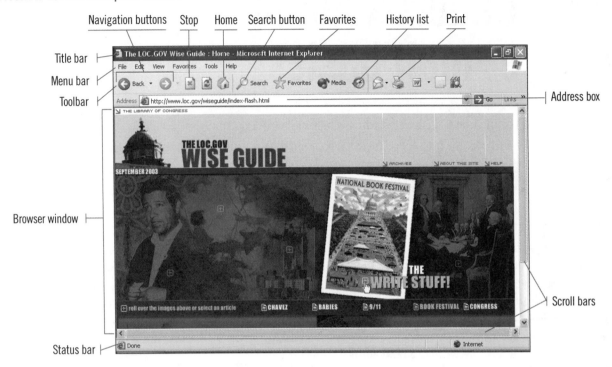

Navigation buttons   Stop   Home   Search button   Favorites   History list   Print

Title bar

Menu bar

Toolbar

Browser window

Status bar

Address box

Scroll bars

FIGURE A-26: A Web page in Internet Explorer and the HTML code used to display it

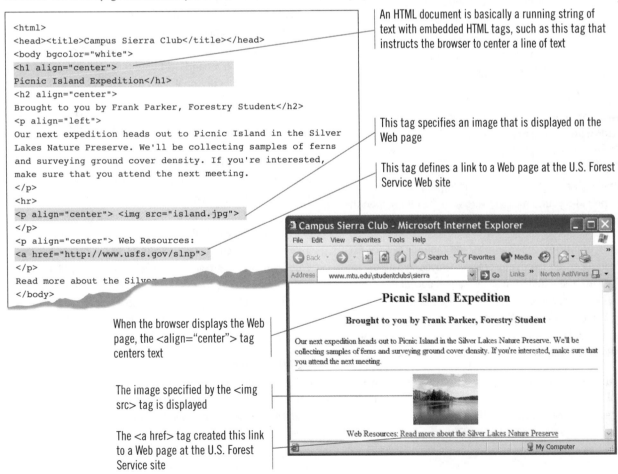

```
<html>
<head><title>Campus Sierra Club</title></head>
<body bgcolor="white">
<h1 align="center">
Picnic Island Expedition</h1>
<h2 align="center">
Brought to you by Frank Parker, Forestry Student</h2>
<p align="left">
Our next expedition heads out to Picnic Island in the Silver
Lakes Nature Preserve. We'll be collecting samples of ferns
and surveying ground cover density. If you're interested,
make sure that you attend the next meeting.
</p>
<hr>
<p align="center"> <img src="island.jpg">
</p>
<p align="center"> Web Resources:
<a href="http://www.usfs.gov/slnp">
</p>
Read more about the Silver
</body>
```

An HTML document is basically a running string of text with embedded HTML tags, such as this tag that instructs the browser to center a line of text

This tag specifies an image that is displayed on the Web page

This tag defines a link to a Web page at the U.S. Forest Service Web site

When the browser displays the Web page, the <align="center"> tag centers text

The image specified by the <img src> tag is displayed

The <a href> tag created this link to a Web page at the U.S. Forest Service site

UNIT A

Understanding e-mail basics

The Internet really took off when people discovered electronic mail. Billions of e-mail messages speed over the Internet each year. E-mail can refer to a single electronic message or to the entire system of computers and software that transmits, receives, and stores e-mail messages. Any person with an e-mail account can send and receive e-mail. Basic e-mail activities are discussed in Table A-1.

DETAILS

- An **e-mail account** provides the rights to a storage area, or mailbox, supplied by an e-mail provider, such as an ISP. Each mailbox has a unique address that typically consists of a user ID, an @ symbol, and the name of the computer that maintains the mailbox. For example, suppose that a university student named Dee Greene has an electronic mailbox on a computer called rutgers.edu. If her user ID is "dee_greene," her **e-mail address** would be dee_greene@rutgers.edu.

- An **e-mail message** is a document that is composed on a computer and transmitted in digital or "electronic" form to another computer. Every message includes a message header and the body of the message, usually displayed in a form, as shown in Figure A-27. Basic e-mail activities include writing, reading, replying to, and forwarding messages. Messages can be printed, kept for later reference, or deleted.

- Any file that travels with an e-mail message is called an **e-mail attachment**. A conversion process called **MIME (Multi-Purpose Internet Mail Extensions)** provides a way of transporting digital photos, sounds, and other media as plain ASCII text that can travel over the Internet as e-mail attachments. An electronic message incorporated in the e-mail header provides your e-mail software with the information that allows it to reconstruct the attachment into its original form.

- After you receive an e-mail message, you can use the Forward feature to pass it on to other people. When you initiate the forward process, the original e-mail message is copied into a new message window, complete with the address of the original sender. You can then enter the address of the person to whom you are forwarding the message. You can also add a note about why you are passing the message along.

- Today, most e-mail software allows you to create e-mail messages in HTML format. Why use HTML format for your e-mail? HTML messages can contain fancy formatting. The only limitation is that your e-mail recipients must have HTML-compliant e-mail software; otherwise, your message will be delivered as ASCII text.

- Although e-mail is delivered quickly, it is important to use proper netiquette when composing a message. **Netiquette (Internet etiquette)** is a series of customs or guidelines for maintaining civilized and effective communications in online discussions and e-mail exchanges. For example, typing in all caps, such as "WHAT DID YOU DO?" is considered shouting and rude.

- An **e-mail system** is the equipment and software that carries and manipulates e-mail messages. It includes computers and software called **e-mail servers** that sort, store, and route mail.

- E-mail is based on **store-and-forward technology**, a communications method in which data that cannot be sent directly to its destination will be temporarily stored until transmission is possible. This technology allows e-mail messages to be routed to a server and held until they are forwarded to the next server or to a personal mailbox.

- Three types of e-mail systems are widely used today: POP, IMAP, and Web-based mail. **POP (Post Office Protocol)** temporarily stores new messages in your mailbox on an e-mail server. See Figure A-28. Most people who use POP have obtained an e-mail account from an ISP. Such an account provides a mailbox on the ISP's **POP server**, which is a computer that stores your incoming messages until they can be transferred to your hard disk. Using POP requires e-mail client software. This software, which is installed on your computer, provides an Inbox and an Outbox. When you ask the e-mail server to deliver your mail, all of the messages stored in your mailbox on the POP server are transferred to your computer, stored on your computer's disk drive, and listed as new mail in your Inbox. You can then disconnect from the Internet, if you like, and read the new mail at your leisure.

  IMAP (Internet Messaging Access Protocol) is similar to POP, except that you have the option of downloading your mail or leaving it on the server. **Web-based e-mail**, the most commonly used, keeps your mail at a Web site rather than transferring it to your computer. Examples of Web-based e-mail are Yahoo mail and Hotmail. Before you can use Web-based e-mail, you'll need an e-mail account with a Web-based e-mail provider.

22 COMPUTER CONCEPTS

FIGURE A-27: Composing a message

When you compose an e-mail message, you'll begin by entering the address of one or more recipients and the subject of the message

You can also specify one or more files to attach to the message

The body of the e-mail message contains the message itself

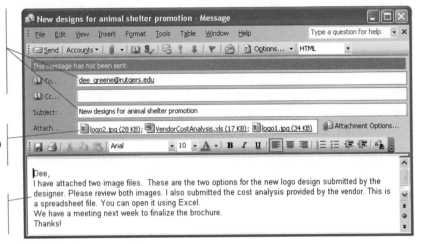

When the message is sent, your e-mail software adds the date and your e-mail address to identify you as the sender

FIGURE A-28: Incoming and outgoing mail

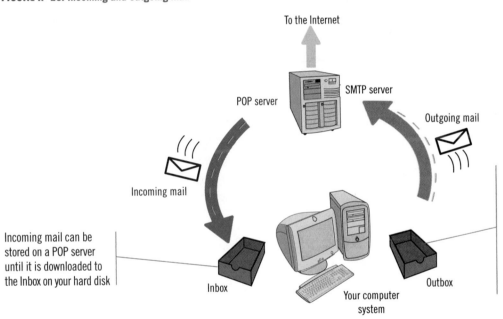

Incoming mail can be stored on a POP server until it is downloaded to the Inbox on your hard disk

An Outbox temporarily holds mesages that you composed and completed, but that haven't been transmitted over the Internet; when you go online, you can send all the mail that's being held in your Outbox; outgoing mail is routed by an SMTP (Simple Mail Transfer Protocol) server, instead of by the POP server

Table A-1: Basic e-mail activities consist of writing, reading, replying to and forwarding messages

FEATURE/ ACTIVITY	USE TO	FEATURE/ ACTIVITY	USE TO
Reply	Send a reply to recipients of an e-mail; includes the original message	Group	Create an e-mail "group" that consists of several e-mail addresses
Forward	Pass an e-mail on to other people	Priority	Assign a priority level to your e-mail messages
Cc:	Send a "carbon copy" of a message to one or more recipients	Sort	Sort e-mail messages by date received, sender name, subject, or priority
Bcc:	Send a "blind carbon copy" of a message to one or more recipients	Automate	Automate replies to messages when you will not be responding for a few days
Address book	Maintain contact information	Block	Refuse messages that arrive from a particular e-mail address

The sequence of events that occurs between the time that you turn on a computer and the time that it becomes ready to accept commands is referred to as the **boot process** or "booting" your computer. Your computer boots up by first loading a small program, called a "bootstrap" program, into memory, then it uses that small program to load a large operating system. Your computer's small bootstrap program is built into special ROM (read-only memory) circuitry housed in the computer's system unit. When you turn on a computer, the ROM circuitry receives power and it begins the boot process.

What is the purpose of the boot process? The boot process involves a lot of flashing lights, whirring noises, and beeping as your computer performs a set of diagnostic tests called the **power-on self-test (POST)**. The good news is that these tests can warn you if certain crucial components of your computer system are out of whack. The bad news is that these tests cannot warn you of impending failures. Also, problems identified during the boot process usually must be fixed before you can start a computing session.

The boot process serves an additional purpose—loading the operating system from the hard disk into memory so that it can help the computer carry out basic operations. Without the operating system, a computer's CPU is basically unable to communicate with any input, output, or storage devices. It can't display information, accept commands, store data, or run any application software. Therefore, loading the operating system is a crucial step in the boot process.

Most of a computer's memory is "volatile" random access memory (RAM), which cannot hold any data when the power is off. Although a copy of the operating system is housed in RAM while the computer is in operation, this copy is erased as soon as the power is turned off. Given the volatility of RAM, computer designers decided to store the operating system on a computer's hard disk. During the boot process, a copy of the operating system is copied into RAM, where it can be accessed quickly whenever the computer needs to carry out an input, processing, output, or storage operation. The operating system remains in RAM until the computer is turned off.

Six major events happen during the boot process:

1. Power up. When you turn on the power switch, the power light is illuminated, and power is distributed to the computer circuitry.

2. Start boot program. The processor begins to execute the bootstrap program that is stored in ROM.

3. Power-on self-test. The computer performs diagnostic tests of several crucial system components.

4. Identify peripheral devices. The operating system identifies the peripheral devices that are connected to the computer and checks their settings.

5. Load operating system. The operating system is copied from the hard disk to RAM.

6. Check configuration and customization. The processor reads configuration data and executes any customized startup routines specified by the user.

What if I turn on a computer and nothing happens? The first step in the boot process is the power-up stage. Power from a wall outlet or battery activates a small power light. If the power light does not come on when you flip the "on" switch, you should check all the power connections and be sure everything is plugged in properly.

What kinds of problems are likely to show up during the power-on self-test? The POST checks your computer's main circuitry, screen display, memory, and keyboard. It can identify when one of these devices has failed, but it cannot identify intermittent problems or impending failures. The POST notifies you of a hardware problem by displaying an error message on the screen or by emitting a series of beeps. A **beep code** provides your computer with a way to signal a problem, even if the screen is not functioning. You can check the documentation or Web site for your computer to find the specific meaning of numeric error codes. The printed or online reference manual for a computer usually explains the meaning of each beep code.

Should I try to fix these problems myself? If a computer displays error messages, emits beep codes, or seems to freeze up during the boot process, you can take some simple steps that might fix it. First, turn the computer off, check all the cables, wait five seconds, then try to start the computer again. Refer to Figure A-29 for a power-up checklist. If you still encounter a boot error after trying to restart the computer several times, contact a technical support person.

What's the long list of stuff that appears on my screen during the boot process? After the POST, the bootstrap program tries to identify all of the devices that are connected to the computer. The settings for each device appear on the screen, creating a list of rather esoteric information.

On occasion, a device gets skipped or misidentified during the boot process. An error message is not produced, but the device doesn't seem to work properly. To resolve this problem, shut down the computer and reboot it. If a device is causing persistent problems, you may need to check the manufacturer's Web site to see if a new software patch will improve its operation.

Do computers have trouble loading the operating system or applying customization settings? Problems during the last stages of the boot process are rare, except when a disk has been inadvertently left in the floppy disk drive. Before computers were equipped with hard disk drives, floppy disks were used to store the operating system and application software. As a legacy from these early machines, today's computers first check the floppy disk drive for a disk containing the operating system. If it doesn't find a disk in the drive, it proceeds to look for the operating system on the hard disk. However, if a floppy disk happens to be left in drive A, the computer will assume that you want to boot from it and will look for the operating system on that disk. The error message "Non-system disk or disk error" is the clue to this problem. Remove the floppy disk and press any key to resume the boot process.

How do I know when the boot process is finished? The boot process is complete when the computer is ready to accept your commands. Usually, the computer displays an operating system prompt or main screen. The Windows operating system, for example, displays the Windows desktop when the boot process is complete.

If Windows cannot complete the boot process, you are likely to see a menu that contains an option for Safe Mode. **Safe Mode** is a limited version of Windows that allows you to use your mouse, monitor, and keyboard, but not other peripheral devices. This mode is designed for troubleshooting, not for real computing tasks. If your computer enters Safe Mode at the end of the boot process, you should use the Shut Down command on the Start menu to shut down and turn off your computer properly. You can then turn on your computer again. It should complete the boot process in regular Windows mode. If your computer enters Safe Mode again, consult a technician.

FIGURE A-29: Power-up checklist

☑ **Make sure that the power cable is plugged into the wall and into the back of the computer.**

☑ **Check batteries if you're using a notebook computer.**

☑ **Try to plug your notebook into a wall outlet.**

☑ **Make sure that the wall outlet is supplying power (plug a lamp into it and make sure that you can turn it on).**

☑ **If the computer is plugged into a surge strip, extension cord, or uninterruptible power supply, make sure that it is turned on and functioning correctly.**

☑ **Can you hear the fan in your desktop computer? If not, the computer's power supply mechanism might have failed.**

Computers are helping athletes optimize their performance. In the mid-1960s researchers first used mainframe computers to perform complex computations for biomechanics, the study of the motion of living things. Biomechanics can be applied to many sport-related activities, such as determining the optimal take-off position for an ice skater's triple jump or discovering the best wrist action for a basketball free-throw. Figure A-30 shows how a computer helps with a golf swing.

On a very simple level, biomechanics views the human body's bones and joints as a series of interconnected lines, called vectors. Your arm, for example, is composed of two vectors connected at the elbow. When you bend your arm, the angle formed by the two vectors decreases. The size of the vectors and the angles they form can be expressed and manipulated mathematically, allowing biomechanics researchers to model the entire human body as a series of vectors. Because the human body doesn't operate in a vacuum, biomechanical analyses must take into account physical factors, such as gravity, mass, speed, and the fluid dynamics of air or water in which the athlete performs. Calculations for all the factors in biomechanical analyses involve many data points and complex equations—definitely a job for computers.

Today, researchers can use powerful processors, wireless electromagnetic sensors, digital video cameras, and sophisticated modeling software to study an athlete's movement. Small sensors are attached to key joints of the athlete's body. At rates up to 120 times per second, each sensor sends its location as X, Y, and Z coordinates to a computer. A computer then uses the sensor data to construct a 3-D animation of the athlete's movements. The data can be superimposed on an animated skeletal model so that athletes and coaches can look for fundamental athletic performance problems. A series of performances can be compared on a split screen display or with strobe-like multiple shots.

Another way to enhance athletic performance is with computer-controlled simulators. Similar to a flight simulator, a sports simulator creates a computer-generated environment that the athlete can manipulate. Simple and inexpensive software-based simulators for sports such as golf, sailing, and BMX racing run on standard personal computers. Most software-based sports simulators are essentially games. Simulators that depict settings based on real

locations, however, help athletes familiarize themselves with a course or track before competing on it. More sophisticated sports simulators include hardware components that simulate the total sports experience. For example, a bobsled simulator developed at The University of California includes a computer-controlled capsule equipped with a screen display, realistic steering controls, an audio system that generates the sound of a sled on a track, and a motion control system designed to realistically roll and vibrate the cockpit. Data from competition tracks in Salt Lake City, Lillehammer, Calgary, and Albertville can be fed into the computer. Based on the driver's steering input, the computer generates an image of the track ahead, sends messages to the motion control system, and returns force-feedback to the driver through the steering handles. Bobsled drivers are typically limited to four or five daily practice runs on a real track, but with the bobsled simulator they can take many practice runs, concentrate on difficult sections of the track, practice on different tracks without traveling, and compare their runs to other drivers.

FIGURE A-30

The same technology powers arcade style golf, racecar, and snowboard simulators. Simulation technology is also filtering down to consumer fitness equipment, such as stationary bicycles and treadmills.

In addition to optimizing performance, computers make it possible to design stronger, lighter, and more efficient sports equipment, such as mountain bikes, athletic shoes, and snowboards. Refer to Figure A-31. Advances in the fields of computerized engineering and materials science have revolutionized equipment design and manufacturing. Until a decade ago, equipment designers created simple 2-D models on a computer screen, and then hand-tooled a product mockup. Today, powerful computer workstations and 3-D CAD (computer-aided design) software help designers plot their ideas in three dimensions, and then send the design to a CAM (computer-aided manufacturing) device that carves out a physical model from light-reactive plastic or wax. In the past, exorbitantly expensive CAD software, CAM devices, and high-end computer workstations prevented many companies from using CAD/CAM technology. Today, CAD software is much more affordable and runs on consumer-level personal computers. Most athletic equipment manufacturers can also afford to maintain their own CAM equipment in house.

Computer use in sports is not without controversy. The use of high-tech computer gear has raised dissent among some sports fans, who question whether the focus of sports has shifted from athletes to their equipment. Computers and materials science experts can supply pole-vaulters with springier poles, golfers with long-range balls and clubs, and cyclists with ever-lighter bikes. In races that may be won by a tenth of a second, equipment rather than human performance can make the difference between first and second place.

Some observers believe that fair competition is possible only if all contestants use the same gear. Is the solution to standardize competition gear? Those opposed to this idea argue that standardized equipment would inhibit innovations that contribute to the evolution of sports. International sports associations tend to agree that within limits, competitors can use the best gear that computers, designers, and engineers can produce. As long as this continues to be the case, expect sports equipment manufacturers to continue exercising their CAD/CAM equipment to produce cutting-edge athletic gear. However, even the best gear can't transform an athlete into a champion, so also expect innovations in the use of technology to analyze athletic performance and increase performance skills.

FIGURE A-31

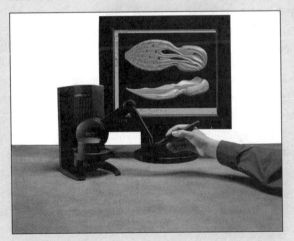

You wake up, put in your contact lenses, and rush over to the computer to check your e-mail. After reading and responding to the messages that came in overnight, you write a few new messages to get the day going, check out world events on several of your favorite news sites, play a quick game of solitaire, and then an hour or two later, remember you haven't yet dressed or had breakfast. Then fast forward to the end of the day…you get home from the job—which may or may not require you to sit at a computer, say a quick hello to your family, and then sit down for a few hours of "leisure" time at the computer.

As computers are becoming more ubiquitous, that is, ever-present in our lives, people are spending more and more time at the keyboard. What are the implications for personal health (physical, emotional, and mental), language usage, and society? How does all this time people are spending at the computer affect society in general? Are we spending too much time online? The Internet is available 24 hours a day, 7 days a week…and as a result people can check their e-mail, stay in touch with work (even when they should be on vacation), research their stocks, and so on any time of the day or night. Is all this time at the computer necessary, or are we computer-addicted?

Computer users who spend excessive amounts of time at the keyboard are prone to a variety of computer-related health issues. Physical health issues include repetitive stress injuries, such as carpal tunnel syndrome. Repetitive stress injuries are caused by repetitive motions, such as using the same arm or wrist motion to enter data, and are not solely computer-related. Other physical health issues include eye strain and fatigue, as well as headaches, which can be the result of sitting for long periods of time looking at a monitor without proper eyewear or at inappropriate distances.

A comprehensive research study on the effects of prolonged daily use of computers, particularly the effects of sitting in front of a monitor, was conducted by researchers at Chiba University in Japan. The study, published in the American Journal of Industrial Medicine (Volume 42, Issue 5, 2002), investigated more than 25,000 workers three times over a 3-year period (1995-1997) using a self-administered questionnaire. The researchers looked at three primary factors: mental, physical, and sleep-related symptoms. Even after adjusting for mitigating factors, they found that there was a significant relationship between the amount of time people sit at a computer and look at a monitor and physical and mental ailments. People working at a computer longer than five hours per day seemed to exhibit the most symptoms. Physical ailments included headache, eyestrain, and joint pain. Mental ailments for people working more than five hours at a computer included increased lethargy, insomnia, anxiety, and fatigue.

The science of ergonomics, which is the study of people and their work environments to improve work conditions and to enhance productivity, has tried to address physical issues related to ubiquitous computing by creating ergonomically-designed workspaces. These workspaces include proper furniture, such as desks that can be adjusted to the needs of the user, special keyboard layouts, and adjustable chairs. Ergonomics also addresses the issue of proper lighting to help reduce eyestrain and headache. The science also provides information on proper posture—a key element in helping to reduce physical injuries.

In addition to physical injuries, healthcare workers are concerned about the emotional and mental issues stemming from excessive computer use. One such problem is that of computer addiction disorder (CAD), sometimes referred to as Internet addiction disorder (IAD). As of this writing, CAD/IAD has not been recognized officially as a psychological or psychiatric diagnosis, but the addiction to computers and computer use is being studied seriously by healthcare professionals.

Apparently, computer usage is affecting not only our physical health but also our language skills. Several major news organizations have reported on the effect of computers in the way students write. Teachers report that essays and school assignments are being submitted with some words written in the language of text messaging (short abbreviations used for communicating over the Internet) rather than full words and correct English. Many teens are incorporating text messaging, which they use when sending instant messages through services such as ICQ and AOL Instant Messaging or when sending text messages on their cell phones, into their school work. For example, "gr8 2 b ur friend cuz u r kewl, c u l8r @ home" may seem like an odd collection of symbols and letters but for a teen it's a simple message: "Great to be your friend because you are cool, see you later at home."

Text messaging is also called Short Message Service. Webopedia defines Short Message Service (SMS) as "the transmission of short text messages to and from a mobile phone, fax machine and/or IP address. Messages must be no longer than 160 alpha-numeric characters and contain no images or graphics." If you only have 160 characters, you tend to get creative, such as using "gr8" for great! Recently, the Oxford University Press added an appendix that includes a glossary of abbreviations used in electronic text messaging to its Concise Oxford Dictionary. These shorthand terms were developed and defined by e-mail users. Some worry that including this glossary of abbreviations in the Concise Oxford Dictionary is a step toward acceptance of these abbreviations as Standard English.

It is a well-known fact that language is always evolving. Each new generation contributes words to its language, words that then become part of the accepted language. However, the Internet generation is pushing the boundaries of written language by suggesting that simply typing "lol" (laughing out loud), "brb" (be right back), and "ttyl" (talk to you later) should be universally accepted as Standard English. Regardless of whether or not these abbreviations are accepted as Standard English, they are clearly impacting language usage by their pervasive intrusion into our written language.

What is the impact on society of ubiquitous computing? Is the computer changing the way we interact with our family and friends? How do you tell your neighbors good news? Bad news? There was a time when you would walk next door or down the block and tell a friend face-to-face about a promotion, a success, or a sad event. With our circles widening in large geographic areas, it's a good thing to be able to stay in touch with people who no longer live down the block. However, are we losing the ability to face people and tell them things personally?

Computer usage will continue to expand. The 24/7 accessibility to computers is changing society—for example, the way businesses do business, the way the economy runs, and the way people work. As it does, we would be wise to consider its impact on our lives.

▼ EXPAND THE IDEAS

1. What are the pertinent health issues for computer users who spend more than 5 hours each day at a keyboard? Research two topics on this issue. Write a short paper summarizing two studies or articles.

2. How well do you know the shorthand used in text messaging? Could you understand an Instant message if it came to you? Have you ever used abbreviations (such as b/c for "because" or w/in for "within")? Write a message that is no longer than 160 characters and that uses text messaging. In a group, exchange papers and see if the messages can be interpreted. Discuss the advantages and disadvantages of using these abbreviations.

3. Research the impact of being available 24/7 to marketers and clients. What are the benefits and drawbacks to such extended accessibility? Who is most affected by this accessibility? Comment on how the 24/7 availability of computers affects our society and what we as a society should do about it, if anything.

End of Unit Exercises

▼ KEY TERMS

Always-on connection
Application software
Beep code
Binary number system
Bit
Blog
Bookmark
Boot process
Browser
Byte
Cable modem
Cable modem service
CD-ROM drive
CD-writer
Central processing unit (CPU)
Chat group
Computer
Computer file
Computer network
Computer program
Computer system
Data
Data file
Desktop computer
Dial-up connection
Display device
Downloading
DSL
DSS
DVD drive
DVD-writer
E-commerce

E-mail
E-mail account
E-mail address
E-mail attachment
E-mail message
E-mail servers
E-mail system
Executable file
Favorites
File
Filename
Filename extension
Floppy disk drive
Handheld computer
Hard disk drive
Hardware
History list
Home page
HTML
HTML tag
HTTP
Hypertext
IMAP
Information
Input
Input device
Instant messaging
Internet
Internet backbone
Internet telephony
IP address
ISDN

ISP
Keyboard
Keyword
LAN (local area network)
Link
Mailing list server
Mainframe computer
Memory
Microcomputer
MIME
Modem
Monitor
Mouse
Netiquette
Network card
Newsgroup
Notebook computer
Online
Operating system
Output
Output device
Packet
Password
PDA
Peer-to-Peer (P2P)
Peripheral device
Personal computer (PC)
Platform
POP
POP server
Power-on self-test (POST)
Printer

Processing
Processor
Router
Safe Mode
Search engine
Server
Server software
Software
Sound card
Speakers
Storage
Storage device
Store-and-forward technology
Stored program
Supercomputer
System software
System unit
Tablet computer
TCP/IP
Uploading
URL
Usenet
User ID
Videogame console
Voice band modem
Web
Web-based e-mail
Web page
Web server
Web site
Workstation

▼ UNIT REVIEW

1. Make sure that you can define each of the key terms in this unit in your own words. Select 10 of the terms with which you are unfamiliar and write a sentence for each of them.

2. Explain the basic functions of a computer: input, processing, storing, and output. Explain why the stored program concept is important to all of this.

3. Identify and describe each of the components of a basic personal computer system.

4. Describe the difference between an operating system and application software.

5. Define computer platform. Then discuss what makes two computer platforms compatible or incompatible.

6. List at least five resources that are provided by the Internet and identify those that are most popular.

7. Make a list of the ways to connect to the Internet presented in this unit and specify characteristics of each.

8. Describe the components of a URL and of an e-mail address.

9. Describe the rules that you should follow when copying text and images from the Internet.

10. Define "browser," then describe how a browser helps you navigate the Web.

▼ FILL IN THE BEST ANSWER

1. The basic functions of a computer are to accept _Input_, process data, store data, and produce output.

2. A computer processes data in the _CENTRAL_ processing unit.

3. The idea of a(n) _Computer_ program means that instructions for a computing task can be loaded into a computer's memory.

4. The _SYSTEM_ unit is the case that holds the main circuit boards, processor, power supply, and storage devices for a personal computer system.

5. A device that is an integral part of a computer but that can be added to a computer is called a(n) _Output_ device.

6. Executable files usually have a(n) _EXE_ extension.

7. A(n) _OPERATING_ system is the software that acts as the master controller for all of the activities that take place within a computer system.

8. The main routes of the Internet are referred to as the Internet _BACKBONE_.

9. Communication between all of the different devices on the Internet is made possible by _TCP_/IP. _TRANSMISSION CONTROL PROTOCOL_

10. Most of the "stuff" that's accessible on the Internet is stored on _SELVEL SOFTWARE_ that are maintained by various businesses and organizations.

11. A dial-up connection requires a device called a(n) _Voice_ band modem.

12. To use a cable Internet connection you need a cable modem and a(n) _NETWORK CARD_.

13. A cable modem provides an always _ON_ connection to the Internet.

14. The process of entering a user ID and password is referred to as _Logging on_.

15. Every Web page has a unique address called a(n) _URL_. _UNIFORM RESOURCE LOCATOR_

16. A browser assembles a Web page on your computer screen according to the specifications contained in the _HTML_ tags.
    Hypertext Markup Language

17. Whenever you start your browser, it displays your _HOME_ page.

18. A(n) _URL_ fetches and displays Web pages.

19. Store-and-forward technology stores messages on an e-mail _WEB SERVERS_ until they are forwarded to an individual's computer.

20. For many e-mail systems, a(n) _POP_ server handles incoming mail, and a(n) _SMTP_ server handles outgoing mail.

▼ INDEPENDENT CHALLENGE 1

When discussing computers and computer concepts it is important to use proper terminology. Unit A presented you with many computer terms that describe computer equipment. If you would like to explore any of the terms in more detail, there are online dictionaries that can help you expand your understanding of these terms.

1. For this independent challenge, write a one-page paper that describes the computer that you use most frequently.

2. Refer to the Key Terms used in this unit and use terms from this unit to describe your computer components and the functions they perform.

3. In your final draft, underline each Key Term that you used in your paper. Follow your professor's instructions for submitting your paper as an e-mail attachment or as a printed document.

▼ INDEPENDENT CHALLENGE 2

Suppose that producers for a television game show ask you to help them create a set of computer-related questions for the next show. You will compose a set of 10 questions based on the information provided in Unit A. Each question should be in multiple-choice format with four possible answers.

1. Write 10 questions: two very simple questions, five questions of medium difficulty, and three difficult questions. Each question should be on an index card.

2. For each question, indicate the correct answer on the back of each card and the page in this book on which the answer can be found.

3. Gather in small groups and take turns asking each other the questions.

▼ INDEPENDENT CHALLENGE 3

 The Computers in Context section of this unit focused on how computers are applied to sports. For this independent challenge, you will write a two- to five-page paper about how computers and technology have influenced and affected sports and athletics based on information that you gather from the Internet.

1. To begin this Independent Challenge, log on to the Internet and use your favorite search engine to find information on current uses of technology in sports and athletics to get an in-depth look at the topic. Are computers granting an unfair advantage to those who can use them to train and enhance performance? Are computers and technology creating equipment that is so superior that it creates an unfair advantage for those who can afford them?

2. Determine the viewpoint that you will present in your paper about computers in sports. You might, for example, decide to present the viewpoint that it all comes down to the skills of the athlete and computers do not provide any unfair advantage. Whatever viewpoint you decide to present, make sure that you can back it up with facts and references to authoritative articles and Web pages.

3. Place citations to your research (include the author's name, article title, date of publication, and URL) at the end of your paper as endnotes, on each page as footnotes, or along with the appropriate paragraphs using parentheses. Follow your professor's instructions for submitting your paper via e-mail or as a printed document.

▼ INDEPENDENT CHALLENGE 4

 A new ISP is getting ready to open in your area, and the president of the company asks you to design a print ad. Your ad must communicate all pertinent information about the ISP.

1. Before starting on the design, use your favorite search engine to find out more about ISPs in your area. Gather information to use in your ad, such as the type of services offered (dial-up, cable modem, etc.), the speed of service, the geographical coverage, price, and special or proprietary services.

2. Make up a name for your ISP. Design a print ad for the company using a computer or freehand tools. Submit your ad design along with a short written summary that describes how this ad reflects the ISP and the services it offers.

▼ STUDENT EDITION LABS

Reinforce the concepts you have learned in this unit through the **E-Mail** Student Edition Lab, available online at the Illustrated Computer Concepts Web site.

▼ SAM LABS

 If you have a SAM user profile, you have access to additional content, features, and functionality. Log in to your SAM account and go to your assignments page to see what your instructor has assigned for this unit.

▼ VISUAL WORKSHOP

The digital divide is defined as the difference in rates of access to computers and the Internet among different demographic groups. With the explosion of the Internet and the technology that drives the information age, forward-thinking social reformers recognized early on the potential for a divide between the "haves" and the "have nots." See Figure A-32. Not-for-profit organizations, concerned with the impact of the digital divide, designed studies to help them analyze the causes and effects of this phenomenon. These studies have been conducted for the past few decades.

FIGURE A-32

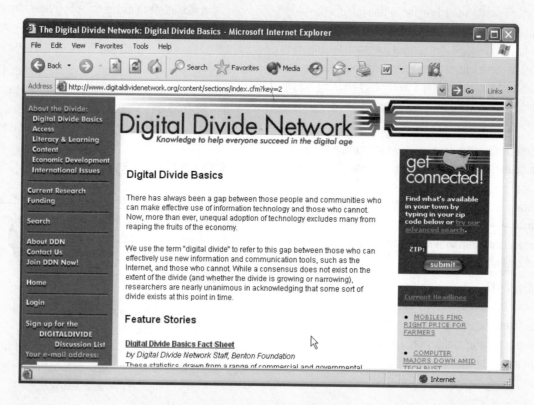

1. Is there a solution to the digital divide? Connect to the Internet and use your favorite search engine to search on the key phrase "digital divide." Find sites that include links to articles and research studies that address the digital divide. Review the findings for two studies or articles. Write a short paper summarizing these studies or articles. In your conclusion, comment on how you feel the digital divide affects our society and what we as a society should do about it, if anything.

2. Could you live without computers? Computers are ubiquitous; beyond the obvious applications, such as using your word processor to write a report, you come in contact with them during the course of your day in simple activities such as shopping in a supermarket or getting cash from your bank's ATM machine. Create a log to track your daily activities that involve computers. Keep the log for one week. At the end of the week, write a summary of any surprises or insights you have as to how computers affect your life.

3. Is there a digital divide in your community? Create a survey that will determine Internet access and computer ownership among people that you know. The survey should consist of 5-10 questions. You want to find out, within a chosen sector, who owns a computer, if they own more than one, what they use the computer(s) for, if they have Internet access, and if they access the Internet from their home or elsewhere. Be sure to survey at least 20 people. The survey should be anonymous but include demographic information. Compile the results of your survey into a chart and write a short summary explaining your findings.

UNIT B

Computer Hardware

This unit discusses computer hardware, with several lessons focusing on the various technologies that enable a computer to store and retrieve data and programs. Storage technology defines how computers store data and program files. You will learn the difference between magnetic, solid state, and optical storage. You will learn about input and output devices such as popular printer and display technologies. You will learn about the components of a computer's expansion bus, including various types of expansion slots and cables and how to use the expansion bus to add devices to a computer. You will learn about a variety of peripheral devices including how to install them, and in the Tech Talk, how the Windows Registry tracks installed devices. You will also have an opportunity to look at computers in the context of the military. The Issue discusses computer recycling.

Introducing storage technology

The basic functions of a computer are to accept input, process data, store data, and produce output. When you want to store data permanently, you save the data to a storage device. Computers can be configured with a variety of storage devices, such as a floppy disk drive, Zip drive, hard disk drive, CD drive, or DVD drive. While one storage technology might provide extremely fast access to data, it might also be susceptible to problems that could wipe out all of your data. A different storage technology might be more dependable, but it might also have the disadvantage of providing relatively slow access to data. Understanding the strengths and weaknesses of each storage technology will enable you to use each device appropriately and with maximum effectiveness.

DETAILS

- The term **storage technology** refers to data storage systems. Each data storage system has two main components: a storage medium and a storage device. A **storage medium** (storage media is the plural) is the disk, tape, memory card, CD, DVD, paper, or other media that holds data. For some examples of storage media, see Figure B-1. A **storage device** is the mechanical apparatus that records and retrieves data from a storage medium. Storage devices include floppy disk drives, Zip drives, hard disk drives, tape drives, CD drives, and DVD drives. For some examples of storage devices, see Figure B-2.

- Data is copied from a storage device into RAM, where it waits to be processed. **RAM** (random access memory) is a temporary holding area for the operating system, the file you are working on (such as a word processing document), and application program instructions. RAM is not permanent storage, in fact RAM is very **volatile**, which means data in RAM can be lost easily. That is why it is important to store data permanently.

- RAM is important to the storage process. You can think of RAM as the connection between your computer's storage devices and its storage media. After data is processed in RAM, it is usually copied to a storage medium for more permanent safekeeping.

- The process of recording or storing data is often referred to as "writing data" or "saving a file" because the storage device writes the data on the storage medium to save it for later use. The process of retrieving data is often referred to as "reading data," "loading data," or "opening a file."

- A computer works with data that has been coded and can be represented by 1s and 0s. When data is stored, these 1s and 0s must be converted into a signal or mark that's fairly permanent but that can be changed when necessary. The data is not literally written as "1" or "0." Instead, the 1s and 0s must be transformed to change the surface of a storage medium. Exactly how this transformation happens depends on the storage technology. For example, floppy disks store data in a different way than CD-ROMs store data.

The science of data representation

Letters, numbers, musical notes, and pictures don't pass from the keyboard through the circuitry of a computer and then jump out onto the screen or printer. So how is it that a computer can work with documents, photos, videos, and sound recordings? The answer to that question is what data representation and digital electronics are all about. Data representation is based on the binary number system, which uses two numbers, 1 and 0, to represent all data. Data representation makes it possible to convert letters, sounds, and images into electrical signals. Digital electronics makes it possible for a computer to manipulate simple "on" and "off" signals, which are represented by the 0s and 1s, to perform complex tasks.

FIGURE B-1: Examples of storage media

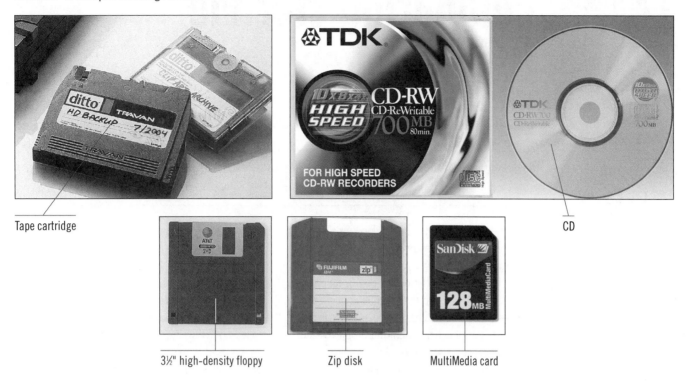

Tape cartridge

CD

3½" high-density floppy

Zip disk

MultiMedia card

FIGURE B-2: Examples of storage devices in a system unit

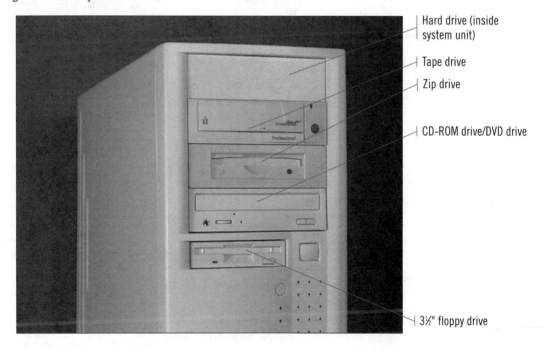

Hard drive (inside system unit)

Tape drive

Zip drive

CD-ROM drive/DVD drive

3½" floppy drive

Comparing storage technologies

Three types of storage technologies are commonly used for personal computers: magnetic, optical, and solid state. Each storage technology has advantages and disadvantages. To compare storage devices, you need to understand how each one works.

DETAILS

● **Magnetic storage**. Hard disk, floppy disk, Zip disk, and tape storage technologies can be classified as magnetic storage, which stores data by magnetizing microscopic particles on the disk or tape surface. The particles retain their magnetic orientation until that orientation is changed, thereby making disks and tape fairly permanent but modifiable storage media. A **read-write head** mechanism in the disk drive reads and writes the magnetized particles that represent data. Figure B-3 shows how a computer stores data on magnetic media.

Before data is stored, the particles on the surface of the disk are scattered in random patterns. The disk drive's read-write head magnetizes the particles and orients them in either a positive or negative direction. These patterns of magnetized particles are interpreted as the 0s and 1s that represent data. Data stored magnetically can be changed or deleted simply by altering the magnetic orientation of the appropriate particles on the disk surface. This feature of magnetic storage provides flexibility for editing data and reusing areas of a storage medium containing data that is no longer needed.

Magnetic media is not very durable. Data stored on magnetic media such as floppy disks can be altered by magnetic fields, dust, mold, smoke particles, heat, and mechanical problems with a storage device. For example, a magnet should never be placed on or near a floppy disk because it will destroy the magnetic particles on the disk. Magnetic media gradually lose their magnetic charge, which results in lost data. Some experts estimate that the reliable life span of data stored on magnetic media is about three years.

● **Optical storage**. CD and DVD storage technologies make use of optical storage, which stores data as microscopic light and dark spots on the disc surface. The dark spots are called **pits**, and it is possible to see the data stored on a CD or DVD storage medium using a high-powered microscope. See Figure B-4. The lighter, non-pitted surface areas of the disc are called **lands**. This type of storage is called optical storage because a low-power laser light is used to read the data stored on an optical disc. When the beam strikes a pit, no light is reflected. When the laser strikes a reflective surface, light bounces back into the read head. The patterns of light and dark between pits and lands are interpreted as the 1s and 0s that represent data. Data recorded on optical media is generally considered to be less susceptible to environmental damage than data recorded on magnetic media. The useful life of a CD-ROM disc is estimated to exceed 200 years.

● **Solid state storage**. A variety of compact storage cards, pens, and sticks can be classified as solid state storage. Solid state media stores data in a non-volatile, erasable, low-power chip. A solid state storage medium stores data in a microscopic grid of cells. See Figure B-5. A card reader transfers data between the card and a computer. Solid state storage provides faster access to data than magnetic or optical storage technology because it includes no moving parts. Solid state storage is very durable—it is virtually impervious to vibration, magnetic fields, or extreme temperature fluctuations. These characteristics make solid state storage a good choice for storing images created by digital cameras and sound files stored on portable listening devices. The capacity of solid state storage does not currently match that of hard disks, CDs, or DVDs. The cost per megabyte of storage is significantly higher than for magnetic or optical storage.

FIGURE B-3: Magnetic storage

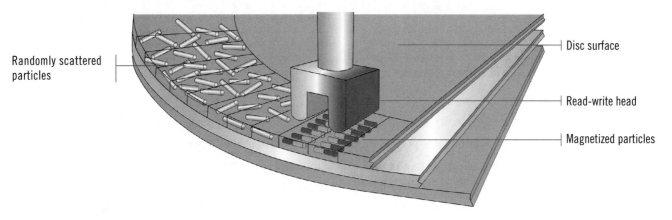

Randomly scattered particles

Disc surface

Read-write head

Magnetized particles

FIGURE B-4: Optical storage

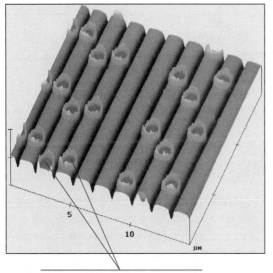

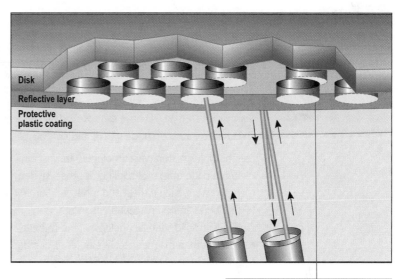

Disk

Reflective layer

Protective plastic coating

The pits on an optical storage disc as seen through an electron microscope; each pit is 1 micron in diameter

When a CD-ROM disc is manufactured, a laser burns pits into a reflective surface; these pits become dark non-reflective areas on the disc

FIGURE B-5: Solid state storage

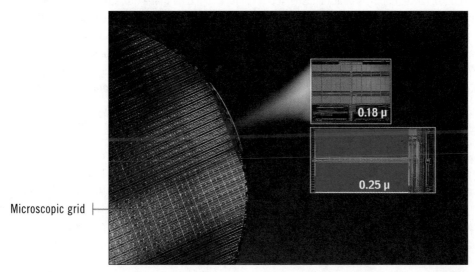

Microscopic grid

0.18 μ

0.25 μ

Comparing storage media and devices

When trying to determine the best storage media for a job, it is useful to apply four criteria: versatility, durability, speed, and capacity. Versatility is the ability of a device and its media to work in more than one way. After storing data using this storage technology, can that data be changed? Durability determines the ability of the device or media to last. How long will it work? How long will the data be accessible? Speed is the time it takes to retrieve or access the data, a factor that is very important in determining how efficiently you work. Finally, capacity is the amount of data each technology can store.

DETAILS

- Versatility. Some storage devices can access data from only one type of medium. More versatile devices can access data from several different media. A floppy disk drive, for example, can access only floppy disks, but a DVD drive can access data DVDs, DVD movies, audio CDs, data CDs, and CD-Rs.

- Durability. Most storage technologies are susceptible to damage from mishandling or other environmental factors, such as heat and moisture. Some technologies are less susceptible than others. Optical and solid state technologies tend to be less susceptible than magnetic technologies to damage that could cause data loss.

- Speed. Not surprisingly, fast storage devices are preferred over slower ones. **Access time** is the average time it takes a computer to locate data on the storage medium and read it. Access time for a personal computer storage device, such as a disk drive, is measured in **milliseconds** (thousandths of a second). Lower numbers indicate faster access times. For example, a drive with a 6 ms access time is faster than a drive with an access time of 11 ms. Random-access devices have the fastest access times.

  Random access (also called "direct access") is the ability of a device to "jump" directly to the requested data. Floppy disk, hard disk, solid state, CD, and DVD drives are random-access devices. A tape drive, on the other hand, must use slower **sequential access**, which reads through the data from the beginning of the tape. The advantage of random access becomes clear when you consider how much faster and easier it is to locate a song on a CD (random access) than on a cassette tape (sequential access).

  Data transfer rate is the amount of data that a storage device can move from the storage medium to the computer per second. Higher numbers indicate faster transfer rates. For example, a CD-ROM drive with a 600 KBps (kilobytes per second) data transfer rate is faster than one with a 300 KBps transfer rate.

- Capacity. **Storage capacity** is the maximum amount of data that can be stored on a storage medium, measured in kilobytes (KB), megabytes (MB), gigabytes (GB), or terabytes (TB). The amount of data that a disk stores—its capacity—depends on its density. **Disk density** refers to the closeness of the data on the disk surface. The higher the disk density, the more data it can store. Higher capacity is almost always preferred. Table B-1 compares the capacity of various storage devices and media.

FYI

Storage media is divided into tracks and then into sectors to create electronic "addressable bins" in which to store data.

Adding storage devices to a computer

Computer users frequently want to upgrade their hard drives to gain capacity or to add CD or DVD drives to make their systems more versatile. The system unit case for a desktop computer contains several storage device "parking spaces" called **drive bays**. See Figure B-6. If you have an empty bay that is the right type and size, you can add a storage device. Bays come in two widths—5 ¼" and 3½". CD and DVD drives require 5¼" bays; a floppy disk drive fits in a 3½" bay. Some drive bays provide access from the outside of the system unit, a necessity for a storage device with removable media, such as floppy disks, CDs, tapes, and DVDs. Internal drive bays are located inside the system unit and are designed for hard disk drives, which don't use removable storage media.

TABLE B-1: Capacities of storage media

DEVICE	CAPACITY	COMMENTS
Floppy disk	1.44 MB	Low capacity means that the disk can hold small files but not large files; not suitable for graphics-intenstive files
SuperDisk	120 MB or 240 MB	SuperDisks are manufactured by Imation; Zip disks are manufactured by Iomega; each holds much more than a floppy; each requires its own proprietary drive; a full system backup requires multiple disks
Zip disk	100 MB, 250 MB, and 750 MB	
Fixed hard disk	80 GB (average)	High storage capacity, fast and convenient, economical storage-cost/megabyte, is susceptible to damage or theft of your computer
External hard drive	80 GB	Fast, but transfer rate depends on computer system; drive can be removed and locked in a secure location
Removable hard disk	2.2 GB (average)	Fast, limited capacity, but disks can be removed and locked in a secure location
CD	700 MB	Limited capacity, can't be reused, long shelf life
CD-RW	700 MB	Limited capacity, reusable
Writable DVD	4.7 GB	Good capacity, standards still in development
Tape	30 GB (average)	Good capacity, reasonable media cost, convenient—you can let backups run overnight, but slow—it can take 15-20 minutes to back up 1 GB of data

FIGURE B-6: Drive bays

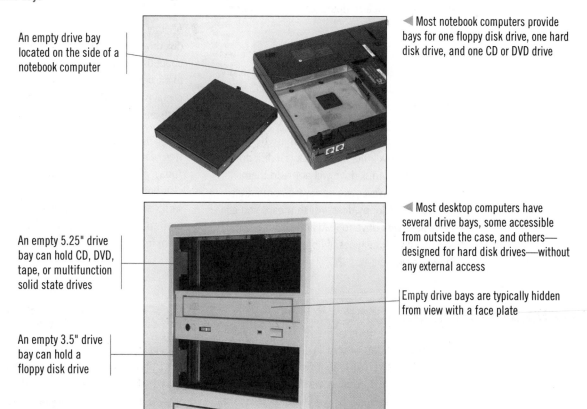

An empty drive bay located on the side of a notebook computer

◀ Most notebook computers provide bays for one floppy disk drive, one hard disk drive, and one CD or DVD drive

An empty 5.25" drive bay can hold CD, DVD, tape, or multifunction solid state drives

An empty 3.5" drive bay can hold a floppy disk drive

◀ Most desktop computers have several drive bays, some accessible from outside the case, and others—designed for hard disk drives—without any external access

Empty drive bays are typically hidden from view with a face plate

Exploring floppy disk technology

A **floppy disk** is a round piece of flexible mylar plastic covered with a thin layer of magnetic oxide and sealed inside a protective casing. If you broke open the disk casing (something you should never do unless you want to ruin the disk), you would see that the mylar disk inside is thin and literally floppy. See Figure B-7. Floppy disks are also referred to as "floppies" or "diskettes." It is not correct to call them "hard disks" even though they seem to have a "hard" or rigid plastic casing.

DETAILS

- Floppy disks provide one type of inexpensive, removable storage for personal computer systems. Floppy disks come in many sizes and capacities. The floppies most commonly used on today's personal computers are 3½" disks with a capacity of 1.44 MB, which means they can store 1,440,000 bytes of data.

- A floppy disk features a **write-protect window**, which is a small square opening that can be covered by a moveable plastic tab on the disk. When you open the window, the disk is "write-protected," which means that a computer cannot write or save data on the disk.

- Two additional storage systems use magnetic technology. **Zip disks**, manufactured by Iomega, are available in 100 MB, 250 MB, and 750 MB versions. **SuperDisks**, manufactured by Imation, have a capacity of 120 MB and 240 MB. Although the increased storage capacity of these types of disks is attractive, they require special disk drives; a standard floppy disk drive will not read them. SuperDisks, however, are backward-compatible with standard floppy disks, which means you can use a SuperDisk drive to read and write to standard floppy disks. Three types of floppy disk drives are shown in Figure B-8.

- The major advantage of floppy disks is their portability. Floppies are still used in many school computer labs so that students can transport their data to different lab machines or to their personal computers.

- A major disadvantage of standard 3½" floppy disks is their relatively low storage capacity. Files that students are creating, such as presentations with graphics and databases, are large. Often, these files will not fit on a 3½" floppy disk, which makes Zip disks, SuperDisks, or CDs that you can read from and write to (called CD-Rs) more attractive.

- Another disadvantage is that a standard 3½" floppy disk drive is not a particularly speedy device. It takes about 0.5 second for the drive to spin the disk up to maximum speed and find a specific sector that contains data. A Zip drive is about 20 times faster, but both are significantly slower than a hard disk drive.

- In the past, floppy disks were extensively used to store data, share files, and distribute software. Today, most software vendors use CDs or DVDs as distribution disks. In addition, local computer networks and the Internet have made it easy to share or distribute files without physically transporting them from one place to another.

What HD DS and HDD mean

Today's floppies are "high-density disks" (HD or HDD). When you see "HD DS" on a box of floppy disks it means "high-density double-sided." Although the storage capacity of a standard floppy disk pales beside that of Zip and SuperDisks, there was a time when floppies stored even less. At one time, floppy disks stored data only on one side. Today, however, most store data on both sides. Read-write heads above and below the disk read both sides so that you don't have to turn the disk over.

FIGURE B-7: A 3½" floppy disk

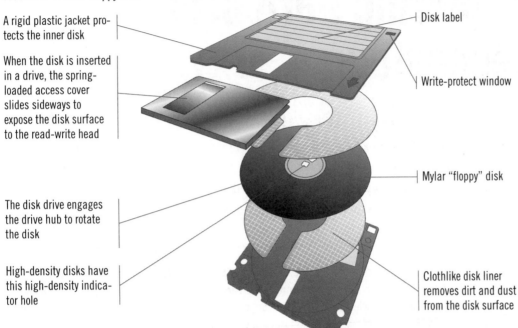

A rigid plastic jacket protects the inner disk

When the disk is inserted in a drive, the spring-loaded access cover slides sideways to expose the disk surface to the read-write head

The disk drive engages the drive hub to rotate the disk

High-density disks have this high-density indicator hole

Disk label

Write-protect window

Mylar "floppy" disk

Clothlike disk liner removes dirt and dust from the disk surface

FIGURE B-8: A floppy disk, a Zip disk, and a SuperDisk

The storage device that records and retrieves data on a floppy disk is a floppy disk drive, shown here with a 3½" floppy disk

A Zip disk requires special disk drives, but is transportable and provides more storage capacity than a floppy disk

A SuperDisk provides an alternative high-capacity, transportable storage option; SuperDisk drives can read standard floppy disks, but a SuperDisk cannot be used in a standard floppy disk drive

Exploring hard disk technology

Hard disk technology is the preferred type of main storage for most computer systems. Hard disks provide more than enough storage capacity for most users and provide faster access to files than floppy disk drives do. In addition, hard disks are more economical than floppy disks. A hard disk typically stores millions of times more data than a floppy disk, but a hard disk drive might cost only three times as much as a floppy disk drive.

DETAILS

● A **hard disk** is one or more platters and their associated read-write heads. A **hard disk platter** is a flat, rigid disk made of aluminum or glass and coated with magnetic iron oxide particles. Personal computer hard disk platters are typically 3½" in diameter. This is the same size as the circular mylar disk in a floppy, but the density of the surface particles on hard disk platters far exceeds that of a floppy disk. The terms "hard disk" and "hard disk drive" are often used interchangeably. The term "fixed disk" is also used to refer to hard disks.

● Hard disk storage capacities of 80 GB and access times of 6 to 11 ms are not uncommon. Computer ads typically specify the capacity and access time of a hard disk drive. So "80 GB 8 ms HD" means a hard disk drive with 80 gigabyte capacity and an access time of 8 milliseconds.

● The access time for a hard disk is significantly faster than that for a floppy disk. Hard disk drive speed is sometimes measured in **revolutions per minute (rpm)**. The faster a drive spins, the more rapidly it can position the read-write head over specific data. For example, a 7,200 rpm drive is able to access data faster than a 5,400 rpm drive.

● Hard disk platters are divided into tracks and sectors into which data is written. You might guess that a hard disk drive would fill one platter before storing data on a second platter. However, it is more efficient to store data at the same track and sector locations on all platters before moving the read-write heads to the next sector. A vertical stack of tracks is called a **cylinder**, which is the basic storage bin for a hard disk drive. Figure B-9 provides more information on how a hard disk drive works.

● A hard drive storage device includes a circuit board, called a **controller**, which positions the disk and read-write heads to locate data. Disk drives are classified according to the type of controller they use. Popular drive controllers include Ultra ATA,

EIDE, and SCSI. **Ultra ATA (AT attachment)** and **EIDE (enhanced integrated drive electronics)** use essentially the same drive technology and feature high storage capacity and fast data transfer. Ultra ATA drives, which are commonly found in today's PCs, are twice as fast as their EIDE counterparts. **SCSI (small computer system interface)** drives provide a slight performance advantage over EIDE drives and are typically found in high-performance workstations and servers.

● The storage technology used on many PCs transfers data from a disk, through the controller, to the processor, and finally to RAM before it is actually processed. **DMA (direct memory access)** technology allows a computer to transfer data directly from a drive into RAM, without intervention from the processor. This architecture relieves the processor of data-transfer duties and frees up processing cycles for other tasks. **UDMA (ultra DMA)** is a faster version of DMA technology. DMA and Ultra ATA are companion technologies. A common storage configuration for PCs pairs an Ultra ATA drive with UDMA data transfer.

● Hard disks are not as durable as many other storage technologies. The read-write heads in a hard disk hover a microscopic distance above the disk surface. If a read-write head runs into a dust particle or some other contaminant on the disk, or if the hard disk is jarred while it is in use, it might cause a **head crash**. A head crash damages some of the data on the disk. To help prevent contaminants from contacting the platters and causing head crashes, a hard disk is sealed in its case.

● Removable hard disks or hard disk cartridges can be inserted and removed from the drive much like floppy disks. Removable hard disks increase the storage capacity of your computer system, although the data is available on only one disk at a time. Removable hard disks also provide security for data by allowing you to remove the hard disk cartridge and store it separately from the computer.

FIGURE B-9: How a hard disk works

The drive spindle supports one or more hard disk platters; both sides of the platter are used for data storage; more platters mean more data storage capacity; hard disk platters rotate as a unit on the spindle to position read-write heads over specific data; the platters spin continuously, making thousands of rotations per minute

▲ Each data storage surface has its own read-write head, which moves in and out from the center of the disk to locate data; the head hovers only a few microinches above the disk surface, so the magnetic field is much more compact than on a floppy disk; as a result, more data is packed into a smaller area on a hard disk platter

Understanding tape storage

Tape is another type of storage technology; it consists of a tape for the storage medium and a tape drive for the storage device. Tape is a sequential, rather than a random-access, storage medium. Data is arranged as a long sequence of bits that begins at one end of the tape and stretches to the other end. As a result, tape access is much slower than hard drive access. In fact, access times for a tape are measured in seconds rather than in milliseconds. A tape may contain hundreds, or in the case of a mainframe, thousands of feet of tape.

The most popular types of tape drives for personal computers use tape cartridges for the storage medium. A **tape cartridge** is a removable magnetic tape module similar to a cassette tape. Figure B-10 shows several different kinds of tape used with personal computer tape drives.

Tape drives are available in either internal or external models. An internal tape drive fits into a standard drive bay. An external model is a standalone device that you can connect to your computer with a cable.

FIGURE B-10

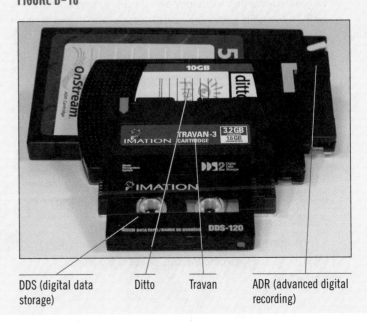

DDS (digital data storage)   Ditto   Travan   ADR (advanced digital recording)

Exploring CD/DVD technology

Optical storage media use one of three technologies: read-only (ROM), recordable, or rewritable. Both **CDs (compact discs)** and **DVDs ("digital video disc" or "digital versatile disc")** use optical storage technologies. The suffix associated with a CD or DVD helps you recognize the type of technology used to create the CD or DVD. The suffixes "ROM," "R," and "RW" denote specific CD and DVD technologies. CD-ROM specifies "read-only" technology, CD-R specifies "CD recordable" technology, and CD-RW specifies "CD rewritable" technology.

Info Web
CD AND DVD

DETAILS

- Optical storage technology provides larger storage capacity than floppy disks, solid state media, Zip disks, or SuperDisks. Standard CD capacity is 700 MB of data. The current capacity of a DVD is about 4.7 GB (4,700 MB).

- **CD drives** and **DVD drives** are storage devices that use laser technology to read data on computer or audio CDs or DVDs respectively. Figure B-11 shows how to place a CD in a CD drive. Figure B-12 illustrates how a CD-ROM drive uses laser technology to read data. CD and DVD drives contain a spindle that rotates the disc over a laser lens. The laser directs a beam of light toward the underside of the disc. Dark "pits" and light "lands" on the disc surface reflect the light differently. As the drive reads the disc, these differences are translated into the 0s and 1s that represent data.

  Most CD drives can read CD-ROM, CD-R, and CD-RW discs. Most DVD drives can read CD and DVD formats. Storing computer data and creating music CDs requires a recordable or rewritable device. As you can see from Table B-2, the most versatile optical storage device is a DVD+R/+RW/CD-RW combo.

- **Read-only (ROM) technology.** A computer CD-ROM or DVD disc contains data that was stamped on the disc surface when it was manufactured, such as commercial software, music, and movies. Examples of CDs and DVDs using read-only optical technology follow:

  CD-DA (compact disc digital audio) is the format for commercial music CDs. Music is typically recorded on audio CDs by the manufacturer.

  DVD-Video (digital versatile disc video) is the format for commercial DVDs that contain feature-length films.

  CD-ROM (compact disc read-only memory) was the original format for storing computer data. Data is stamped on the disc at the time it is manufactured.

  DVD-ROM (digital versatile disc read-only memory) contains data stamped onto the disc surface at the time of manufacture.

For all of these examples, data cannot be added, changed, or deleted from these discs.

- **Recordable technology (R)** uses a laser to change the color in a dye layer sandwiched beneath the clear plastic disc surface. The laser creates dark spots in the dye that are read as pits. The change in the dye is permanent, so data cannot be changed once it has been recorded. Usually, you can record your data in multiple sessions, that is, you add two files to your CD-R disc today and then add more files to thse same disc tomorrow. Examples of CDs and DVDs using recordable optical technology follow:

  CD-R (compact disc recordable) discs store data using recordable technology. The data on a CD-R cannot be erased or modified once you record it. However, most CD-R drives allow you to record your data in multiple sessions.

  DVD+R (digital versatile disc recordable) discs store data using recordable technology similar to a CD-R, but with DVD storage capacity.

- **Rewritable technology (RW)** uses "phase change" technology to alter a crystal structure on the disc surface. Altering the crystal structure creates patterns of light and dark spots similar to the pits and lands on a CD. The crystal structure can be changed from light to dark and back again many times, making it possible to record and modify data much like on a hard disk. Examples of CDs and DVDs using rewritable optical technology follow:

  CD-RW (compact disc rewritable) discs store data using rewritable technology. Stored data can be recorded and erased multiple times, making it a very flexible storage option.

  DVD+RW (digital versatile disc rewritable) discs store data using rewritable technology similar to CD-RW, but with DVD storage capacity.

- A rewritable CD or DVD drive is not a good replacement for a hard disk drive. The process of accessing, saving, and modifying data on a rewritable disc is relatively slow compared to the speed of hard disk access.

FIGURE B-11: Inserting a CD-ROM

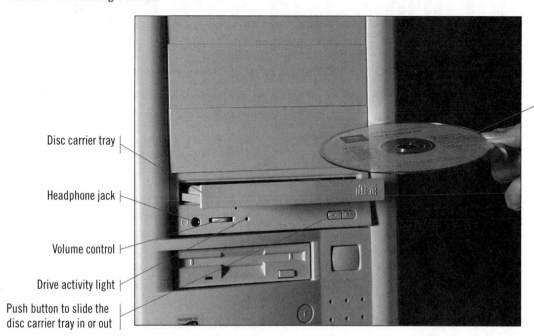

Disc carrier tray

Headphone jack

Volume control

Drive activity light

Push button to slide the disc carrier tray in or out

Data is stored on the bottom of a CD-ROM disc in one continuous track that spirals out from the center of the disc; the track is divided into equal-length sectors; the printed side of the disc does not contain data; it should be face up when you insert the disc because the lasers read the bottom of the disc

FIGURE B-12: How a CD-ROM drive works

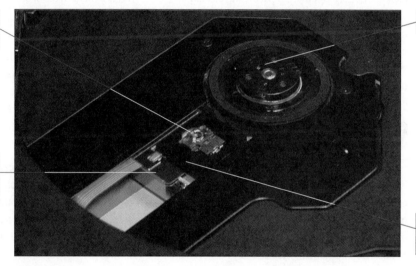

Laser lens directs a beam of light to the underside of the CD-ROM disc

Tracking mechanism positions a disc track over the laser lens

Drive spindle spins the disc

Laser pickup assembly senses the reflectivity of pits and lands

TABLE B-2: CD and DVD drive capabilities

	PLAY AUDIO CDS	PLAY DVD MOVIES	READ CD DATA	READ DVD DATA	CREATE MUSIC CDS	STORE DATA ON CDS	STORE DATA ON DVDS
CD-ROM drive	X		X				
CD-R drive	X		X		X	X	
CD-RW drive	X		X		X	X	
DVD/CD-RW drive	X	X	X	X	X	X	
DVD+R/+RW/CD-RW drive	X	X	X	X	X	X	X

Exploring solid state storage

Solid state storage is portable, provides fast access to data, and uses very little power. It is an ideal solution for storing data on mobile devices and transporting data from one device to another. Solid state storage is widely used in consumer devices, such as digital cameras, MP3 music players, notebook computers, PDAs, and cell phones.

DETAILS

● A variety of compact storage cards can be classified as solid state storage, which stores data in a non-volatile, erasable, low-power chip. The chip's circuitry is arranged as a grid, and each cell in the grid contains two transistors that act as gates. When the gates are open, current can flow and the cell has a value that represents a "1" bit. When the gates are closed, the cell has a value that represents a "0" bit. Very little power is required to open or close the gates, which makes solid state storage ideal for battery-operated devices, such as digital cameras. Once the data is stored, it is non-volatile—the chip retains the data without the need for an external power source. Some solid state storage requires a device called a **card reader** to transfer data to or from a computer; others plug directly into a computer's system unit.

● Consumers today can select from a variety of solid state storage media. See Figure B-13.

A **USB flash drive**, such as Sony's MicroVault, is a portable storage device featuring a built-in connector that plugs directly into a computer's USB port. A USB flash drive requires no card reader, making it easily transportable from one computer to another. Nicknamed "pen drives" or "keychain drives," USB flash drives are about the size of a highlighter pen and so durable that you can literally carry them on your key ring. When connected to your computer's USB port, you can open, edit, delete, and run files stored on a USB flash drive just as though those files were stored on your computer's hard disk.

CompactFlash (CF) cards are about the size of a matchbook and provide high storage capacities and access speeds. CompactFlash cards include a built-in controller that reads and writes data within the solid state grid. The built-in controller removes the need for control electronics on the card reader, so the device that connects to your computer to read the card's data is simply an adapter that collects data from the card and shuttles it to the computer's system unit. With their high storage capacities and access speeds, CompactFlash cards are ideal for use on high-end digital cameras that require megabytes of storage for each photo.

MultiMedia cards (MMC) offer solid state storage in a package about the size of a postage stamp. Initially used in mobile phones and pagers, use of MultiMedia cards has spread to digital cameras and MP3 players. Like CompactFlash cards, MultiMedia cards include a built-in controller, so MMC readers are electronically simple and very inexpensive.

SecureDigital (SD) cards are based on MultiMedia card technology, but feature significantly faster data transfer rates and include cryptographic security protection for copyrighted data and music. SecureDigital cards are popular for MP3 storage.

SmartMedia cards were originally called "solid state floppy disk cards" because they look much like a miniature floppy disk. Unlike other popular solid state storage, SmartMedia cards do not include a built-in controller, which means that the SmartMedia reader manages the read/write process. These cards are the least durable of the solid state storage media and should be handled with care.

FIGURE B-13: Popular solid state storage options

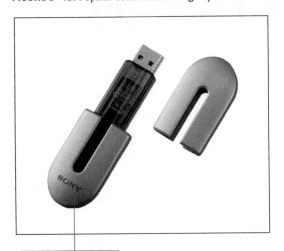

Sony's MicroVault USB
flash drive: 32-512 MB
capacities

CompactFlash card:
8 MB-1 GB capacities

MultiMedia card:
32-256 MB capacities

SecureDigital card:
32 MB-1 GB capacities

SmartMedia card:
32-128 MB capacities

Why use solid state storage?

A solid state memory card in a digital camera can hold data for hundreds of snap-shots. You can remove the card from the camera and insert it into a card reader that's connected to a computer. Once the card is connected to your computer, you can transfer the files to your hard drive so the photos can be edited using the computer's graphics software and transmitted via the computer's Internet connection. Or, moving data the other way, you can download MP3 music files and store them on a solid state memory card. Then you can insert the card into a portable MP3 player so you can hear your favorite tunes while you're on the go. Solid state storage is also ideal for portable computing, that is, transporting data from one computer to another. For example, you can transfer data from your home computer to a solid state storage media and then bring that storage media to a computer in your school lab or your workplace. Whether you are using the solid state memory card with a camera, an MP3 player, or for some other portable computing needs, the data on the memory card can be erased so the card can be reused.

Examining input devices

Most computer systems include a keyboard and pointing device as the primary input devices for basic data input. Although you don't have to be a great typist to use a computer effectively, you should be familiar with the computer keyboard and its special keys. The most popular pointing devices for personal computers include mice, trackballs, pointing sticks, trackpads, and joysticks. Using a pointing device requires some practice in order to become skillful.

DETAILS

● Most computers are equipped with a keyboard. You can even find keyboards on handheld devices—entering text and numbers is an important part of most computing tasks. A computer keyboard includes the basic **typing keypad** with keys or buttons with letters and numbers as well as several keys with characters and special words to control computer-specific tasks. You use the keys to input commands, respond to prompts, and type the text of documents. Figure B-14 illustrates a variety of keyboards you might encounter on various computing devices. Virtually every computer user interface requires you to use a keyboard.

In addition to the basic typing keypad, desktop and notebook computer keyboards include a **navigation keypad** with keys such as the Home, End, and arrow keys, which you can use to efficiently move the screen-based insertion point or cursor. An **insertion point** (or **cursor**) indicates where the characters you type will appear. The insertion point appears on the screen as a flashing vertical bar. The cursor appears on the screen as a flashing underline. You can change the location of the cursor or insertion point using the arrow keys or the mouse.

Function keys at the top of many keyboards are designed for computer-specific tasks. For example, [F1] often opens a Help window. Most desktop computer keyboards also include a calculator-style **numeric keypad**.

Modifier keys, the [Ctrl], [Alt], and [Shift] keys are located at the periphery of the typing keypad. You can use the [Ctrl], [Alt], and [Shift] keys in conjunction with the other keys on the keyboard to expand the repertoire of available commands. Instead of using the mouse, you might use the [Alt] or [Ctrl] key in combination with letter keys to access menu options. Such combinations are called **keyboard shortcuts**.

● A **pointing device** allows you to manipulate an on-screen pointer and other screen-based graphical controls. A standard desktop computer includes a mouse as its primary pointing device. Many computer owners also add a mouse to their notebook computers. A **mouse** includes one or more buttons that can be "clicked" to input commands. To track its position, a mouse uses one of two technologies: mechanical or optical. See Figure B-15. Most computer owners prefer the performance of an optical mouse because it provides more precise tracking, greater durability, less maintenance, and more flexibility to use the mouse on a wide variety of surfaces without a mouse pad.

● Pointing sticks, trackpads, and trackballs are typically used with notebook computers as an alternative to a mouse. See Figure B-16. A **pointing stick**, or **TrackPoint**, looks like the tip of an eraser embedded in the keyboard of a notebook computer. It is a space-saving device that you can push up, down, or sideways to move the on-screen pointer. A **trackpad** is a touch-sensitive surface on which you can slide your fingers to move the on-screen pointer. A **trackball** looks like a mechanical mouse turned upside down. You use your fingers or palm to roll the ball and move the pointer.

A joystick looks like a small version of a car's stick shift. Moving the stick provides input to on-screen objects, such as a pointer or a character in a computer game. Joysticks, can include several sticks and buttons for arcade-like control when playing computer games.

● Additional input devices, such as scanners, digital cameras, and graphics tablets, are handy for working with graphical input. Microphones and electronic instruments provide input capabilities for sound and music.

FIGURE B-14: Computer keyboards

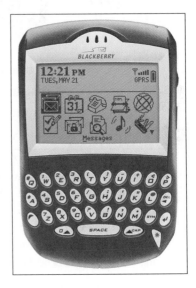

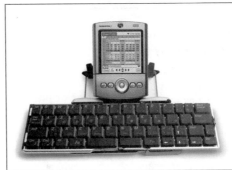

FIGURE B-15: Mechanical and optical mice

◄ A mechanical mouse (left) reads its position based on the movement of a ball that rolls over a mouse pad placed on a desk; an optical mouse (right) uses an onboard chip to track a light beam as it bounces off a surface, such as a desk, clipboard, or mouse pad

FIGURE B-16: Alternative pointing devices

Pointing stick   Trackpad   Trackball   Joystick

Comparing display devices

DISPLAY DEVICES

A computer display system is the main output device for a computer. Two key components of a computer display system are a graphics card and a display device, such as a monitor or screen. Display devices use one of three technologies: CRT, LCD, and gas plasma. See Figure B-17.

DETAILS

- For many years, CRT monitors were the only display devices available for desktop computers. **CRT (cathode ray tube)** technology uses gun-like mechanisms to direct beams of electrons toward the screen and activate individual dots of color that form an image—much like a color TV. CRT monitors offer an inexpensive and dependable computer display.

- Today, an alternative to CRT monitors, are LCD monitors. **LCD (liquid crystal display)** technology produces an image by manipulating light within a layer of liquid crystal cells. LCDs are standard equipment on notebook computers. The advantages of an LCD monitor include display clarity, low radiation emission, portability, and compactness. Standalone LCDs, referred to as "LCD monitors" or "flat panel displays," are available for desktop computers as a replacement for CRT monitors. They are, however, more expensive than CRT monitors.

- A third display device technology is used in gas plasma screens. **Plasma screen technology** creates an on-screen image by illuminating miniature colored fluorescent lights arrayed in a panel-like screen. The name "plasma" comes from the type of gas that fills fluorescent lights and gives them their luminescence. Like LCD screens, plasma screens are compact, light-weight, and more expensive than CRT monitors.

- Image quality is determined by screen size, dot pitch, resolution, and color depth. **Screen size** is the measurement in inches from one corner of the screen diagonally across to the opposite corner. Typical monitor screen sizes range from 13" to 21". On most monitors, the viewable image does not stretch to the edge of the screen. Instead, a black border makes the viewing area smaller than the screen size. Many computer ads include a measurement of the **viewable image size (vis)**. For example, a 15" monitor might have an approximately 13.9" vis.

  A monitor's **viewing angle width** indicates how far to the side you can still clearly see the screen image. A wide viewing angle indicates that you can view the screen from various positions

without compromising image quality. CRT and plasma screens offer the widest viewing angles. Graphics artists tend to prefer CRT screens, which display uniform color from any angle.

- **Dot pitch (dp)** is a measure of image clarity. A smaller dot pitch means a crisper image. Technically, dot pitch is the distance in millimeters between like-colored pixels, the small dots of light that form an image. A dot pitch between .26 and .23 is typical for today's monitors.

- The computer's graphics card sends an image to the monitor at a specific **resolution**, defined as the maximum number of horizontal and vertical pixels that are displayed on the screen. Standard resolutions include 800 × 600 and 1024 × 768. Even higher resolutions, such as 1600 × 1200, are possible given enough memory on the graphics card and a monitor capable of displaying that resolution. At higher resolutions, the computer displays a larger work area, such as an entire page of a document, but text and other objects appear smaller. The two screen shots in Figure B-18 help you compare a display at 800 × 600 resolution with a display at 1024 × 768 resolution.

- The number of colors that a monitor and graphics card can display is referred to as **color depth** or "**bit depth**." Most PCs have the capability to display millions of colors. When you set the resolution at 24-bit color depth (sometimes called "True Color"), your PC can display more than 16 million colors and produce what are considered photographic-quality images. Windows allows you to select resolution and color depth.

- Although you can set the color depth and resolution of your notebook computer display, you might not have as many options as you do with a desktop computer. Typically, the graphics card circuitry is built into the motherboard of a notebook computer, making it difficult to upgrade and gain more video memory for additional resolution and color depth.

FIGURE B-17: Display device technology options

CRT

LCD

Gas Plasma

FIGURE B-18: Comparing screen resolutions

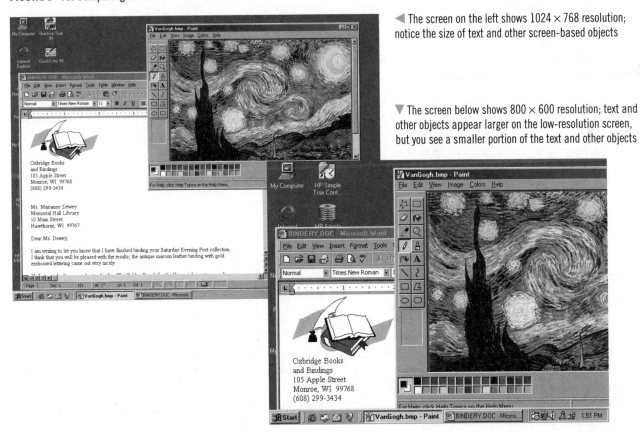

◀ The screen on the left shows 1024 × 768 resolution; notice the size of text and other screen-based objects

▼ The screen below shows 800 × 600 resolution; text and other objects appear larger on the low-resolution screen, but you see a smaller portion of the text and other objects

Graphics cards

A **graphics card** (also called a "graphics board" or a "video card") contains circuitry that generates the signals for displaying an image on the screen. It also contains special video memory, which stores screen images as they are processed before they are displayed. The amount of video memory is the key to how fast a screen updates for fast action games, 3-D modeling, and graphics-intensive desktop publishing. In addition to video memory, most graphics cards contain special graphics accelerator technology to further boost performance. Graphics circuitry can be built into a computer's motherboard or supplied as a small circuit board, like the one in Figure B-19, that plugs into the motherboard.

FIGURE B-19: A PC graphics card

Comparing printers

Printers are one of the most popular output devices available for personal computers. Printers differ in resolution and speed, both of which affect the print quality and price. Today's best-selling printers typically use ink jet or laser technology. Printer technologies for specialized applications include dot matrix, solid ink, thermal transfer, and dye sublimation.

DETAILS

● The quality or sharpness of printed images and text depends on the printer's resolution, the density of the grid of dots that create an image. Printer resolution is measured by the number of dots it can print per linear inch, abbreviated as **dpi**. At normal reading distance, a resolution of about 900 dots per inch appears solid to the human eye, but a close examination of color sections will reveal a dot pattern. Expensive coffee-table books are typically produced on printers with 2,400 dpi or higher.

● Printer speeds are measured either by pages per minute (ppm) or characters per second (cps). Color printouts typically take longer than black-and-white printouts. Pages that contain mostly text tend to print more rapidly than pages that contain graphics. Ten pages per minute is a typical speed for a personal computer printer.

● In addition to printer speed, a printer's **duty cycle** determines how many pages a printer is able to churn out. Printer duty cycle is usually measured in pages per month. For example, a personal laser printer has a duty cycle of about 3,000 pages per month (ppm)—that means roughly 100 pages per day.

● Ink jet printers outsell all of the others because most ink jet printers are small, lightweight, and inexpensive, yet produce very good quality color output. An **ink jet printer** has a nozzle-like print head that sprays ink onto paper to form characters and graphics. You must periodically replace the black ink cartridge and a second cartridge that carries the colored inks. See Figure B-20. Ink jet printers have excellent resolution, which can range from 600 dpi to 2,880 dpi, depending on the model.

● A **laser printer** (see Figure B-21) uses the same technology as a photocopier to produce dots of light on a light-sensitive drum. Personal laser printers produce six to eight ppm (pages per minute) at a resolution of 600 dpi. Professional models pump out 15 to 25 ppm at 1,200 dpi. Laser printers are a popular technology for situations that require high-volume output or good-quality printouts.

● When PCs first began to appear in the late 1970s, dot matrix printers were the technology of choice, and they are still available today. A **dot matrix printer** (see Figure B-22) produces characters and graphics by using a grid of fine wires. A fast dot

matrix device can print at speeds up to 455 cps or about five pages per minute. Unlike laser and ink-jet technologies, a dot matrix printer actually strikes the paper and, therefore, can print multipart carbon forms. Today dot matrix printers are used primarily for "back-office" applications that demand low operating cost and dependability but not high print quality.

● A **solid ink printer** melts sticks of crayon-like ink and then sprays the liquefied ink through the print head's tiny nozzles. The ink solidifies before the paper can absorb it, and a pair of rollers finishes fusing the ink onto the paper. A solid ink printer produces vibrant colors on most types of paper and is used for professional graphics applications.

● A **thermal transfer printer** uses a page-sized ribbon that is coated with cyan, magenta, yellow, and black wax. The print head consists of thousands of tiny heating elements that melt the wax onto specially coated paper or transparency film (the kind used for overhead projectors). This type of printer excels at printing colorful transparencies for presentations, but the fairly expensive per-page costs and the requirement for special paper make this a niche market printer that is used mainly by businesses.

● A **dye sublimation printer** uses technology similar to wax transfer. The difference is that the page-sized ribbon contains dye instead of colored wax. Heating elements in the print head diffuse the dye onto the surface of specially coated paper. Dye sublimation printers produce excellent color quality. The high per page cost, however, makes these printers too pricey for the average consumer.

● A large memory capacity is required to print color images and graphics-intensive documents. For example, a laser printer might have between 2 MB and 32 MB of memory. Some printers accept additional memory, if you find that your printer requires more memory for the types of document you typically print.

● A computer sends data for a printout to the printer along with a set of instructions on how to print that data. **Printer Control Language (PCL)** is the most widely used language for communication between computers and printers, but **PostScript** is an alternative printer language that many publishing professionals prefer.

FIGURE B-20: Ink jet printer

▶ Most ink jet printers use **CMYK color**, which requires only cyan (blue), magenta (pink), yellow, and black inks to create a printout that appears to have thousands of colors

FIGURE B-21: Laser printer

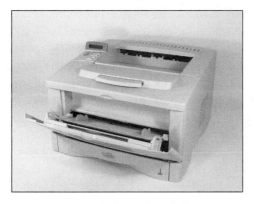

▲ Laser printers are a popular technology when high-volume output or good-quality printouts are required; electrostatically charged ink is applied to the drum, then transferred to paper

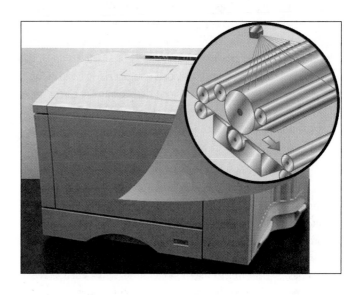

FIGURE B- 22: Dot matrix printer

▲ Dot matrix printers can print text and graphics; some even print in color using a multicolored ribbon; with a resolution of 140 dpi, a dot matrix printer produces low-quality output with clearly discernible dots forming letters and graphics

Print head contains a matrix of thin wires

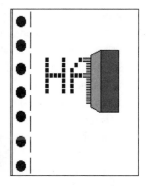

▲ As the print head moves across the paper, the wires strike the ribbon and paper in a pattern prescribed by your PC

Understanding expansion slots, cards, and ports

Within a computer, data travels from one component to another over circuits called a **data bus**. One part of the data bus runs between RAM and the microprocessor; the other part runs between RAM and various storage devices. The segment of the data bus between RAM and peripheral devices is called the **expansion bus**. As data moves along the expansion bus, it may travel through expansion slots, cards, ports, and cables. This lesson takes a closer look at slots, cards, and ports; the next lesson looks at cables.

DETAILS

- An **expansion slot** is a long, narrow socket on the motherboard into which you can plug an expansion card. The motherboard is the main board in the computer that holds the components that control the processing functions. An **expansion card** is a small circuit board that provides a computer the ability to control a storage device, an input device, or an output device. Expansion cards are also called "expansion boards," "controller cards," or "adapters." To insert an expansion card, you slide it into an expansion slot, where it can be secured with a small screw. See Figure B-23.

- Most desktop computers have four to eight expansion slots, but some of the slots usually contain factory installed expansion cards. A graphics card (sometimes called a "video card") provides a path for data traveling to the monitor. A **modem card** provides a way to transmit data over phone lines or cable television lines. A **sound card** carries data out to speakers and headphones, or back from a microphone. A **network card** allows you to connect your computer to a local area network. You might add other expansion cards if you want to connect a scanner or download videos from a camera or VCR.

- A desktop computer may have up to three types of expansion slots. Each expansion card is built for only one type of slot. ISA, PCI, and AGP slots are different lengths so you can easily identify them by opening your computer's system unit and looking at the motherboard. See Figure B-24. **ISA (industry standard architecture)** slots are an old technology, used today only for some modems and other relatively slow devices. **PCI (peripheral component interconnect)** slots offer fast transfer speeds and a 32-bit or 64-bit data bus. This type of slot typically houses a graphics card, sound card, video capture card, modem, or network interface card. **AGP (accelerated graphics port)** slots provide a high-speed data pathway that is primarily used for graphics cards.

- Most notebook computers are equipped with a special type of external slot called a **PCMCIA slot (personal computer memory card international association)**. Typically, a notebook computer has only one of these slots, but the slot can hold more than one PC card (also called "PCMCIA expansion cards" or "Card Bus cards"). PCMCIA slots are classified according to their thickness. Type 1 slots accept only the thinnest PC cards, such as memory expansion cards. Type II slots accept most of the popular PC cards such as those that contain modems, sound cards, and network cards. Type III slots commonly included with today's notebook computers accept the thickest PC cards, which contain devices such as hard disk drives. A Type III slot can also hold two Type 1 cards, two Type II cards, or a Type 1 and a Type II card. Figure B-25 shows a PCMCIA slot and a PC card.

- An **expansion port** is any connector that passes data in and out of a computer or peripheral device. See Figure B-26. Ports are sometimes called "jacks" or "connectors," but the terminology is inconsistent. An expansion port is often housed on an expansion card so that it is accessible through an opening in the back of the computer's system unit. A port might also be built into the system unit case of a desktop or notebook computer. The built-in ports on a computer usually include a mouse port, keyboard port, serial port, and USB port. Ports that have been added with expansion cards usually protrude through rectangular cutouts in the back of the case.

- USB ports are probably the most popular ports for connecting peripheral devices. Most computers feature several USB ports, which provide connectivity for lots of USB devices. On many computer models USB ports are conveniently located on the front of the system unit so that peripherals can be easily connected and disconnected. Many kinds of peripheral devices—including mice, scanners, and joysticks—are available with USB connections. Several types of storage devices, such as USB Flash drives, also use USB connections. Windows automatically recognizes most USB devices, which makes installation simple.

FIGURE B-23: Inserting an expansion card

FIGURE B-24: Types of expansion slots

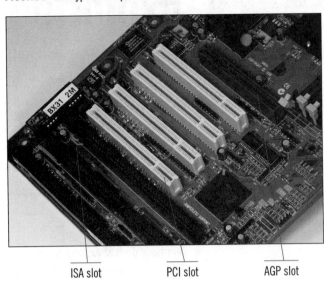

ISA slot   PCI slot   AGP slot

FIGURE B-25: PC card for a notebook computer

PC card

FIGURE B-26: Expansion ports on a typical desktop computer

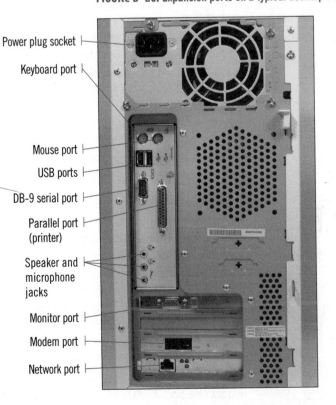

Power plug socket

Keyboard port

Mouse port

USB ports

DB-9 serial port

Parallel port
(printer)

Speaker and
microphone
jacks

Monitor port

Modem port

Network port

Exploring peripheral devices

All computers use peripheral devices to input, output, and store data. **Peripheral devices** are equipment that you connect to the computer to enhance its functionality. They are hardware components that are "outside," or in addition to, the main computer. They are connected to the main computer through the use of expansion slots, cards, ports, and cables.

DETAILS

- Peripheral devices expand and modify your system. Although the keyboard, printer, monitor, disk drives, and mouse can be considered peripheral devices, most people do not consider them to be peripheral devices because they are necessary to perform basic computer functions. Figure B-27 shows examples of several peripheral devices. A **computer projection device** is an output device that produces a large display of the information shown on the computer screen. A **scanner** is an input device that converts a page of text or images just into a digital format. **Multifunction devices** work both as input and output devices to combine the functions of a printer, scanner, copier, fax, and answering machine. A **digital camera** is an input device that records an image in digital format. A **graphics tablet** is an input device that accepts input from a pressure-sensitive stylus and converts strokes into images on the screen. A **Web cam** is an input device used to capture live video and transmit it over the Internet. A trackball and **joystick** are pointing devices that you use as alternative input devices to a mouse. TrackPoints and touchpads are alternative input devices often found on notebook computers.

- In order for a peripheral device to work, a connection must be made between it and the motherboard, often the connection is made using a cable. To install a peripherial device, you must match the peripheral device and a port on the computer. If the right type of port is not available, you might have to add an expansion card. Figure B-28 describes the cable connectors you might need in order to connect a peripheral device to your PC. If a cable is supplied with a peripheral device, you can usually figure out where to plug it in by matching the shape of the cable connector to the port. If you need to purchase a cable, be sure the cable matches the available ports.

- Remember, when you install a peripheral device, you are basically creating a connection for data to flow between the device and the computer. The installation might simply require connecting a cable, or it might require installing an expansion card. If you own a desktop computer, you might have to open the system unit. Before doing so, make sure you unplug the computer and ground yourself—that means that you are releasing static electricity by using a special grounding wristband or by touching both hands to a metal object before opening the system unit.

- Today's PCs include a feature called **Plug and Play** (also known as **PnP**) that automatically takes care of technical details for installing just about every popular peripheral device. Once the peripheral device is connected to the motherboard, PnP should recognize the new device. If not, you'll probably have to install device driver software.

- Each peripheral device requires software called a **device driver** to set up communication between your computer and the device. The directions supplied with your new peripheral device will include instructions on how to install the device driver if it does not happen automatically with PnP. Typically, you'll use the device driver disk or CD once to get everything set up, then you can put the disk away. Be sure to keep the driver disk or CD in a safe place, however, because if you ever need to restore your computer or reinstall the device, you may need to install the driver again. If the peripheral device still doesn't work, check the manufacturer's Web site for a device driver update, or call the manufacturer's technical support department.

FIGURE B-27: Examples of peripheral devices

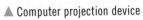
▲ Computer projection device

▲ Scanner

▲ Multifunction device

▲ Digital camera

▲ Graphics tablet

▲ Web cam

FIGURE B-28: Personal computer cables and connectors

	CONNECTOR	DESCRIPTION	DEVICES
	Serial DB-9	Connects to serial port, which sends data over a single data line one bit at a time at speeds of 56 Kbps	Mouse or modem
	Parallel DB-25M	Connects to parallel port, which sends data simultaneously over 8 data lines at speeds of 12,000 Kbps	Printer, external CD drive, Zip drive, external hard disk drive, or tape backup device
	USB	Connects to universal serial bus (USB), which sends data over a single data line and can support up to 127 devices. USB-1 carries data at speeds up to 12,000 Kbps; USB-2, at 480,000 Kbps	Modem, keyboard, joystick, scanner, mouse, external hard disk drive, MP3 player
	SCSI C-50F	Connects to SCSI port, which sends data simultaneously over 8 or 16 data lines at speeds between 40,000 Kbps and 640,000 Kbps; supports up to 16 devices	Internal or external hard disk drive, scanner, CD drive, tape backup device
	IEEE 1394	Connects to the FireWire port, which sends data at 400,000 Kbps	Video camera, DVD player
	VGA HDB-15	Connects to the video port	Monitor

The Windows Registry

To many computer owners, the Windows Registry is simply a mysterious "black box" that is mentioned occasionally in articles about computer troubleshooting. It is certainly possible to use a computer without intimate knowledge of the Registry, but it is useful to understand that the Registry is the "glue" that binds together many of the most important components of a PC: the computer hardware, peripheral devices, application software, and system software. See Figure B-29. After reading this Tech Talk section, you should have a basic understanding of the Registry and its role in the operation of a computer system.

Why does a PC need the Registry? You know that you use application software to direct the operations that a computer carries out. For some operations, particularly those that involve hardware, the application software communicates with the operating system. The operating system might communicate with device drivers or, in some cases, it can communicate directly with a peripheral device.

In order to act as an intermediary between software and peripheral devices, your operating system needs information about these components: where they are located, what's been installed, how they are configured, and how you want to use them. A special type of memory called **CMOS memory** holds the most essential data about your computer's processing and storage hardware, but the **Windows Registry** keeps track of your computer's peripheral devices and software so that the operating system can access the information it needs to coordinate the activities of the entire computer system. Some examples of specific data that the Registry tracks include your preferences for desktop colors, icons, pointers, shortcuts, and display resolution; the sounds that are assigned to various system events, such as clicking and shutting down; the capability of your CD-ROM drive for playing audio CDs and autorunning computer CDs; the options that appear on a shortcut menu when you right-click an object; your computer's network card settings and protocols; and the location of the uninstall routines for all installed hardware and software.

FIGURE B-29: Items tracked by the Windows Registry

User preferences for desktop colors, icons, pointers, short-cuts, and display resolution

Sounds that are assigned to various system events, such as clicking and shutting down

The capability of your CD-ROM drive for playing audio CDs and autorunning computer CDs

The options that appear on a shortcut menu when you right-click an object

The computer's network card settings and protocols

The location of the uninstall routines for all installed software.

The contents of the Registry are stored in multiple files in the Windows/System folder of your computer's hard disk and are combined into a single database when Windows starts. Although each version of Windows uses a slightly different storage scheme, the basic organization and function of the Registry is similar in all versions.

Windows stores the entire contents of the Registry in two files: System.dat and User.dat. System.dat includes configuration data for all the hardware and software installed on a computer. User.dat contains user-specific information, sometimes called a "user profile," which includes software settings and desktop settings.

The Registry has a logical structure that appears as a hierarchy of folders, as shown in Figure B-30. There are six main folders in the Registry, and their names begin with HKEY. Each folder contains data that pertains to a particular part of a computer system.

You indirectly change the Registry whenever you install or remove hardware or software. Device drivers and the Windows Plug and Play feature automatically update the Registry with essential information about the hardware's location and configuration. The setup program for your software provides similar update services for newly installed software.

You can also make changes to the Windows Registry by using the dialog boxes for various configuration routines provided by the operating system and application software. For example, if you want to change the desktop colors for your user profile, you can do so by selecting the Settings option from the Start menu, clicking Control Panel, and then selecting the Display option. Any changes that you make to the settings in the Display Properties dialog box (Figure B-31) will be recorded in the Windows Registry.

FIGURE B-30: The Windows Registry is organized as a hierarchy of folders and files

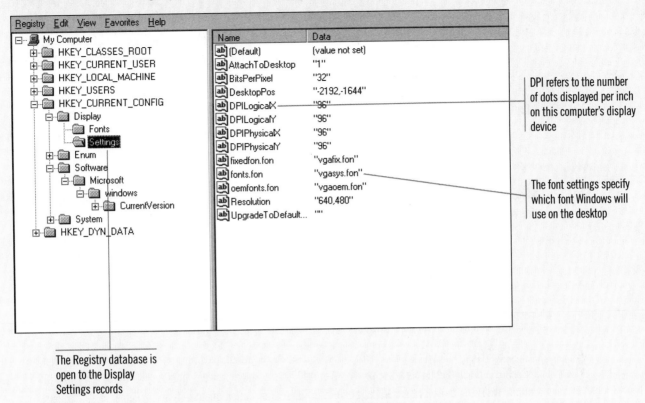

DPI refers to the number of dots displayed per inch on this computer's display device

The font settings specify which font Windows will use on the desktop

The Registry database is open to the Display Settings records

FIGURE B-31: Changes that you make when using the Display Properties dialog box automatically update the corresponding entries in the HKEY_CURRENT_CONFIG folder of the Registry

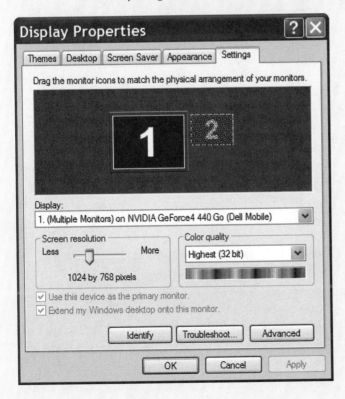

The military, an early pioneer in computer and communication technologies (see Figure B-32), continues to be the driving force behind technologies that have revolutionized everyday life. During World War II, the U.S. military initiated a classified research program, called Project PX, to develop an electronic device to calculate artillery firing tables; each table required weeks of grueling manual calculations. Project PX produced ENIAC (Electrical Numerical Integrator And Calculator), one of the first general-purpose electronic computers. When ENIAC was completed in 1946, the war was over, but ENIAC's versatile architecture could be used for other calculations, such as designing hydrogen bombs, predicting weather, and engineering wind tunnels. ENIAC's technology evolved into the computers used today.

After Project PX, the military continued to support computer research. Like most large corporations, the military used mainframe computers to maintain personnel, inventory, supply, and facilities records and distributed this data to terminals at other locations via rudimentary networks. Because all data communication flowed through the mainframe, a single point of failure for the entire system was a possible risk. A malfunction or an enemy "hit" could disrupt command and control, sending the military into chaos. To eliminate this risk, the armed forces created the Advanced Research Projects Agency (ARPA) to design a distributed communications system that could continue operating without a centralized computer. The result was ARPANET, which paved the way for the data communications system we know today as the Internet.

The U.S. Department of Defense (DoD) currently maintains two data communications networks: SIPRNet, which is a classified (secret-level) network and NIPRNet, which provides unclassified services. The DoD's public Web site, called DefenseLINK, provides official information about defense policies, organizations, budgets, and operations.

Computers and communications technology have also become an integral part of high-tech military operations (see Figure B-33). U.S. Apache helicopters, for example, are equipped with computer-based Target Acquisition Designation Sights, laser range finder/designators, and Pilot Night Vision Sensors. These arcade-style controls are also used by tank drivers in the U.S. Army's 4th Infantry Division. Each vehicle in this "Digitized Division" is equipped with a Force 21 Battle Command Brigade and Below system, which works like a battlefield Internet to transmit data from one vehicle to another using wireless communication regarding the location of friendly and enemy forces.

FIGURE B-32

Much like a video game, the Force 21 touch screen shows friendly troops in blue, and a global positioning satellite (GPS) system updates their positions automatically. Enemy troops spotted by helicopters are shown as red icons. To get information on any friendly or enemy vehicle, a soldier can simply touch one of these blue or red icons. To send text messages—much like cell phone and computer instant messaging—a soldier touches the Message button.

The built-in GPS system provides location and route information, much like sophisticated mapping programs in luxury cars. Force 21 computers are installed in shock-resistant cases and equipped with a cooling system that eliminates the need for a fan, which might pull in dust, dirt, or water. The computers run Sun Microsystem's Solaris operating system because it is less vulnerable to viruses and intrusion attacks than Microsoft Windows. To prevent enemy capture and use, Force 21 computers have a self-destruct mechanism that can be triggered remotely.

In addition to pilots and tank drivers, battlefield soldiers will soon be equipped with "wearable" computer and communications equipment. The $2 billion Land Warrior program will provide high-tech weaponry, such as the Integrated Helmet Assembly Subsystem for soldiers. IHAS is a helmet-mounted device that displays graphical data, digital maps, thermal images, intelligence information, and troop locations. It also includes a weapon-mounted video camera, so that soldiers can view and fire around corners and acquire targets in darkness.

The military has also conducted research in computer simulations that are similar to civilian computer games. "Live" military training is dangerous—weapons are deadly and equipment costs millions of dollars. With computer simulations, however, troops can train in a true-to-life environment without physical harm or equipment damage. Flying an F-16 fighter, for example, costs about $5,000 an hour, but flying an F-16 simulator costs only $500 per hour. The military uses simulators to teach Air Force pilots to fly fighter jets, Navy submarine officers to navigate in harbors, and Marine infantry squads to handle urban combat.

Military trainers agree that widespread use of computer games helps prepare troops to adapt quickly to real situations. A 24-year-old preflight student at Pensacola Naval Air Station modified the Microsoft Flight Simulator game to re-create a T-34C Turbo Mentor plane's controls. After logging 50 hours on the simulator, the student performed so well on a real plane that the Navy used his simulation to train other pilots. Today, a growing cadre of computer and communications specialists is needed to create and maintain increasingly complex military systems.

An army once depended on its infantry, but today's high-tech army depends equally on its database designers, computer programmers, and network specialists. Even previously low-tech military jobs, such as mechanics and dietitians, require some computer expertise. New recruits are finding military computer systems easy to learn, based on their knowledge of civilian technologies, such as the Internet and computer games.

FIGURE B-33

Although most citizens agree that an adequate national defense is necessary, the cost of defense-related equipment, personnel, and research remains controversial. In 1961, President Dwight Eisenhower warned "We must guard against the acquisition of unwarranted influence, whether sought or unsought, by the military-industrial complex." Many socially motivated citizens and pacifists protested diverting tax dollars from social and economic programs to the military-industrial complex that Eisenhower cautioned against. In retrospect, however, military funding contributed to many technologies we depend on today. For example, detractors tried to convince the government that Project PX was doomed to failure, but without ENIAC research, computers might not exist today. Skeptics saw no future for the fruits of ARPANET research, but it led to the Internet, which has changed our lives significantly.

Why Recycle Computers?

Keeping up with technology means replacing your computer every few years, but what should you do with your old, outdated computer? According to the National Safety Council, an estimated 300 million computers will be obsolete by the year 2007. A recycling company called Back Thru the Future Micro Computer, Inc. (BTTF) estimates that 63 million computers will be retired in 2005 alone, compared with 20 million that became obsolete in 1998. BTTF estimates that printer ink cartridges are discarded at the rate of almost eight cartridges every second in the United States alone. A recycling company called GreenDisk estimates that about 1 billion floppy disks, CDs, and DVDs end up in landfills every year.

U.S. landfills already hold more than 2 million tons of computer parts, which contain toxic substances such as lead, phosphorus, and mercury. A computer monitor can contain up to six pounds of lead. An Environmental Protection Agency (EPA) report sums up the situation: "In this world of rapidly changing technology, disposal of computers and other electronic equipment has created a new and growing waste stream." See Figure B-34.

Many computers end up in landfills because their owners were unaware of potential environmental hazards and simply tossed them in the garbage. In addition, PC owners typically are not provided with information concerning the options for disposing of their old machines. Instead of throwing away your old computer, you might be able to sell it; donate it to a local school, church, or community program; have it hauled away by a professional recycling firm; or send it back to the manufacturer.

With the growing popularity of Internet auctions and dedicated computer reclamation sites, you might be able to get some cash for your old computer. At Web sites, such as the Computer Recycle Center (www.recycles.com), you can post an ad for your "old stuff." Off the Web, you can find several businesses, such as Computer Renaissance, that refurbish old computers and sell them in retail stores.

Donating your old computer to a local organization doesn't actually eliminate the disposal problem, but it does delay it. Unfortunately, finding a new home for an old computer is not always easy. Most schools and community organizations have few resources for repairing broken equipment, so if your old computer is not in good working order, it could be more of a burden than a gift. In addition, your computer might be too old to be compatible with the other computers that are used in an organization. It helps if you can donate software along with your old computer. To provide a legal transfer, include the software distribution disks, manuals, and license agreement. And remember, once you donate the software, you cannot legally use it on your new computer unless it is freeware or shareware. If you cannot find an organization to accept your computer donation, look in your local Yellow Pages or on the Internet for an electronics recycling firm that will haul away your computer and recycle any usable materials.

FIGURE B-34

In recent years, about half the states in the U.S. have taken some legislative action to curtail the rampant disposal of obsolete computer equipment. For example, Massachusetts implemented a statewide ban in 2000 on disposing computers in landfills, which helped spur recycling efforts. New Jersey's tough regulations on electronics disposal, which became effective in December 2002, apply to more than 220 pounds or 100 kilograms, which is about eight monitors. Under those regulations, disposal must be at an approved New Jersey facility and disposal records must be kept for three years. Failure to comply can result in a $2,000 fine for each violation. Many lawmakers in the United States, Japan, and the European Union believe that more legislation is necessary but they can't agree on an implementation plan. Basic to the issue is the question of "Who pays?" Should it be the taxpayer, the individual, or the computer manufacturer?

Taxpayers typically pick up the tab for electronic waste disposal through municipal trash pick-up fees or local taxes. For example, the Silicon Valley Toxics Coalition estimates that California taxpayers will spend more than $1 billion to manage electronic waste between 2002 and 2006. But is this approach fair to individual taxpayers who generate very little electronic waste?

To make consumers responsible for the cost of recycling the products they buy, some lawmakers suggest adding a special recycling tax to computers and other electronic devices. A proposal in South Carolina, for example, would impose a $5 fee on the sale of each piece of electronic equipment containing a CRT and require the state treasurer to deposit the fees into a recycling fund for electronic equipment.

Other lawmakers propose to make manufacturers responsible for recycling costs and logistics. Some companies currently participate in voluntary extended producer responsibility programs. Hewlett-Packard, 3M, Nortel, Frigidaire, IBM, Sony, and Xerox, for example, provide recycling options for some products and components. Sony recently implemented a take-back program in Minnesota that allows residents to recycle all Sony products at no cost for the next five years.

IBM recently implemented its PC Recycling Service program, which allows you to ship any make of computer, including system units, monitors, printers, and optional attachments, to a recycling center for a nominal fee. These programs and others are important steps in the effort to keep our planet green.

▼ EXPAND THE IDEAS

1. Have you ever thrown away an old computer or other electronic device? If so, how did you dispose of it? Did you donate it, pass it along, or just throw it in the garbage? Write a short essay explaining what your options were at the time, any thoughts about recycling or donating you might have had, and exactly how you got rid of the old computer.

2. Research options for recycling electronic equipment in your local area. Create a chart showing ways to get rid of an old computer, include the positive and negative aspects of each option. Include specific details for recycling or donating the computers, such as names or addresses.

3. Would it be fair for consumers to pay a recycling tax on any electronic equipment that they purchase? Research the current trends. Include any important legislation or pending legislation in your area or around the world that you feel is relevant. Compile your findings in a short report. Include your opinion in the conclusion.

End of Unit Exercises

▼ KEY TERMS

Access time
AGP
Bit depth
Card reader
CD
CD-DA
CD drive
CD-R
CD ROM
CD-ROM disc
CD-RW
CMOS memory
CMYK color
Color depth
CompactFlash (CF) card
Computer projection device
Controller
CRT
Cursor
Cylinder
Data bus
Data transfer rate
Device driver
Digital camera
Disk density
DMA
Dot matrix printer
Dot pitch
Dpi

Drive bay
Duty cycle
DVD
DVD drive
DVD+R
DVD-ROM
DVD+RW
DVD-Video
Dye sublimation printer
EIDE
Expansion bus
Expansion card
Expansion port
Expansion slot
Floppy disk
Function key
Graphics card
Graphics tablet
Hard disk
Hard disk platter
Head crash
Ink jet printer
Insertion point
ISA
Joystick
Keyboard shortcut
Lands
Laser printer
LCD

Magnetic storage
Millisecond
Modem card
Modifier key
Mouse
Multifunction device
MultiMedia card (MMC)
Navigation keypad
Network card
Numeric keypad
Optical storage
PCI
PCMCIA slot
Peripheral device
Pits
Plasma screen technology
Plug and Play (PnP)
Pointing stick
PostScript
Printer control language (PCL)
RAM
Random access
Read-write head
Recordable technology
Resolution
Revolutions per minute (rpm)
Rewritable technology
Scanner
Screen size

SCSI
SecureDigital (SD) card
Sequential access
SmartMedia card
Solid ink printer
Solid state storage
Sound card
Storage capacity
Storage device
Storage medium
Storage technology
SuperDisk
Tape
Tape cartridge
Thermal transfer printer
Touchpad
Trackball
Trackpad
TrackPoint
Typing keypad
UDMA
Ultra ATA
USB flash drive
Viewable image size (vis)
Viewing angle width
Volatile
Web cam
Windows Registry
Write-protect window
Zip disk

▼ UNIT REVIEW

1. Make sure that you can use your own words to define the bold terms that appear throughout the unit.

2. Describe the advantages and disadvantages of magnetic storage, solid state storage, and optical storage.

3. Create a grid with each type of storage device written across the top. Make a list of the corresponding media down the left side of the grid. Working down each column, place an X in cells for any of the media that can be read by the device listed at the top of the column.

4. Summarize important uses for each type of storage technology.

5. Summarize display devices. Be sure to include advantages and disadvantages.

6. Create a table to summarize what you know about the printer technologies that were discussed in this unit.

7. List any peripheral devices that are attached to your computer. Describe what each one does. Be sure to identify each one as input, output, or storage.

8. If possible, open your computer and count the number of expansion slots that are not currently in use and how many are in use.

9. Look at the front of your computer and identify the devices that are in the drive bays.

10. Count the number of cables coming out of the back of your computer. Using Figure B-28 identify each type of cable.

▼ FILL IN THE BEST ANSWER

1. Data on an optical storage medium is stored as _____Pits_____ and lands.

2. _____Access_____ time is the average time that it takes a computer to locate data on a storage medium and read it.

3. A computer can move directly to any file on a(n) (eg. c.d) _____Random_____ access device, but must start at the beginning and read through all of the data on a(n) (eg. tape) _____Sequential_____ access device.

4. Higher disk _____density_____ provides increased storage capacity.

5. "HD DS" means _____Hard Disk_____.

6. EIDE, Ultra ATA, and SCSI refer to the type of _____controller_____ used by a hard disk drive.

7. CD-R technology allows you to _____record_____ data on a disk, then change that data.

8. A variety of compact storage cards, pens, and sticks can be classified as _____solid state_____ storage which store data in a non-volatile, erasable, low-power chip.

9. The _____expansion_____ bus carries data from RAM to peripheral devices.

10. AGP, PCI, and ISA are types of expansion _____slot_____, which are part of a personal computer's motherboard.

11. Many peripheral devices come packaged with device _____driver_____ software.

12. A scanner is a type of _____input_____ device.

13. Most people set their monitors to a(n) _____resolution_____ of 800 × 600 or 1024 × 768.

14. The number of colors that a monitor can display is referred to as bit _____depth_____.

15. The advantages of an LCD _____monitor_____ include display clarity, low radiation emission, and portability.

16. The most popular printers for personal computers are _____ink jet printers_____, which are inexpensive and produce good-quality color printouts.

17. Today's PCs include a feature called Plug and _____play_____ that automatically takes care of technical details for installing peripheral devices.

18. A _____modifier_____ key such as the [Ctrl] key is used in conjunction with other keys to expand the abilities of each key.

19. TrackPoints and touchpads are alternative _____mouse_____ devices often found on notebook computers.

20. A read-write _____head_____ is a mechanism in the disk drive that reads and writes the magnetized particles that represent data.

▼ INDEPENDENT CHALLENGE 1

You know that you're really a tech wizard when you can decipher every term and acronym in a computer ad. But even the most knowledgeable computer gurus sometimes need a dictionary for new terms.

1. For this independent challenge, photocopy a full page from a current computer magazine that contains an ad for a computer system. On the copy of the ad, use a colored pen to circle each descriptive term and acronym.

2. On a separate sheet of paper, or using a word processor, list all of the terms that you circled and write a definition for each term. If you encounter a term that was not defined in the unit, use a computer dictionary or refer to the Webopaedia Web site (www.webopedia.com) to locate the correct definition.

3. Prepare your list to submit to your instructor. Add a summary paragraph indicating why you would or would not purchase the computer in the ad and additional information that you need before making a decision.

▼ INDEPENDENT CHALLENGE 2

Storage technology has a fascinating history. Mankind has evolved many ways to retain and store data. From the ancient days when Egyptians were writing on papyrus to modern day holographic technologies, societies have found ways to retain more and more information in permanent and safe ways.

1. To complete this independent challenge you will research the history of storage technologies and create a timeline that shows the developments. Be sure to include such items as 78-rpm records and 8-track tapes. Your research should yield some interesting technologies and systems.

2. For each technology, list the media, the device used to retrieve the information, two significant facts about the technology, the era in which it was used or popular, and what lead to its demise or obsolescence, or why it is still popular.

3. You can create the timeline using images or just words. This is a creative project. Your best research, artistic, and communication skills come together to create this timeline.

▼ INDEPENDENT CHALLENGE 3

It is important that you are familiar with the type of computer you use daily. You may need to consult your technical resource person to help you complete this independent challenge.

1. Identify the components on your computer. What type of computer are you using? What kind of system unit do you have?

2. What peripheral devices are attached to your computer? List the name, manufacturer, and model number of each device if available.

3. Draw a sketch of your computer. Label each component and identify what it does.

▼ INDEPENDENT CHALLENGE 4

 For this project, use your library and Web resources to research information in order to compare printers.

1. Use the information in this unit as well as your own resources to create a comparative table of printers.

2. Your column heads might address these questions: What types are available? What technology is used? What is the duty cycle? What is the cost range? What is the average cost per page? Who is the market for this type of printer?

3. Provide a summary statement indicating which printer you would buy and why, based on the information in your table.

▼ INDEPENDENT CHALLENGE 5

 In this unit you learned about peripheral devices. Some of these are standard peripheral devices such as monitors and printers. If your office is tight for space, you might consider purchasing a multifunction device. For this project, use your library and Web resources to research information about multifunction devices.

1. Research and find the types of multifunction devices available. Categorize them by their functions: scanners, fax, phone, copiers, color or black-and-white printing, laser or inkjet. Different manufacturers bundle different capabilities into their devices. The more features a unit has, typically, the more expensive it will be.

2. Research and find the manufacturers and model numbers for three devices you would consider buying. Write a comparison of the features, strengths, and weaknesses of each model.

▼ INDEPENDENT CHALLENGE 6

 The Issue section of this unit focused on the potential for discarded computers and other electronic devices to become a significant environmental problem. For this independent challenge, you will write a short paper about recycling computers based on information that you gather from the Internet.

1. To begin this independent challenge, consult the Internet and use your favorite search engine to search for and find Web pages to get an in-depth overview of the issue.

2. Determine the specific aspect of the issue that you will present in your paper. You might, for example, decide to focus on the toxic materials contained in computers that end up in landfills. Or you might tackle the barriers that discourage the shipment of old computers across national borders. Whatever aspect of the issue you decide to present, make sure that you can back up your discussion with facts and references to authoritative articles and Web pages.

3. You can place citations to these pages (include the author's name, article title, date of publication, and URL) at the end of your paper as endnotes, on each page as footnotes, or along with the appropriate paragraphs using parentheses. Follow your professor's instructions for submitting your paper via e-mail or as a printed document.

▼ STUDENT EDITION LABS

Reinforce the concepts you have learned in this unit through the **Using Input Devices, Peripheral Devices,** and **Maintaining a Hard Drive** Student Edition Labs, available online at the Illustrated Computer Concepts Web site.

▼ SAM LABS

 If you have a SAM user profile, you have access to additional content, features, and functionality. Log in to your SAM account and go to your assignments page to see what your instructor has assigned for this unit.

▼ VISUAL WORKSHOP

If you thought a holograph was just the image of Princess Leia saying "Obi-Wan Kenobi, you are my only hope," think again. Holographic storage devices are in development as a means to respond to the growing need for large-volume data storage. Holographic technologies promise data retrieval speeds far exceeding magnetic or optical storage and capacities far beyond anything currently available. Researchers are working to make this technology an affordable reality. Figure B-35 shows a Web page from InPhase Technologies, a company specializing in holographic technologies.

FIGURE B-35

1. Use your favorite search engine to find and read the May 2000 edition of Scientific American (www.sciam.com), which included a feature article about holographic storage. Write a brief summary of the article and, based on what you read, explain the basics of how holographic memory works.

2. Research the current trends in holographic development. Are there any existing applications? How far has the technology come? What companies are working to develop these technologies? How far are we from using holocubes for data storage?

3. Write a scenario that includes the requirements and applications for holographic storage. Under what circumstances do you think such technologies would be useful, and what types of data do you think would best take advantage of this new technology?

UNIT C Computer Software

OBJECTIVES

Introduce computer software

Explain how computers interpret software

Explore operating systems

Compare operating systems

Define document production software

Define spreadsheet software

Define database software

Define graphics software

Define business and science software

Define entertainment and education software

Understand licenses and copyrights

Tech Talk: Installing Software

Computers in Context: Journalism

Issue: Is Piracy a Problem?

A computer's versatility is possible because of software—the instructions that tell a computer how to perform a specific type of task. This unit begins with the components of a typical software package and explains how these components work together. Next, you will learn about a computer's most important system software, its operating system. You will get an overview of software applications, including document production, spreadsheets, database, graphics, music, video editing, and games. Finally, the unit wraps up with important practical information on software copyrights and licenses. The Tech Talk reviews how to install and uninstall software. You will also have an opportunity to look at computers in the context of journalism. The Issue discusses software piracy.

Introducing computer software

In common practice, the term "software" is used to describe a commercial product that can be distributed on floppy disks, DVDs, CDs, or made available as a Web download. Computer software determines the tasks that a computer can help you accomplish, such as create documents and presentations, prepare your tax return, or design the floor plan for a new house. You will learn about the components of computer software and how these components work together to help you complete tasks.

DETAILS

- Software is categorized as either application software or system software. **Application software** helps you carry out tasks—such as creating documents, crunching numbers, and editing photographs—using a computer. **System software**—your computer's operating system, device drivers, and utilities—helps your computer carry out its basic operating functions. Figure C-1 shows the types of software that fall into the system software and application software categories.

- **Software** consists of computer programs, support programs, and data files that work together to provide a computer with the instructions and data necessary for carrying out a specific type of task, such as document production or Web browsing.

- Software typically includes files that contain computer programs. A **computer program**, or "program," is a set of self-contained instructions that tells a computer how to solve a problem or carry out a task. A key characteristic of a computer program is that it can be started or "run" by a computer user.

- At least one of the files included in a software package contains an executable program designed to be launched, or started, by users. On PCs, these programs are stored in files that typically have .exe filename extensions and are sometimes referred to as **executable files** or **user-executable files**. When using a Windows PC, you can start an executable file by clicking its icon, selecting it from the Start menu, or entering its name in the Run dialog box.

- Other files supplied with a software package contain programs that are not designed to be run by users. These **support programs** contain instructions for the computer to use with the main user-executable file. A support program can be "called," or activated, by the main program as needed. For example, when you use the spelling checker in a word processing program, the word processing program calls on support programs to run the spelling checker. In the context of Windows software, support programs often have filename extensions such as .dll and .ocx.

- A **data file** contains any data that is necessary for a task, but that is not supplied by the user. For example, word processing software checks spelling by comparing the words in a document with the words in a dictionary file. This dictionary file is a data file that is supplied by the software, not by the user. Data files supplied with a software package have filename extensions such as .txt, .bmp, and .hlp.

- The use of an executable file plus several support programs and data files offers a great deal of flexibility and efficiency for software developers. See Figure C-2. Support programs and data files can usually be modified without changing the main executable file. This modular approach can significantly reduce the time required to create and test the main executable file, which usually contains a long and fairly complex program. The modular approach also allows software developers to reuse their support programs and adapt preprogrammed support programs for use in their software.

- Most software is designed to provide a task-related environment, which includes a screen display, a means of collecting commands and data from the user, the specifications for processing data, and a method for displaying or outputting data. Figure C-3 is a simple computer program that converts a Fahrenheit temperature to Celsius and displays the result.

FIGURE C-1: Software categories

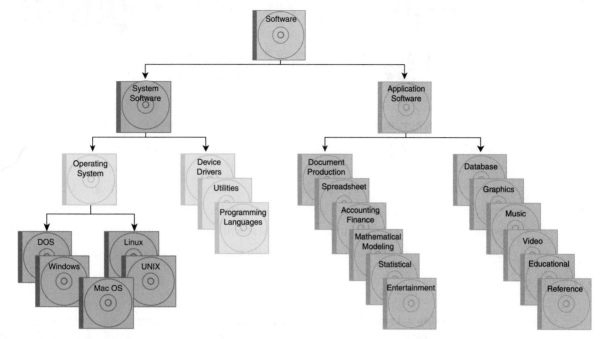

FIGURE C-2: Installed files for a software program

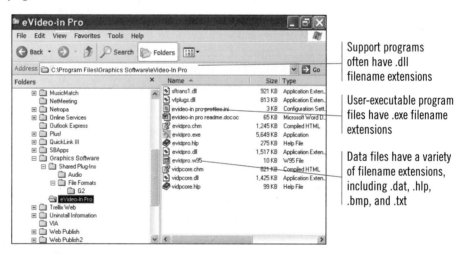

Support programs often have .dll filename extensions

User-executable program files have .exe filename extensions

Data files have a variety of filename extensions, including .dat, .hlp, .bmp, and .txt

FIGURE C-3: A simple computer program

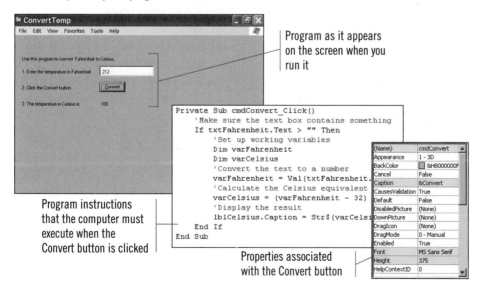

Program as it appears on the screen when you run it

Program instructions that the computer must execute when the Convert button is clicked

Properties associated with the Convert button

Explaining how computers interpret software

Computer programmers write the instructions for the computer programs and support programs that become the components of a computer software product. The finished software product is then distributed by the programmers themselves, or by software publishers, companies that specialize in packaging, marketing, and selling commercial software. Most businesses, organizations, and individuals purchase commercial software to avoid the time and expense of writing their own. Learning how programmers write the instructions and how a computer's processor translates these instructions will help you understand how software works.

DETAILS

- A **programming** or **computer language** provides the tools that a programmer uses to create software. These languages help the programmer produce a lengthy list of instructions called **source code**. Most programmers today prefer to use **high-level languages**, such as C++, Java, COBOL, and Visual Basic, which have some similarities to human languages and produce programs that are fairly easy to test and modify.

- A computer's processor interprets the programmer's instructions, but the processor can only understand **machine language**—the instruction set that is "hard wired" within the processor's circuits. Instructions written in a high-level language must be translated into machine language before a computer can use them.

- Translating instructions from a high-level language into machine language can be accomplished by two special types of programs: compilers and interpreters. Figure C-4 gives you an idea of what happens to high-level instructions when they are converted into machine language instructions. A simple instruction to add two numbers becomes a long series of 0s and 1s in machine language.

- A **compiler** converts high-level instructions into a compiled program, which is a new file containing machine language instructions. A compiler translates all of the instructions in a program as a single batch, and the resulting machine language instructions, called **object code**, are placed in a new file.

- As an alternative to a compiler, an **interpreter** converts one instruction at a time while the program is running. An interpreter reads the first instruction in a script, converts it into machine language, and then sends it to the processor. The interpreter continues in this way to convert instructions until all instructions are interpreted. See Figure C-5. An interpreted program runs more slowly than a compiled program because the translation process happens while the program is running.

- Figure C-6 illustrates how a video editing program, such as eVideo-In Pro works when installed on a computer that is running Windows. The files included in this software package interact with the hardware when you select commands to edit videos.

FIGURE C-4: Converting a high-level instruction to machine code

High-level Language Instruction	Machine Language Equivalent	Description of Machine Language Instructions
Answer = FirstNumber + SecondNumber	10001000 00011000 010000000	Load FirstNumber into Register 1
	10001000 00010000 00100000	Load SecondNumber into Register 2
	00000000 00011000 00010000	Perform ADD operation
	10100010 00111000	Move the number from the accumulator to the RAM location called Answer

FIGURE C-5: The interpreter converts instructions one instruction at a time

▶ An interpreter converts high-level instructions into machine language instructions while the program is running

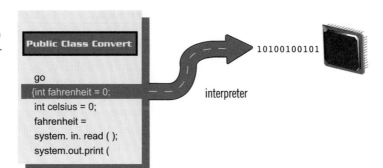

interpreter

◀ An interpreted program runs more slowly than a compiled program because the translation process happens while the program is running

FIGURE C-6: How software works

1. When you start the eVideo-In Pro software, the instructions in the file eVidpro.exe are loaded from disk into RAM and then sent to the processor

2. eVidpro.exe is a compiled program, so its instructions are immediately executed by the processor

3. As processing begins, the eVideo-In Pro window opens and the graphical controls for video editing tasks appear; the program waits for you to select a control by clicking it with the mouse

eVidpro.exe

eVidpro.exe

4. Based on your selection, eVidpro.exe follows its instructions and performs the actions you specify; many of the instructions for these actions are included in the main executable file; if not, eVidpro.exe calls a support program, such as Sftrans.dll

5. If you access eVideo-In Pro Help, eVidpro.exe loads the data file eVidpro.hlp

6. eVidpro.exe continues to respond to the controls you select until you click the Close button, which halts execution of the program instructions, closes the program window, and releases the space the program occupied in RAM for use by other programs or data

Sftrans.dll

eVidpro.hlp

Exploring operating systems

The term **operating system (OS)** is defined as system software that acts as the master controller for all of the activities that take place within a computer system. If you understand how an operating system works, you will understand how your computer performs its many functions. For example, when you issue a command using application software, the application software tells the operating system what to do. See Figure C-7. While you interact with application software, your computer's operating system is busy behind the scenes.

DETAILS

● In the context of a computer system, the term **resource** refers to any component that is required to perform work. For example, the processor is a resource. RAM, storage space, and peripherals are also resources. The operating system manages a computer's resources by interacting with application software, device drivers, and hardware.

● Figure C-8 illustrates some common operating system tasks. Your operating system stores and retrieves files from your disks and CDs. It remembers the names and locations of all your files and keeps track of empty spaces where new files can be stored. It communicates with device driver software so that data can travel smoothly between the computer and the peripheral resources. If a peripheral device or driver is not performing correctly, the operating system makes a decision about what to do; usually it displays an on-screen warning about the problem.

● Many activities called "processes" compete for the attention of your computer's processor. To manage all of these competing processes, your computer's operating system helps the processor switch tasks. When you want to run more than one program at a time, the operating system has to allocate specific areas of memory for each program. See Figure C-9.

● While multiple programs are running, the OS must ensure that instructions and data from one area of memory don't "leak" into an area allocated to another program. If an OS fails to protect each program's memory area, data can get corrupted, programs can "crash," and your computer will display error messages.

● Your computer's operating system ensures that input and output proceed in an orderly manner, using queues to collect data and buffers to hold data while the computer is busy with other tasks. By using a keyboard buffer, for example, your computer never misses one of your keystrokes, regardless of how fast you type.

● Many operating systems also influence the "look and feel" of your software by determining the kinds of menus, toolbars, and controls that are displayed on the screen, and how these objects react to your input. Most operating systems today support a **graphical user interface**, which provides a way to point and click a mouse to select menu options and manipulate graphical objects that are displayed on the screen. Graphical user interface is sometimes abbreviated "GUI" and referred to as a "gooey."

● In some computers—typically handhelds and videogame consoles—the entire operating system is small enough to be stored in ROM. For nearly all personal computers, servers, workstations, mainframes, and supercomputers, the operating system program is quite large, so most of it is stored on a hard disk. The operating system's small **bootstrap program** is stored in ROM and supplies the instructions needed to load the operating system's core into memory when the system boots. This core part of the operating system, called the **kernel**, provides the most essential operating system services, such as memory management and file access. The kernel stays in memory all the time your computer is on. Other parts of the operating system, such as customization utilities, are loaded into memory as they are needed. **Utilities** are tools you can use to control and customize your computer equipment and work environment. Table C-1 lists some OS utilities.

● **DOS** stands for Disk Operating System. It was developed by Microsoft, introduced on the original IBM PC in 1982. Although IBM called this operating system PC-DOS, Microsoft marketed it to other companies under the name MS-DOS. Today, users rarely interact with DOS. Operating systems for today's computers are discussed in the next lesson.

FIGURE C-7: How the operating system interacts with application software

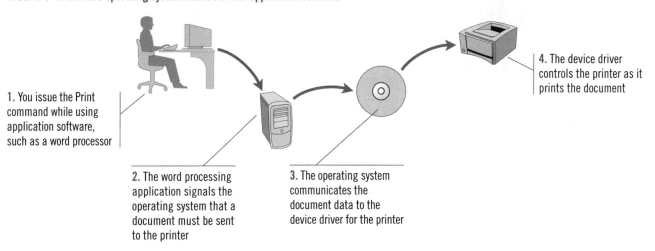

1. You issue the Print command while using application software, such as a word processor

2. The word processing application signals the operating system that a document must be sent to the printer

3. The operating system communicates the document data to the device driver for the printer

4. The device driver controls the printer as it prints the document

FIGURE C-8: Operating system tasks

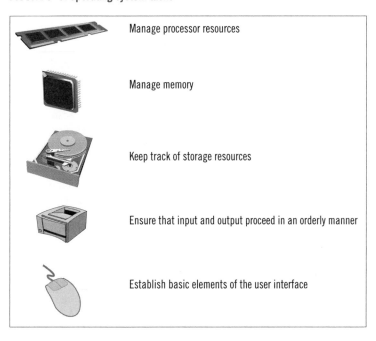

Manage processor resources

Manage memory

Keep track of storage resources

Ensure that input and output proceed in an orderly manner

Establish basic elements of the user interface

FIGURE C-9: The operating system and RAM

RAM

Operating System

Document

Word Processing Software

Photo Data

Graphics Software

TABLE C-1: Examples of Windows operating system utilities

UTILITY USED TO	WHAT WINDOWS PROVIDES
Launch programs	When you start your computer, Windows displays a "desktop" that contains a collection of graphical objects, such as the Start menu, which you can manipulate to start programs.
Manage files	Windows Explorer allows you to view a list of files, move them to different storage devices, copy them, rename them, and delete them.
Get help	Windows provides a Help system that you can use to find out how various commands work.
Customize the user interface	The Control Panel, accessible from the Start menu, provides utilities that help you customize your screen display and work environment.
Configure equipment	The Windows Control Panel also provides access to utilities that help you set up and configure your computer's hardware and peripheral devices.

Comparing operating systems

The operating system is the master controller of your computer system. It determines how you interact with your computer. This lesson discusses categories of operating systems and compares the main features of popular operating systems.

DETAILS

● Operating systems are informally categorized using one or more of the following terms:

A **single-user operating system** expects to deal with one set of input devices—those that can be controlled by one user at a time. Operating systems for handheld computers and many personal computers fit into the single-user category.

A **multiuser operating system** is designed to deal with input, output, and processing requests from many users at the same time. One of its most difficult responsibilities is to schedule all of the processing requests that must be performed by a centralized computer, often a mainframe.

A **network operating system**, or **server operating system**, provides communications and routing services that allow computers to share data, programs, and peripheral devices. While a multiuser OS and a network OS may sound the same, a multiuser operating system schedules requests for processing on a centralized computer; a network operating system simply routes data and programs to each user's local computer, where the actual processing takes place.

A **desktop operating system** is one that's designed for either a desktop or notebook personal computer. The computer that you typically use at home, at school, or at work is most likely configured with a desktop operating system. Typically, these operating systems are designed to accommodate a single user, but may also provide networking capability. Some operating system vendors characterize their products as "home" or "professional" versions. The home version typically has fewer network management tools than the professional version.

Today's desktop operating systems invariably provide multitasking services. A **multitasking operating system** provides process and memory management services that allow two or more programs to run simultaneously. Most of today's personal computers use operating systems that offer multitasking services.

● **Microsoft Windows** is installed on over 80% of the world's personal computers. Since its introduction in 1985, Windows has evolved through several versions. Microsoft currently offers several types of operating systems. Home, Professional, and

Workstation editions are designed for personal computers. Server editions are designed for LAN, Internet, and Web servers. Embedded editions are designed for handheld devices, such as PDAs and mobile phones.

● Like Windows, **Mac OS** has been through a number of revisions. Its current version is OS X (version 10).

● Both Mac OS for the Apple Macintosh computer and Windows base their user interfaces on the graphical interface model that was pioneered at Xerox. A quick comparison of Figure C-10 and Figure C-11 shows that both Windows and Mac interfaces use a mouse to point and click various icons and menus. Both interfaces feature rectangular work areas for multitasking services and provide basic networking services. Many of the most prolific software publishers produce one version of their software for Windows and another version for Mac OS.

● The **UNIX** operating system was developed in 1969 at AT&T's Bell Labs. It gained a good reputation for its dependability in multiuser environments. Many versions of it became available for mainframes and microcomputers.

● In 1991, Linus Torvalds developed the **Linux** operating system (see Figure C-12), based on a version of UNIX. Linux is rather unique because it is distributed under the terms of a General Public License (GPL), which allows everyone to make copies for their own use, to give it to others, or to sell it. This licensing policy has encouraged programmers to develop Linux utilities, software, and enhancements. Linux is primarily distributed over the Web.

● **Palm OS** and **Windows Mobil OS** are the two dominant operating systems of handheld computers. PDA and desktop operating systems provide many similar services, but because PDAs tend to be used for less sophisticated tasks, their simpler and smaller operating systems can be stored in ROM. A PDA's operating system is ready almost instantly when the unit is turned on and provides built-in support for touch screens, handwriting input, wireless networking, and cellular communications. **Windows XP Tablet Edition** is the operating system supplied with just about every tablet computer. Its main feature is handwriting recognition, which accepts printed input from the touch-sensitive screen.

FIGURE C-10: Microsoft Windows

Icons represent computer hardware and software

The Start button provides access to a menu of programs, documents, and utilities

◄ The Windows operating system gets its name from the rectangular work areas that appear on the screen-based desktop; each work area can display a different document or program, providing a visual model of the operating system's multitasking capabilities

Two different programs can run in two separate windows

The taskbar indicates which programs are running

FIGURE C-11: Mac OS

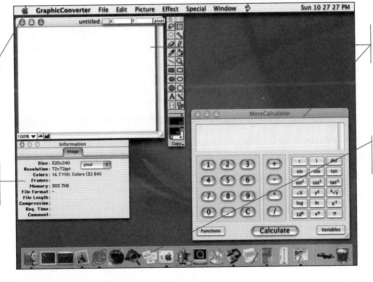

The Apple logo provides access to a menu

Menus and other on-screen objects are manipulated by using a mouse

Two different programs can run in two separate windows

Icons represent computer hardware components and software

FIGURE C-12: Linux

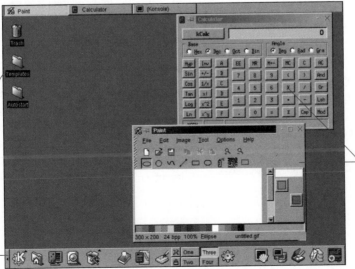

Desktop icons look similar to those on the Windows and Macintosh desktops

A horizontal option bar combines features of the Windows Start menu, Control Panel, and taskbar

◄ Linux users can choose from several graphical interfaces; this is the popular KDE (K Desktop Environment)

Two different programs can run in two separate windows

Defining document production software

Whether you are writing a 10-page paper, writing software documentation, designing a brochure for your new startup company, or laying out the school newspaper, you will probably use some form of **document production software**. This software assists you with composing, editing, designing, printing, and electronically publishing documents.

DETAILS

● Document production software can be classified as one of three types:

Word processing software is used to produce documents such as reports, letters, and manuscripts. Word processing software gives you the ability to compose a document on the screen before you commit it to paper. Refer to Figure C-13. Microsoft Word is an example of word processing software.

Desktop publishing software (DTP) takes word processing software one step further by helping you use graphic design techniques to enhance the format and appearance of a document. Although today's word processing software offers many page layout and design features, desktop publishing software provides more sophisticated features to help you produce professional-quality output for publications. QuarkXPress is an example of destktop publishing software.

Web authoring software helps you design and develop Web pages that you can publish electronically on the Internet. Web authoring software provides easy-to-use tools for composing the text for a Web page, assembling graphical elements, and automatically generating HTML tags. Macromedia Dreamweaver is an example of Web authoring software.

● A description of common features of document production software follows:

Alignment: determines the position of text as left, right, centered, or fully justified

Autocorrect: automatically changes a typo, such as "teh" to "the"

Find and replace: finds all occurrences of a word or phrase and lets you replace it with another word or phrase, such as changing May to August

Formatting options: allows you to change font, font size, and font style

Line spacing: determines the space between lines of type, such as single space

Mail merge: creates personalized letters by automatically combining information in a mailing list with a form letter

Spelling checker/grammar checker: marks words in a document as misspelled if they do not match words in the spelling dictionary; points out potential grammatical trouble spots, such as run-on sentences

Style: saved set of formatting options that you apply to text; you can create character, paragraph, table, and list styles

● The **format** for a document refers to how all text, pictures, titles, and page numbers are arranged on the page. The look of your document will depend on formatting factors, such as font style, paragraph style (see Figure C-14), and page layout. You can vary the font style by selecting different fonts, such as Arial and Comic Sans MS, and character formatting attributes, such as bold, italic, underline, superscript, and subscript. You can also select a color and size for a font. The font size for the text in a typical paragraph is set at 8, 10, or 12 pt. Titles can be as large as 72 pt.

● **Page layout** refers to the physical position of each element on a page. A **header** is text that you specify to appear in the top margin of every page automatically. A **footer** is text that you specify to appear in the bottom margin of every page automatically. **Clip art** is a collection of drawings and photos designed to be inserted into documents. A **table** is a grid-like structure that can hold text or pictures. For printed documents, tables are a popular way to provide easy-to-read columns of data and to position graphics. For Web pages, tables provide one of the few ways to position text and pictures precisely.

● Some software allows you to divide each page into several rectangular-shaped **frames** that you can fill with either text or pictures. See Figure C-15. Frames provide you with finer control over the position of elements on a page, such as a figure and a caption on top of it. Since frames are helpful for complex page layout, DTP software is usually frame oriented.

FIGURE C-13: Microsoft Word

As you type, the spelling checker compares your words with a list of correctly spelled words; words not included in the list are marked with a wavy line as possible misspellings

Even after you type an entire document, adjusting the size of your right, left, top, and bottom margins is simple

Mountain.doc - Microsoft Word
File Edit View Insert Format Tools Table Window Help
Type a question for help
Normal + Arial
Arial
12
100%
Mountain climbing was once the doman of professional explorers, whose bodies and minds were honed to a long assault against weather, ice, and rock. Expeditions attacked Mount Everest beginning in 1922. It was not until 1953 that Edmund Hillary and his guide, Tenzing Norkay, reached the summit. Hillary was knighted for this accomplishment.
Sir Edmund Hillary would be amazed to discover that today Mount Everest is something of a tourist destination. Guided "adventure" tours head toward the summit like cruise ships plying Caribbean ports. This $65,000 trek is not without risk. In 1996 a sudden storm killed eight climbers.
Back in 1923, British mountaineer, George Mallory was asked, why climb Everest? His reply, "Because it's there." A new answer to this question, "Because we can" is largely attributable to high-tech mountain gear. Polypropylene and Gore-Tex clothing provide light; yet warm protection from the
Page 1 Sec 1 1/1 At 1" Ln 1 Col 1 REC TRK EXT OVR English (U.S

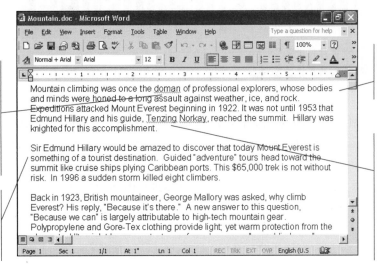

Document production software uses word wrap to fit your text automatically within the margins

Proper nouns and scientific, medical, and technical words are likely to be flagged as misspelled even if you spell them correctly because they do not appear in the spelling checker's dictionary

FIGURE C-14: Applying a style

The style called Document Title specifies Times New Roman font, size 18, bold, and centered

Mountain Climbing.doc - Microsoft Word
File Edit View Insert Format Tools Table Window Help
Type a question for help
Arial
12
100%
Clear Formatting
Arial
Document Title
Heading 1
Heading 2
Heading 3
Normal
More...
Attack on Everest
Page 1 Sec 1 1/1 At 1" Ln 1 Col 1 REC TRK EXT OVR English (U.S

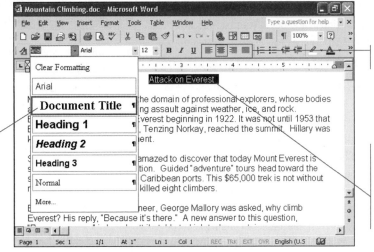

Paragraph alignment buttons

Applying the formats assigned to a style simply requires you to highlight the text, then click a style from the list, such as the Document Title style

FIGURE C-15: Using frames

One frame holds the centered title and author's byline

A frame can be positioned anywhere on the page, even in the center of two text columns

Wrapping text around a frame adds interest to the layout

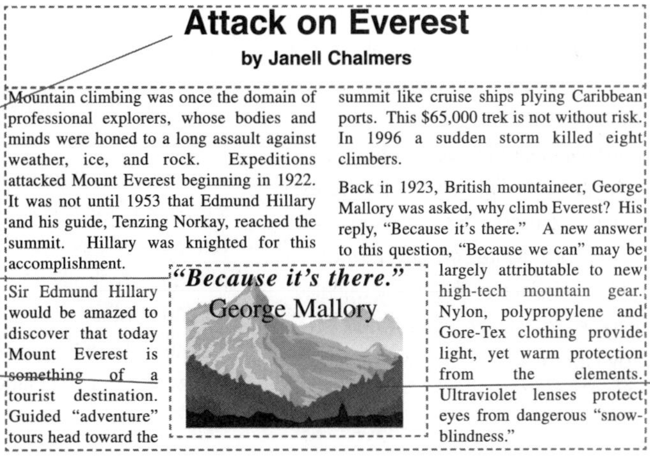

Attack on Everest
by Janell Chalmers
Mountain climbing was once the domain of professional explorers, whose bodies and minds were honed to a long assault against weather, ice, and rock. Expeditions attacked Mount Everest beginning in 1922. It was not until 1953 that Edmund Hillary and his guide, Tenzing Norkay, reached the summit. Hillary was knighted for this accomplishment.
Sir Edmund Hillary would be amazed to discover that today Mount Everest is something of a tourist destination. Guided "adventure" tours head toward the summit like cruise ships plying Caribbean ports. This $65,000 trek is not without risk. In 1996 a sudden storm killed eight climbers.
Back in 1923, British mountaineer, George Mallory was asked, why climb Everest? His reply, "Because it's there." A new answer to this question, "Because we can" may be largely attributable to new high-tech mountain gear. Nylon, polypropylene and Gore-Tex clothing provide light, yet warm protection from the elements. Ultraviolet lenses protect eyes from dangerous "snow-blindness."
"Because it's there."
George Mallory

Graphical elements such as photos, diagrams, graphs, and pie charts can be incorporated in your documents using frames

Defining spreadsheet software

Spreadsheet software is used for numerical calculations based on simple equations or more complex formulas. Spreadsheets are ideal for projects that require repetitive calculations: budgeting, maintaining a grade book, balancing a checkbook, tracking investments, calculating loan payments, and estimating project costs. Spreadsheet software can turn your data into a variety of colorful graphs and charts.

DETAILS

- A **spreadsheet** uses rows and columns of numbers to create a model or representation of a real situation. For example, your checkbook register is a type of spreadsheet because it is a numerical representation of the cash flowing in and out of your bank account. **Spreadsheet software** provides tools to create electronic spreadsheets.

FYI

Spreadsheet software is useful for what-if analyses, such as, "Is it better to take out a 30-year mortgage at 5.0% interest or a 15-year mortgage at 4.5% interest?"

- You use spreadsheet software to create an on-screen **worksheet** like the one shown in Figure C-16. A worksheet is based on a grid of columns and rows. Each **cell** in the grid can contain a value, label, or formula and has a unique **cell reference**, or "address," derived from its column and row location. For example, A1 is the cell reference for the upper-left cell in a worksheet because it is in column A and row 1. You can select any cell and make it the active cell by clicking it. Once a cell is active, you can enter data into it. A **value** is a number that you want to use in a calculation. A **label** is any text that is used to describe data.

QUICK TIP

You can format the labels and values on a worksheet by changing fonts and font size, selecting a font color, and selecting a font style, such as bold.

- The values contained in a cell can be manipulated by formulas that are placed in other cells. A **formula** works behind the scenes to tell the computer how to use the contents of cells in calculations. You can enter a simple formula in a cell to add, subtract, multiply, or divide numbers. Figure C-17 illustrates how a formula might be used in a simple spreadsheet to calculate savings. More complex formulas can be designed to perform just about any calculation you can imagine. You can enter a formula "from scratch" by typing it into a cell, or you can

use a **function**, which is a predefined formula built into the spreadsheet software.

- When you change the contents of any cell in a worksheet, all of the formulas are recalculated. This **automatic recalculation** feature assures you that the results in every cell are accurate with regard to the information currently entered in the worksheet. Your worksheet is also automatically updated to reflect any rows or columns that you add, delete, or copy within the worksheet.

- In order for automatic recalculation to be accurate, you must understand and implement proper cell referencing in your formulas. Unless you specify otherwise, a cell reference is a **relative reference**—a reference that can change if cells are deleted or inserted and the data or a formula moves. See Figure C-18. If you don't want a cell reference to change, you can use an absolute reference. An **absolute reference** never changes when you delete or insert cells or copy or move formulas. Understanding when to use absolute references is one of the key aspects to developing spreadsheet design expertise.

- Most spreadsheet software includes a few templates or wizards for predesigned worksheets, such as invoices, income-expense reports, balance sheets, and loan payment schedules. Additional templates are available on the Web. These templates are typically designed by content professionals and contain all of the necessary labels and formulas. To use a template, you simply plug in the values for your calculation.

FIGURE C-16: An on-screen worksheet

Each column is lettered

Cell A1

Each row is numbered

Values in these cells can be used for calculations

Labels, such as Expenses and Profit, identify data

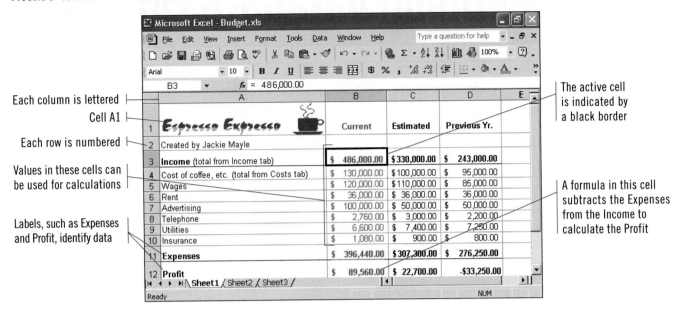

The active cell is indicated by a black border

A formula in this cell subtracts the Expenses from the Income to calculate the Profit

FIGURE C-17: How formulas work

▶ When a cell contains a formula, it displays the result of the formula, rather than the formula itself

The number that appears in cell B6 was calculated by the spreadsheet based on the formula typed in the cell

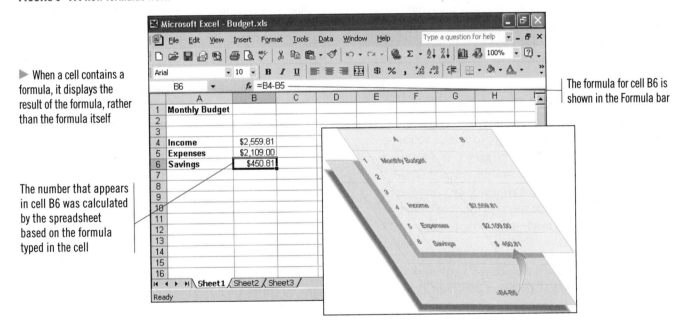

The formula for cell B6 is shown in the Formula bar

FIGURE C-18: Relative vs. absolute references

▶ Relative references within a formula can change when you insert or delete rows and columns or when you copy or move formulas; an absolute reference is "anchored" so that it always refers to a specific cell

Two blank rows

The original formula =B4-B5 uses relative references

When row 3 is deleted, the Income and Expenses values move up one row, which means that these values have new cell references; the formula changes to =B3-B4 to reflect the new cell references

Defining database software

Database software helps you enter, find, organize, update, and report information stored in a database. Databases can be stored on personal computers, LAN servers, Web servers, mainframes, and even handheld computers. This lesson provides an overview of databases and how database software manages the data stored in databases.

DETAILS

● The term **database** has evolved from a specialized technical term into a part of our everyday vocabulary. In the context of modern usage, a database is simply a collection of data that is stored on one or more computers. A database can contain any sort of data, such as a university's student records, a library's card catalog, a store's inventory, an individual's address book, or a utility company's customers.

● Database software stores data as a series of records, which are composed of fields that hold data. A **record** holds data for a single entity—a person, place, thing, or event. A **field** holds one item of data relevant to a record. You can envision a record as a Rolodex or index card and a series of records as a **table** as shown in Figure C-19.

● Database software provides tools to work with more than one collection of records, as long as the records are somehow related to each other. For example, in a jazz music database, one table of database records might contain data about songs with fields such as those shown in Figure C-19. Another table of records might contain biographical data about musicians, including name, birth date, and home town. It might even include a field for the performer's photo. These two sets of records can be related by the name of the performing artist, as shown in Figure C-20.

● Database software provides the tools you need to define fields for a series of records. Figure C-21 shows a simple form you might use to specify the fields for a database. After you've defined fields for a series of records, you can enter the data for each record. Your database software provides a simple-to-use data entry form that allows you to easily fill in the data for each field.

● Instead of typing data into a database, you can also import data from a commercial database, such as a customer mailing list— you can even download databases from the Web, and then import the data into fields you have defined with your database software.

● Many databases contain hundreds or thousands of records. If you want to find a particular record or a group of records, scrolling through every record is much too cumbersome. Instead, you can enter a **query**—a search specification that prompts the computer to look for records in a particular field— and the computer will quickly locate the records. Most database software provides one or more methods for making queries.

● A **query language**, such as **SQL (Structured Query Language)**, provides a set of commands for locating and manipulating data. To locate all performances of Summertime before 1990 from a Jazz Songs database, you might enter a query such as: Select * from JazzSongs where SongTitle = 'Summertime' and Date < '1990'

● Some database software provides **natural language query** capabilities. To make a query, you can simply enter a question, such as: Who performed Summertime before 1990? As an alternative to a query language or a natural language query, the database software might allow you to **query by example (QBE)**, simply by filling out a form with the type of data you want to locate.

● Database software can help you print reports, export data to other programs (such as to a spreadsheet where you can graph the data), convert the data to other formats (such as HTML so that you can post the data on the Web), and transmit data to other computers. Whether you print, import, copy, save, or transmit the data you find in databases, it is your responsibility to use it appropriately. Never introduce inaccurate information into a database. Respect copyrights, giving credit to the person or organization that compiled the data. You should always respect the privacy of the people who are the subject of the data. Unless you have permission to do so, do not divulge names, social security numbers, or other identifying information that might compromise someone's privacy.

FIGURE C-19: Defining a database

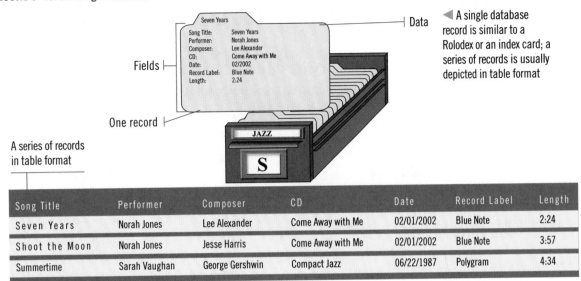

Fields

One record

Data

A series of records
in table format

A single database
record is similar to a
Rolodex or an index card; a
series of records is usually
depicted in table format

Song Title	Performer	Composer	CD	Date	Record Label	Length
Seven Years	Norah Jones	Lee Alexander	Come Away with Me	02/01/2002	Blue Note	2:24
Shoot the Moon	Norah Jones	Jesse Harris	Come Away with Me	02/01/2002	Blue Note	3:57
Summertime	Sarah Vaughan	George Gershwin	Compact Jazz	06/22/1987	Polygram	4:34

FIGURE C-20: Related records

JAZZ PERFORMERS

Performer	Birth Date	Home Town
Ella Fitzgerald	04/25/1918	Newport News, VA
Norah Jones	03/30/1979	New York, NY
Billie Holiday	04/07/1915	Baltimore, MD

The two sets of records are related
by the Performer field; the relationship
allows you to select Norah Jones from
the Jazz Performers records and jump
to any record in the Jazz Songs records
that Norah Jones performed

JAZZ SONGS

Song Title	Performer	Composer	CD	Date	Record Label	Length
Seven Years	Norah Jones	Lee Alexander	Come Away with Me	02/01/2002	Blue Note	2:24
Shoot the Moon	Norah Jones	Jesse Harris	Come Away with Me	02/01/2002	Blue Note	3:57
Summertime	Sarah Vaughan	George Gershwin	Compact Jazz	06/22/1987	Polygram	4:34

FIGURE C-21: Specifying fields

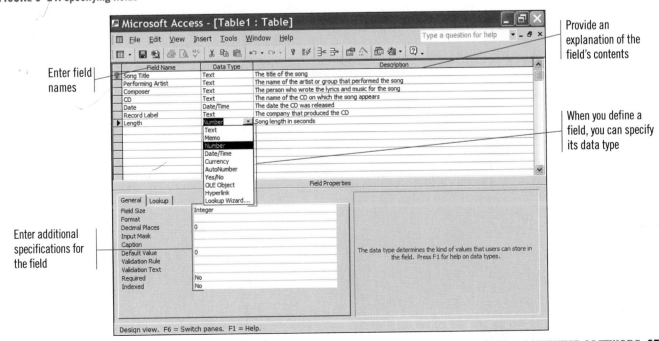

Enter field
names

Enter additional
specifications for
the field

Provide an
explanation of the
field's contents

When you define a
field, you can specify
its data type

Defining graphics software

In computer lingo, the term **graphics** refers to any picture, drawing, sketch, photograph, image, or icon that appears on your computer screen. **Graphics software** is designed to help you create, display, modify, manipulate, and print graphics. Many kinds of graphics software exist, and each one typically specializes in a particular type of graphic. If you are really interested in working with graphics, you will undoubtedly end up using more than one graphics software package, such as those described in this lesson.

DETAILS

- **Paint software** (sometimes called "image editing software") provides a set of electronic pens, brushes, and paints for painting images on the screen. Graphic artists, Web page designers, photographers, and illustrators use paint software as their primary computer-based graphics tool.

- **Photo editing software** includes features specially designed to fix poor-quality photos by modifying contrast and brightness, cropping out unwanted objects, and removing "red eye." Photos can also be edited using paint software, but photo editing software typically provides tools and wizards that simplify common photo editing tasks.

- **Drawing software** provides a set of lines, shapes, and colors that can be assembled into diagrams, corporate logos, and schematics. The drawings created with this type of software tend to have a "flat" cartoon-like quality, but they are very easy to modify and look good at just about any size. Figure C-22 provides more information on paint, photo editing, and drawing software.

- **3-D graphics software** provides a set of tools for creating "wireframes" that represent three-dimensional objects. A wireframe acts much like the framework for a pop-up tent. Just as you would construct the framework for the tent, then cover it with a nylon tent cover, 3-D graphics software can cover a wireframe object with surface texture and color to create a graphic of a 3-D object. See Figure C-23.

- **CAD software** (computer-aided design software) is a special type of 3-D graphics software designed for architects and engineers who use computers to create blueprints and product specifications. Scaled-down versions of professional CAD software provide simplified tools for homeowners who want to redesign their kitchens, examine new landscaping options, or experiment with floor plans.

- **Presentation software** provides all of the tools you need for combining text, graphics, graphs, animations, and sound into a series of electronic **slides**. See Figure C-24. You can display the electronic slides on a color monitor for a one-on-one presentation or use a computer projection device for group presentations. You can also output the presentation as overhead transparencies, paper copies, or 35-mm slides.

FIGURE C-22: Images created using paint, photo editing, and drawing software

▲ Paint software works well with realistic art and photos

▲ Photo editing software includes special features for touching up photographs

▲ Drawing software tends to create two-dimensional "cartoon-like" images

FIGURE C-23: Images created using 3-D graphics tools

▼ 3-D graphics software provides tools for creating a wireframe that represents a three-dimensional object

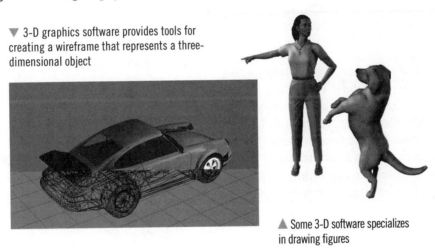

▲ Some 3-D software specializes in drawing figures

FIGURE C-24: A computer-based presentation

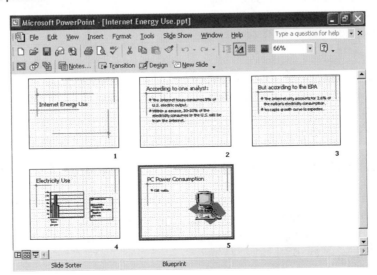

Defining business and science software

The terms business software and science software provide a broad umbrella for several types of software that are designed to help businesses and organizations accomplish routine or specialized tasks. These types of software provide a structured environment dedicated to a particular number-crunching task, such as money management, mathematical modeling, or statistical analysis.

Info Web

NUMERIC
SOFTWARE

DETAILS

- **Accounting and finance software** helps you keep a record of monetary transactions and investments. In this software category, **personal finance software** is geared toward individual finances. **Tax preparation software** is a specialized type of personal finance software designed to help you gather your annual income and expense data, identify deductions, and calculate your tax payment.

- Some accounting and finance software is geared toward business. If you're an entrepreneur, **small business accounting software** can be a real asset. These easy-to-use programs don't require more than a basic understanding of accounting and finance principles. This type of software helps you invoice customers and keep track of what they owe. It stores additional customer data, such as contact information and purchasing history. Inventory functions keep track of the products that you carry. Payroll capabilities automatically calculate wages and deduct federal, state, and local taxes.

- **Vertical market software** is designed to automate specialized tasks in a specific market or business. Examples include patient management and billing software specially designed for hospitals, job estimating software for construction businesses, and student record management software for schools. Today, almost every business has access to some type of specialized vertical market software designed to automate, streamline, or computerize key business activities.

- **Horizontal market software** is generic software that can be used by just about any kind of business. **Payroll software** is a good example of horizontal market software. Almost every business has employees and must maintain payroll records. No matter what type of business uses it, payroll software must collect similar data and make similar calculations in order to produce payroll checks and W2 forms. Accounting software and project management software are additional examples of horizontal market software. **Accounting software** helps a business keep track of the money flowing in and out of various accounts. **Project management software** is an important tool for planning large projects, scheduling project tasks, and tracking project costs.

- **Groupware**, another umbrella term in the world of business software, is designed to help several people collaborate on a single project using network or Internet connections. It usually provides the capability to maintain schedules for all of the group members, automatically select meeting times for the group, facilitate communication by e-mail or other channels, distribute documents according to a prearranged schedule or sequence, and allow multiple people to contribute to a single document.

- One type of science-related software is **statistical software**, which helps you analyze large sets of data to discover relationships and patterns. It is a helpful tool for summarizing survey results, test scores, experiment results, or population data. Most statistical software includes graphing capability so that you can display and explore your data visually.

- **Mathematical modeling software**, such as MathCAD and Mathematica, provides tools for solving a wide range of math, science, and engineering problems. See Figure C-25. Students, teachers, mathematicians, and engineers, in particular, appreciate how this software helps them recognize patterns that can be difficult to identify in columns of numbers.

Why spreadsheet software is not always the best software for businesses

Spreadsheet software provides a tool to work with numeric models by using values, labels, and formulas. The advantage of spreadsheet software is its flexibility. You can create customized calculations according to your exact specifications. The disadvantage of spreadsheet software is that, aside from a few pre-designed templates, you are responsible for entering formulas and selecting functions for calculations. If you don't know the formulas, or don't understand the functions, you would do much better to purchase a business software package with those functions to meet your specific needs.

FIGURE C-25: Mathematical modeling software

$$\text{Solve}\left[\frac{P_x - q_x}{P_x - r_x} == \frac{P_y - q_y}{P_y - r_y} == \frac{P_z - q_z}{P_z - r_z}, \{q_x, q_y\}\right] /. \{P_x \rightarrow 0, P_y \rightarrow 0, P_z \rightarrow 1, q_z \rightarrow -1\}$$

▲ Mathematical modeling software helps you visualize the product of complex formulas; the points from a sphere are graphed onto a plane to demonstrate the principles behind the Astronomical Clock of Prague

FIGURE C-26

▲ **Microsoft Office Professional Edition 2003**
Word
Excel
Outlook
PowerPoint
Access

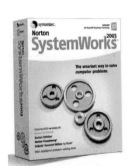

▲ **Norton SystemWorks**
Norton AntiVirus
Norton Utilities
Norton Password Manager
Norton CleanSweep
Norton GoBack Personal
    Edition

▲ **Adobe Creative Suite**
Adobe Illustrator CS
Adobe Photoshop CS
Adobe InDesign CS
Adobe GoLive CS
Adobe Acrobat
    Professional

What is a software suite?

A **software suite** is a collection of application software sold as a single package. See Figure C-26. Office suites, such as Microsoft Office, Star Office, Open Office, and WordPerfect Office, typically include applications to boost basic productivity: word processing, spreadsheet, and e-mail software. Graphics suites, such as Adobe Creative Suite, Macromedia Studio MX 2004, and CorelDRAW Graphics Suite, typically include paint, draw, and Web graphics tools. Software suites are available in many application categories, such as productivity, antivirus, and graphics.

Purchasing a software suite is usually much less expensive than purchasing the applications separately. Another advantage is usability. Because all the applications in a suite are produced by the same software publisher, they tend to use similar user interfaces and provide an easy way to transport data from one application to another. The disadvantage of a software suite is that it might include applications you don't need. If that is the case, you should calculate the price of the applications you do need and compare that to the cost of the suite.

Defining entertainment and education software

The computer can provide entertainment in many formats, including listening to music, watching videos, and playing games. Computer games are the most popular type of entertainment software. Software classified as educational can also be entertaining. When these software categories often overlap, the product is called edutainment.

DETAILS

● It is easy to make your own digital voice and music recordings and store them on your computer's hard disk. Windows and Mac OS operating system utilities typically supply the necessary **audio editing software**, including Sound Recorder on PCs (see Figure C-27), and iTunes on iMacs. Audio editing software typically includes playback as well as recording capabilities. A specialized version of this software called karaoke software integrates music files and on-screen lyrics.

● **MP3** is a music compression file format that stores digitized music in such a way that the sound quality is excellent, but the file size remains relatively small—small enough to be easily downloaded from the Web. To listen to MP3 music on your computer, you need an **MP3 player**. Versions of MP3 player software are available for many handheld computers and for personal computers running Windows, Mac OS, and Linux.

● **Ear training software** targets musicians and music students who want to learn to play by ear, develop tuning skills, recognize notes and keys, and develop other musical skills. **Notation software** is the musician's equivalent of a word processor. It helps musicians compose, edit, and print the notes for their compositions. For non-musicians, **computer-aided music software** is designed to generate unique musical compositions simply by selecting the musical style, instruments, key, and tempo. **MIDI sequencing software** and software synthesizers are an important part of the studio musician's toolbox. They're great for sound effects and for controlling keyboards and other digital instruments.

● **Video editing software** provides a set of tools for transferring video footage from a camcorder to a computer, clipping out unwanted footage, assembling video segments in any sequence, adding special visual effects, and adding a sound track. Despite an impressive array of features, video editing software is relatively easy to use, as explained in Figure C-28.

● Computer games are generally classified into subcategories, such as multiplayer, role-playing, action, adventure, puzzles, simulations, and strategy/war games. Multiplayer games provide an environment in which two or more players can participate in the same game. Players can use Internet technology to band together in sophisticated visual environments. Massively multiplayer games operate on multiple Internet servers, each one with the capacity to handle thousands of players at peak times.

● Since it was established in 1994, the Entertainment Software Rating Board (ESRB) has rated more than 7,000 video and computer games. ESRB ratings have two parts: rating symbols that suggest what age group the game is best for, and content descriptors that tell you about content elements that may be of interest or concern. Rating symbols, shown in Figure C-29, can usually be found on the game box.

● **Educational software** helps you learn and practice new skills. For the youngest students, educational software teaches basic arithmetic and reading skills. Instruction is presented in game format, and the levels of play are adapted to the player's age and ability. For older students and adults, software is available for educational endeavors such as learning languages, training yourself to use new software, learning how to play the piano or guitar, preparing for standardized tests, improving keyboarding skills, and even learning managerial skills for a diverse workplace.

● **Reference software** provides you with a collection of information and a way to access that information. The reference software category spans a wide range of applications from encyclopedias to medical references, from map software to trip planners, and from cookbooks to telephone books. An encyclopedia on CD-ROM or the Web has several advantages over its printed counterpart. For example, in addition to containing text, graphics, and audio, it might also contain video clips and interactive timelines. Finding information is easier, since you can search using keywords or click hyperlinks to access related articles.

Info Web
MUSIC SOFTWARE

FIGURE C-27: Audio editing software

Menus provide additional digital editing features, such as speed control, volume adjustments, clipping, and mixing

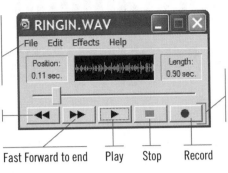

Audio editing software, such as Sound Recorder, provides controls much like a tape recorder

Rewind to beginning

Fast Forward to end | Play | Stop | Record

Info Web
VIDEO EDITING SOFTWARE

FIGURE C-28: Video editing software

▶ Video editing software, such as Adobe Premiere, helps you import a series of video clips from a camera or VCR, arrange the clips in the order of your choice, add transitions between clips, and add an audio track

The video and sound clips that you import for the project are displayed in a list so that you can easily select them in sequence

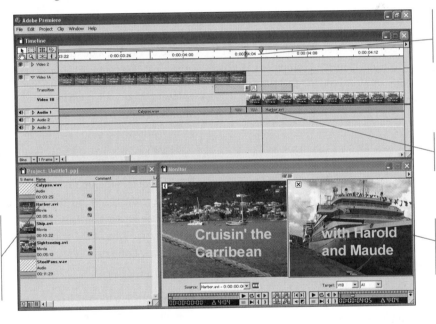

Use the timeline to indicate the sequence for your video clips and transitions

Arrange the audio tracks to synchronize with each video clip

Preview your video to see how the clips, transitions, and soundtrack all work together

Info Web
SOFTWARE RATINGS

FIGURE C-29: ESRB ratings and symbols

EARLY CHILDHOOD
Suitable for ages 3 and older. Contains no material that parents would find inappropriate.

TEEN
Suitable for 13 and older. May contain violent content, mild or strong language, and/or suggestive themes.

ADULTS ONLY
Content suitable only for adults. May include graphic depictions of sex and/or violence.

EVERYONE
Suitable for ages 6 and older. May contain minimal violence, some comic mischief, or crude language.

MATURE
Suitable for 17 and older. May contain mature sexual themes or more intense violence or language.

RATING PENDING
Product has been submitted, but a rating has not yet been assigned.

Understanding licenses and copyrights

Once you purchase a software package, you might assume that you can install it and use it in any way that you like. In fact, your "purchase" entitles you to use the software only in certain prescribed ways. In most countries, computer software, like a book or movie, is protected by a copyright. In addition to copyright protection, computer software is often protected by the terms of a software license. Copyright laws provide fairly severe restrictions on copying, distributing, and reselling software. However, a license agreement may offer some rights to consumers as well.

Info Web

SOFTWARE COPYRIGHT

DETAILS

- A **software license**, or "license agreement," is a legal contract that defines the ways in which you may use a computer program. For personal computer software, you will find the license on the outside of the package, on a separate card inside the package, on the CD packaging, or in one of the program files.

- Typically, computer owners purchase the right to use software that is distributed under a **single-user license** that limits use of the software to only one person at a time. Schools, organizations, and businesses sometimes purchase a site license, multiple-user license, or concurrent-use license, which allows more than one person to use the software. A **site license** is generally priced at a flat rate and allows software to be used on all computers at a specific location. A **multiple-user license** is priced per user and allows the allocated number of people to use the software at any time. A **concurrent-use license** is priced per copy and allows a specific number of copies to be used at the same time.

- Most legal contracts require signatures before the terms of the contract take effect. This requirement becomes unwieldy with software; imagine having to sign a license agreement and return it before you can use a new software package. To circumvent the signature requirement, software publishers typically use two techniques to validate a software license: shrink-wrap licenses and installation agreements. When you purchase computer software, the distribution disks, CDs, or DVDs are usually sealed in an envelope, plastic box, or shrink wrapping. A **shrink-wrap license** goes into effect as soon as you open the packaging. Figure C-30 explains more about the mechanics of a shrink-wrap license.

- An **installation agreement** is displayed on the screen when you first install the software. After reading the software license on the screen, you can indicate that you accept the terms of the license by clicking a designated button usually labeled "OK," "I agree," or "I accept."

- Software licenses are often lengthy and written in legalese, but your legal right to use the software continues only as long as you abide by the terms of the software license. Therefore, you should understand the software license for any software you use. When you read a software license agreement, look for answers to the following questions: Am I buying the software or licensing it? When does the license go into effect? Under what circumstances can I make copies? Can I rent the software? Can I sell the software? What if the software includes a distribution CD and a set of distribution disks? Does the software publisher provide a warranty? Can I loan the software to a friend?

- A **copyright** is a form of legal protection that grants the author of an original work an exclusive right to copy, distribute, sell, and modify that work, except under special circumstances described by copyright laws. Exceptions include the purchaser's right to copy software from a distribution disk or Web site to a computer's hard disk in order to install it; to make an extra, or backup, copy of the software in case the original copy becomes erased or damaged; and to copy and distribute sections of a software program for use in critical reviews and teaching.

- Most software displays a **copyright notice**, such as "© 2004 eCourseWare," on one of its screens. However, because this notice is not required by law, programs without a copyright notice are still protected by copyright law. People who circumvent copyright law and illegally copy, distribute, or modify software are sometimes called software pirates, and their illegal copies are referred to as pirated software.

FIGURE C-30: A shrink-wrap license

▶ When software has a shrink-wrap license, you agree to the terms of the software license by opening the package; if you do not agree with the terms, you should return the software in its unopened package

Reviewing software copyright protections

Commercial software is typically sold in computer stores or at Web sites. Although you buy this software, you actually purchase only the right to use it under the terms of the software license. A license for commercial software typically adheres closely to the limitations provided by copyright law, although it might give you permission to install the software on a computer at work and on a computer at home, provided that you use only one of them at a time.

Shareware is copyrighted software marketed under a try before you buy policy. It typically includes a license that permits you to use the software for a trial period. To use it beyond the trial period, you must send in a registration fee. A shareware license usually allows you to make copies of the software and distribute them to others. If they choose to use the software, they must send in a registration fee as well. These shared copies provide a low-cost marketing and distribution channel.

Registration fee payment relies on the honor system, so unfortunately many shareware authors collect only a fraction of the money they deserve for their programming efforts. Thousands of shareware programs are available, encompassing just about as many applications as commercial software.

Freeware is copyrighted software that is available without a fee. Because the software is protected by copyright, you cannot do anything with it that is not expressly allowed by copyright law or by the author. Typically, the license for freeware permits you to use the software, copy it, and give it away, but does not permit you to alter it or sell it. Many utility programs, device drivers, and some games are available as freeware.

Open source software makes the uncompiled program instructions available to programmers who want to modify and improve the software. Open source software may be sold or distributed free of charge, but it must, in every case, include the uncompiled source code. Linux is an example of open source software, as is FreeBSD—a version of UNIX designed for personal computers.

Public domain software is not protected by copyright because the copyright has expired or the author has placed the program in the public domain, making it available without restriction. Public domain software may be freely copied, distributed, and even resold. The primary restriction on public domain software is that you are not allowed to apply for a copyright on it.

Installing Software

No matter how you obtain a new software package, you must install it on your computer before you can use it.

Printed on the software package, or on the software publisher's Web site, are the **system requirements**, which specify the operating system and minimum hardware capacities for a software product to work correctly. When you **install** software, the new software files are placed in the appropriate folders on your computer's hard disk, and then your computer performs any software or hardware configurations necessary to make sure the program is ready to run.

Windows software typically contains a **setup program** that guides you through the installation process. Figure C-31 shows you what to expect when you use a setup program.

FIGURE C-31: Installing from distribution media

1.
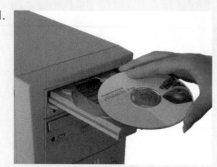

▲ Insert the distribution disk, CD, or DVD. The setup program should start automatically. If it does not, look for a file called *Setup.exe* and then run it.

2.
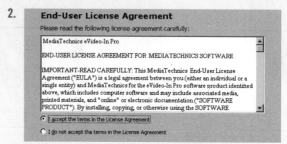

▲ Read the license agreement, if one is presented on the screen. By agreeing to the terms of the license, you can proceed with the installation.

3.
| ● Full Installation |
| ○ Custom Installation |

▲ Select the installation option that best meets your needs. If you select a full installation, the setup program copies all files and data from the distribution medium to the hard disk of your computer system. A full installation provides you with access to all features of the software.

If you select a custom installation, the setup program displays a list of software features for your selection. After you select the features you want, the setup program copies only the selected program files, support programs, and data files to your hard disk. A custom installation can save space on your hard disk drive.

4.
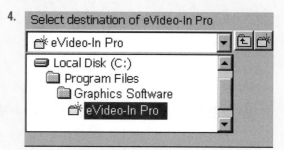

▲ Follow the prompts provided by the setup program to specify a folder to hold the new software program. You can use the default folder specified by the setup program or a folder of your own choosing. You can also create a new folder during the setup process.

5.

▲ If the software includes multiple distribution CDs, insert each one in the specified drive when the setup program prompts you.

6.
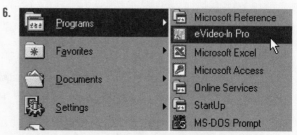

▲ When the setup is complete, start the program you just installed to make sure it works.

Downloadable software can be provided in several different formats. Some automatically install themselves, whereas others require manual procedures. A downloadable file typically is set up as a self-installing executable file, self-executing zip file, or non-executing zip file. Figure C-32 shows you what to expect when you download a program to install.

From time to time, you might also want to uninstall some of the software that exists on your computer. Operating systems, such as Windows and Mac OS, provide access to an **uninstall routine** that deletes the software's files from various directories on your computer's hard disk. The uninstall routine also removes references to the program from the desktop and from operating system files, such as the file system and, in the case of Windows, from the Windows Registry.

FIGURE C-32: Installing downloaded software

1.

▲ At the distribution Web site, locate any information pertaining to installing the software. Read it. You might also want to print it.

2.

▲ Click the download link.

3.
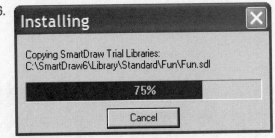

▲ If you are downloading from a trusted site and have antivirus software running, click the Open button in the File Download dialog box.

4.
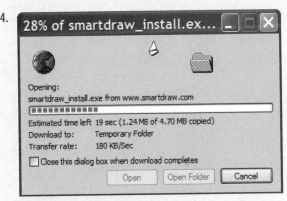

▲ Wait for the download to finish.

5.

▲ Specify a folder to hold the new software program. You can use the default folder specified by the setup program or a folder of your own choosing. You can also create a new folder during the setup process.

6.

<!-- Installing dialog -->
Installing

Copying SmartDraw Trial Libraries:
C:\SmartDraw6\Library\Standard\Fun\Fun.sdl

75%

Cancel

▲ Wait for the setup program to uncompress the downloaded file and install the software in the selected directory. During this process, respond to license agreement and other prompts. When the installation is complete, test the software to make sure it works.

The news business is all about gathering and disseminating information as quickly as possible (see Figure C-33). In the ancient world, news spread by word of mouth, relayed by bards and merchants who traveled from town to town—in essence, they were the first reporters to "broadcast" the news. Throughout history, technology has played a major role in how news reporting has evolved into the modern 24-hour "live" news networks. Johann Gutenberg's printing press (ca. 1450), the first technological breakthrough in the news business, made it feasible to publish news as printed notices tacked to walls in the town square. As paper became more economical, resourceful entrepreneurs sold broadsheets to people eager for news, and the concept of a newspaper was born. The first regularly published newspapers appeared in Germany and Holland in 1609, and the first English newspaper, the *Weekly News*, was published in 1622.

But the news spread slowly. In the early 1800s, it took four weeks for newspapers in New York to receive reports from London. With the advent of the telegraph in 1844, however, reporters from distant regions could "wire" stories to their newspapers for publication the next day. The first radio reporters in the 1920s offered live broadcasts of sports events, church services, and variety shows. Before the 1950s, black-and-white newsreels shown in movie theaters provided the only visual imagery of news events; and it was television that gave viewers news images on a nightly basis.

Technology has benefited print journalism in many ways. For decades, typesetters transferred reporters' handwritten stories into neatly set columns of type. Today, reporters use computers and word processing software to type their stories and run a preliminary check of spelling and grammar. Stories are submitted via a computer network to editors, who use the same software to edit stories so they fit space constraints. The typesetting process has been replaced by desktop publishing software and computer to plate (CTP) technology. Digital pages produced with desktop publishing software are sent to a raster image processor (RIP), which converts the pages into dots that form words and images. A platesetter uses lasers to etch the dots onto a physical plate, which is then mounted on the printing press to produce printed pages. CTP is much faster and more flexible than typesetting, so publishers can make last-minute changes to accommodate late-breaking stories.

Personal computers have added a new dimension to the news-gathering process. Reporters who were once limited to personal interviews, observation, and fact gathering at libraries, can now make extensive use of Internet resources and e-mail. Web sites and online databases provide background information on all sorts of topics. Other resources include newsgroups and chat rooms, where reporters can monitor public opinion on current events and identify potential news sources.

FIGURE C-33

Most major networks maintain interactive Web sites that offer online polls and bulletin boards designed to collect viewers' opinions. Although online poll respondents are not a representative sample of the population, and the statistics are not scientifically valid, they can help news organizations gauge viewer opinions and determine whether news coverage is comprehensive and effective.

E-mail has changed the way reporters communicate with colleagues and sources. It's often the only practical method for contacting people in remote locations or distant time zones, and it's useful with reluctant sources, who feel more comfortable providing information under the cloak of anonymous Hotmail or Yahoo! accounts. "Vetting" e-mail sources—verifying credentials such as name, location, and occupation—can be difficult, however, so reporters tend not to rely on these sources without substantial corroboration.

For broadcast journalism, digital communications play a major role in today's "live on the scene" television reporting. Most news organizations maintain remote production vans, sometimes called "satellite news gathering (SNG) trucks," that travel to the site of breaking news. These complete mobile production facilities include camera control units, audio and video recording equipment, and satellite or microwave transmitters. They need only to raise their antennas to begin to broadcast.

On-the-scene reporting does not always require a truck full of equipment. Audiovisual editing units and video cameras have gone digital, making them easier to use and sized to fit in a suitcase. A new breed of "backpack journalists" carries mini-DV cameras, notebook computers, and satellite phones. Jane Ellen Stevens, a pioneer backpack journalist specializing in science and technology, has reported since 1997 from remote locations, such as a space camp in Russia. Backpack journalists can connect their minicams to notebook computers with a firewire cable, transfer their video footage to the hard disk, and then edit the footage using consumer-level video editing software. The resulting video files, compressed for transmission over a satellite phone, are sent to newsroom technicians, who decompress and then broadcast them—all in a matter of seconds. One drawback of backpack journalists' use of minicams and compression is that the video quality usually isn't as crisp as images filmed with studio cameras. News organizations with high standards were hesitant to use this lower quality video, but have found that viewers would rather see a low-quality image now than a high-quality image later. To many viewers, a few rough edges just make the footage seem more compelling, more "you are there."

Computers, the Internet, and communications technology make it possible to instantly broadcast live reports across the globe, but live reporting is not without controversy. A reporter who arrives at the scene of a disaster with microphone in hand has little time for reflection, vetting, and cross-checking, so grievous errors, libelous images, or distasteful video footage sometimes find their way into news reports.

Jeff Gralnick, former executive producer for ABC News, remarks, "In the old days, we had time to think before we spoke. We had time to write, time to research and time to say, 'Hey, wait a minute.' Now we don't even have the time to say, 'Hey, wait a nanosecond.' Just because we can say it or do it, should we?" Technology has given journalists a powerful arsenal of tools for gathering and reporting the news, but has also increased their accountability for accurate, socially responsible reporting.

context

Is Piracy a Problem?

Software is easy to steal. You don't have to walk out of a Best Buy store with a Quicken Deluxe box under your shirt. You can simply borrow your friend's distribution CDs and install a copy of the program on your computer's hard disk. It seems so simple that it couldn't be illegal. But it is. Software piracy takes many forms. End-user piracy includes friends loaning distribution disks to each other and installing software on more computers than the license allows.

Counterfeiting is the large-scale illegal duplication of software distribution media and sometimes even its packaging. According to Microsoft, many software counterfeiting groups are linked to organized crime and money-laundering schemes that fund a diverse collection of illegal activities. Counterfeit software is sold in retail stores and online auctions—often the packaging looks so authentic that buyers have no idea they have purchased illegal goods.

Internet piracy uses the Web as a way to illegally distribute unauthorized software. Some pirated software has even been modified to eliminate serial numbers, registration requirements, expiration dates, or other forms of copy protection. The Business Software Alliance (BSA) estimates that more than 800,000 Web sites illegally sell or distribute software. In many countries, including the United States, software pirates are subject to civil lawsuits for monetary damages and criminal prosecution, which can result in jail time and stiff fines. Nonetheless, software piracy continues to have enormous impact. According to the Software and Information Industry Association (SIIA), a leading anti-piracy watchdog, revenue losses from business software piracy typically exceed $2 billion per year. This figure reveals only part of the piracy problem—it does not include losses from rampant game and educational software piracy, which are estimated to exceed $12 billion a year.

A small, but vocal, minority of software users, such as members of GNU (which stands for "Gnu's Not UNIX"), believes that data and software should be freely distributed. Richard Stallman writes in the GNU Manifesto, "I consider that the golden rule requires that if I like a program I must share it with other people who like it. Software sellers want to divide users and conquer them, making each user agree not to share with others. I refuse to break solidarity with other users in this way. I cannot in good conscience sign a nondisclosure agreement or a software license agreement."

As a justification of high piracy rates, some observers point out that people in many countries simply might not be able to afford software priced for the U.S. market. This argument could apply to China, where the average annual income is equivalent to about $3,500, and in North Korea, where the average income is only $900. A Korean who legitimately purchases Microsoft Office for $250 would be spending more than one-quarter of his or her annual income.

Most countries with a high incidence of software piracy, however, have strong economies and respectable per capita incomes. To further discredit the theory that piracy stems from poverty, India—which has a fairly large computer-user community, but a per capita income of only $1,600—is not among the top 10 countries with high rates of software piracy.

Is software piracy really damaging? Who cares if you use Microsoft Office without paying for it? Software piracy is damaging because it has a negative effect on the economy. Software production makes a major contribution to the United States economy, employing more than 2 million people and accounting for billions of dollars in corporate revenue. Software piracy in the United States is responsible for tens of thousands of lost jobs, millions in lost wages, and lost tax revenues. Decreases in software revenues can have a direct effect on consumers, too. When software publishers must cut corners, they tend to reduce customer service and technical support. As a result, you, the consumer, get put on hold when you call for technical support, find fewer free technical support sites, and encounter customer support personnel who are only moderately knowledgeable about their products. The bottom line—software piracy negatively affects customer service.

As an alternative to cutting support costs, some software publishers might build the cost of software piracy into the price of the software. The unfortunate result is that those who legitimately license and purchase software pay an inflated price.

If economic factors do not account for the pervasiveness of software piracy, what does? Some analysts suggest that people need more education about software copyrights and the economic implications of piracy. Other analysts believe that copyright enforcement must be increased by implementing more vigorous efforts to identify and prosecute pirates.

▼ EXPAND THE IDEAS

1. Do you believe that software piracy is a serious issue? Write a two-page paper supporting your position. Include the opposing side's arguments in your report. Be sure to include your resources.

2. Do you think there are ways that software publishers can control piracy in the United States? In other countries? Do you know of any recent attempts at doing so? Work in a small group to brainstorm ideas and research recent trends or events. Compile your ideas and findings into a short presentation to give to the class. Include handouts for the audience and cite any sources you used.

3. Do you think that most software pirates understand that they are doing something illegal? Design a marketing campaign that could be used to educate the public about the issue. Create a poster that could be used in the campaign.

4. Should software publishers try to adjust software pricing for local markets? How would you propose such a pricing structure? How would these policies be enforced? Can you think of any other industry that adjusts prices for local markets? Write a two-page paper discussing your proposals and explaining your findings. Be sure to cite your sources.

End of Unit Exercises

▼ KEY TERMS

3-D graphics software
Absolute reference
Accounting and finance software
Accounting software
Application software
Audio editing software
Automatic recalculation
Bootstrap program
CAD software
Cell
Cell reference
Clip art
Commercial software
Compiler
Computer-aided software design
Computer language
Computer program
Computer programmer
Concurrent-use license
Copyright
Copyright notice
Data file
Database
Database software
Desktop operating system
Desktop publishing software
Drawing software
DOS
Ear training software
Educational software

Executable file
Field
Footer
Format
Formula
Frames
Freeware
Function
Graphical user interface (GUI)
Graphics
Graphics software
Groupware
Header
High-level language
Horizontal market software
Install
Installation agreement
Interpreter
Kernel
Label
Linux
Mac OS
Machine language
Mathematical modeling software
Microsoft Windows
Midi sequencing software
MP3
MP3 player
Multiple-user license
Multitasking operating system

Multiuser operating system
Natural language query
Network operating system
Notation software
Object code
Open source software
Operating system
Page layout
Paint software
Palm OS
Payroll software
Personal finance software
Photo editing software
Presentation software
Programming language
Project management software
Public domain software
Query
Query by example
Query language
Record
Reference software
Relative reference
Resource
Server operating system
Setup program
Shareware
Shrink-wrap license
Single-user license
Single-user operating system

Site license
Slide
Small business accounting
    software
Software
Software license
Software suite
Source code
Spreadsheet
Spreadsheet software
SQL
Statistical software
Support program
System requirements
System software
Table
Tax preparation software
Uninstall routine
UNIX
User-executable file
Utilities
Value
Vertical market software
Video editing software
Web authoring software
Windows Mobil OS
Windows XP tablet edition
Word processing software
Worksheet

▼ UNIT REVIEW

1. Use your own words to define each of the bold terms that appear throughout the unit. List 10 of the terms that are least familiar to you and write a sentence for each of them.

2. Make sure that you can list and describe the three types of files that are typically supplied on a software distribution disk.

3. Explain the difference between a compiler and an interpreter.

4. List three types of system software and at least five categories of application software.

5. Describe how an operating system manages resources.

6. Sketch a simple worksheet like one you might find in a spreadsheet software program and label the following: columns, rows, cell, active cell, values, labels, formulas, and Formula bar.

7. List three types of "number crunching" software that you can use instead of spreadsheet software and tell how you might use each one.

8. Describe when you would use each type of graphics software described in this unit.

9. Create a table with these column headings: single-user, multiuser, network, multitasking, and desktop operating system. List Linux, UNIX, Mac OS, and each version of Windows down the side of the table. Use a check mark to indicate which characteristics fit each operating system.

10. In your own words, explain what each of the ESRB ratings mean and how they would help you purchase software.

▼ FILL IN THE BEST ANSWER

1. Software can be divided into two major categories: application software and _SYSTEM_ software.

2. Software usually contains support programs and data files, in addition to a main _EXECUTABLE_ file that you run to start the software.

3. Instructions that are written in a(n) _HIGH_-level language must be translated into _MACHINE_ language before a computer can use them.

4. A(n) _Compiler_ translates all of the instructions in a program as a single batch, and the resulting machine language instructions are placed in a new file.

5. To run more than one program at a time, the operating system must allocate specific areas of _Memory_ for each program.

6. A(n) _graphical_ user interface provides a way for a user to interact with the software using a mouse and graphical objects on the screen.

7. A(n) _Multiuser_ operating system is designed to deal with input, output, and processing requests from many users.

8. A(n) _Network_ operating system provides communications and routing services that allow computers to share data, programs, and peripheral devices.

9. Palm OS and Windows Mobil OS are two of the most popular operating systems for _handheld_ computers.

10. Linux is an example of open _source_ software.

11. Various kinds of document _production_ software provide tools for creating and formatting printed and Web-based documents.

12. _Graphics_ software helps you work with wireframes, CAD drawings, photos, and slide presentations.

13. In a spreadsheet the rows are identified with _VALUE_ and the columns are identified with _TEXT_.

14. _VERTICAL_ market software is designed to automate specialized tasks in a specific market or business.

15. _Clip_ art is a collection of drawings and photos designed to be inserted into documents.

16. _MP3_ is a music compression file that stores digitized music in such a way that quality is excellent but the file size is relatively small.

17. _COPYRIGHT_ laws provide software authors with the exclusive right to copy, distribute, sell, and modify their work, except under special circumstances.

18. _Shareware_ is copyrighted software their is marketed with a "try before you buy" policy.

19. A(n) _Site_ license is generally priced at a flat rate and allows software to be used on all computers at a specific location.

20. Public _Domain_ software is not copyrighted, making it available for use without restriction, except that you cannot apply for a copyright on it.

▼ INDEPENDENT CHALLENGE 1

How you acquire software varies based on the software and your needs. If you have a home computer and own or have purchased software, complete the following independent challenge by writing a short paper discussing the issues raised below.

1. What software is installed on your computer? How did you acquire the software? What type of software does each package fall into based on the categories outlined in this unit?

2. Explain the differences between commercial software, shareware, open source software, freeware, and public domain software. Do you have any of these? If so, which ones? Why did you select one type over the other?

3. If possible, describe one experience installing software, describe the process of installing software from a distribution CD, and contrast it with the process of installing downloaded software.

4. Have you used software that has an ESRB rating? Based on your experience with the software, did you find that the rating was adequate and fair? Why or why not?

▼ INDEPENDENT CHALLENGE 2

When you use a software package, it is important to understand the legal restrictions on its use. For this independent challenge, make a photocopy of the license agreement for any software package. Read the license agreement, then answer these questions:

1. Is this a shrink-wrap license? Why or why not?

2. After you pay your computer dealer for the program covered by this license, who owns the program?

3. Can you legally have one copy of the program on your computer at work and another copy of the program on your computer at home if you use the software only in one place at a time?

4. Can you legally sell the software? Why or why not?

5. Under what conditions can you legally transfer possession of the program to someone else?

6. If you were the owner of a software store, could you legally rent the program to customers if you were sure they did not keep a copy after the rental period was over?

7. Can you legally install this software on one computer, but give more than one user access to it?

8. If you use this program for an important business decision and later find out that a mistake in the program caused you to lose $500,000, what legal recourse is provided by the license agreement?

▼ INDEPENDENT CHALLENGE 3

 There are so many software packages on the market today that it is often overwhelming to make a wise purchasing decision. The breadth of software available in each category is quite large, and no two packages claim all the same features. Do you base your decision to buy a new application package on word of mouth? Reviewer comments in professional magazines? Trying it out? To complete this independent challenge, you will research a type of software package that you intend to purchase.

1. Determine the type of package you want to select (graphics, DTP, word processing, Web development, e-mail, scheduling, or data management) and which operating system you plan to use.

2. Locate vendor ads either on the Internet or in local papers or trade magazines that sell software.

3. Read comparison reviews of the products. Create a chart detailing the features and prepare a competitive analysis of the three top candidates for your purchase.

4. Write a short summary of your findings, indicating which package you would buy and why.

▼ INDEPENDENT CHALLENGE 4

Copyrights and software piracy are very relevant issues for software users, developers, and educators. There is constant debate among all stakeholders as to the best models for software distribution, and how developers, publishers, or programmers should be compensated. To begin this project, log on to the Internet and use your favorite search engine or consult the Copyright and Piracy InfoWeb and link to the recommended Web pages to get an in-depth overview of the issue. Armed with this background, select one of the following viewpoints and statements and argue for or against it:

Viewpoints:

a. Free software advocates: As an enabling technology, software should be freely distributed, along with its modifiable source code.

b. Librarians: Copyright laws, especially the Digital Millennium Copyright Act, minimize the needs of the public and go too far in their efforts to protect the rights of software authors.

c. Software Publishers Association: Strong copyright laws and enforcement are essential for companies to publish and support high-quality software.

Directions:

1. Write a two- to five-page paper about this issue based on information you gather from the Internet.

2. Be sure to cite your sources and list them as part of the paper.

3. Follow your professor's instructions for formatting and submitting your paper.

▼ INDEPENDENT CHALLENGE 5

The Computers in Context section of this unit focused on computer and communications technology used by reporters and journalists. Technology has had a major effect on "backpack journalists" who use small-scale digital devices to gather and report the news.

Log on to the Internet and use your favorite search engine to collect information on the advantages and disadvantages of backpack journalism. In your research, you should explore technical issues, such as the cost of equipment, video quality, and transmission capabilities. Also explore ethical issues pertaining to on-the-spot news reporting.

1. Create an outline of the major points you researched.

2. Summarize your research in a two- to four-page paper. Make sure you cite sources for your material.

3. Follow your professor's instructions for formatting and submitting your paper.

▼ STUDENT EDITION LABS

Reinforce the concepts you have learned in this unit through the **Using Windows, Word Processing, Spreadsheets, Databases, Presentation Software, Installing and Uninstalling Software,** and **Advanced Spreadsheets** Student Edition Labs, available online at the Illustrated Computer Concepts Web site.

▼ SAM LABS

If you have a SAM user profile, you have access to additional content, features, and functionality. Log in to your SAM account and go to your assignments page to see what your instructor has assigned for this unit.

Figure C-34 shows images from handheld computer and tablet PC screens. The image on the left is the Palm OS, the image on the right is the Windows Mobile OS; and the image below is the Windows operating system designed specifically for tablet PCs.

FIGURE C-34

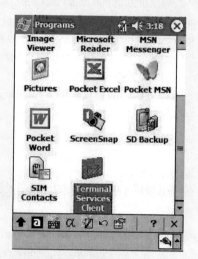

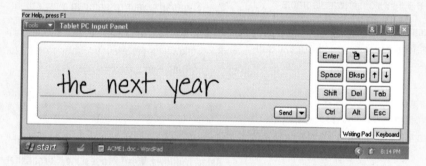

Log on to the Internet. Find Web sites that discuss each of the three operating systems shown above.

1. In your research find five facts about each of the operating systems. Write a brief statement explaining the similarities and differences among these operating systems.

2. Which devices are supported by each of these operating systems?

3. Which utilities are built into these operating systems? Are the utilities similar to utilities you find in personal computer desktop operating systems? Explain the differences.

4. List three applications that are supported by these operating systems. Are these available for personal computer desktop computers also? If so, list one major difference, if any, in the functionality of the software.

UNIT D
Digital Electronics and File Management

OBJECTIVES

Introduce digital data representation

Introduce integrated circuits

Explore processor performance factors

Understand computer memory: RAM

Explore computer memory

Introduce computer file basics

Understand file locations

Explore file management

Understand logical file storage

Use files

Understand physical file storage

Tech Talk: How a Processor Executes Instructions

Computers in Context: Astronomy

Issue: New Chip Technologies

In this unit, you will learn how data representation and digital electronics work together to make computers tick. You will learn about two of the most important components in a computer—the processor and memory. You will learn how they work and how they affect computer performance. You will learn about the different types of memory and how memory works to store and process data. You will get a general introduction to computer files and learn some very practical information about filenames. You will learn techniques for organizing computer files so that they are easy to access and update. You will also learn how an operating system stores, deletes, and tracks files. The Tech Talk section explains the details of how a processor executes instructions. You'll have the opportunity to look at computers in the context of astronomy. The Issue discusses new chip technologies and their impact on the future of computing.

Introducing digital data representation

FYI

If you need to brush up on binary numbers, refer to the Working with Binary Numbers lab in Unit B.

Data representation refers to the form in which information is conceived, manipulated, and recorded. Because a computer is an electronic digital device, it uses electrical signals to represent data. A **digital device** works with discrete data or digits, such as 1 and 0, "on" and "off," or "yes" and "no." Data exists in the computer as a series of electronic signals represented as 1s and 0s, each of which is referred to as a **bit**. Most computer coding schemes use eight bits to represent each number, letter, or symbol. A series of eight bits is referred to as a **byte**. This lesson looks more closely at the coding schemes used in digital representation.

DETAILS

- Just as Morse code uses dashes and dots to represent the letters of the alphabet, computers use sequences of bits to represent numbers, letters, punctuation marks, music, pictures, and videos. **Digital electronics** makes it possible for a computer to manipulate simple "on" and "off" signals to perform complex tasks. The **binary number system** allows computers to represent virtually any number simply by using 0s and 1s, which translate into electrical "on" and "off" signals.

- Digital computers use many different coding schemes to represent data. The coding scheme used by a computer depends on whether the data is numeric data or character data.

- **Numeric data** consists of numbers representing quantities that might be used in arithmetic operations. For example, your annual income is numeric data, as is your age. Computers represent numeric data using the binary number system, also called "base 2." The binary number system has only two digits: 0 and 1. These digits can be converted to electrical "ons" or "offs" inside a computer. The number 2 cannot be used in the binary number system; so instead of writing *2* you would write *10*, which you would pronounce as *one zero*. See Figure D-1.

- **Character data** is composed of letters, symbols, and numerals that will not be used in arithmetic operations. Examples of character data include your name, address, and hair color. Character data is also represented by a series of 1s and 0s.

- Several types of codes are used to represent character data, including ASCII, EBCDIC, and Unicode. **ASCII (American Standard Code for Information Interchange)** requires only seven bits for each character. For example, the ASCII code for an uppercase

"A" is 1000001. ASCII provides codes for 128 characters, including uppercase letters, lowercase letters, punctuation symbols, and numerals. A superset of ASCII, called **Extended ASCII**, uses eight bits to represent each character. See Figure D-2. The eighth bit provides codes for 128 additional characters, which are usually boxes, circles, and other graphical symbols. **EBCDIC (Extended Binary-Coded Decimal Interchange Code)** is an alternative 8-bit code, usually used by older IBM mainframe computers. **Unicode** uses 16 bits and provides codes for 65,000 characters, a real bonus for representing the alphabets of multiple languages. Most personal computers use Extended ASCII code, although Unicode is becoming increasingly popular.

- Because computers represent numeric data with binary equivalents, ASCII codes that represent numbers might seem unnecessary. Computers, however, sometimes distinguish between numeric data and numerals. For example, you don't use your social security number in calculations, so a computer considers it character data composed of numerals, not numbers.

- To work with pictures and sounds, a computer must **digitize** the information that makes up the picture (such as the colors) and the information that makes up the sound (such as the notes) into 1s and 0s. Computers convert colors and notes into numbers, which can be represented by bits and stored in files as a long series of 1s and 0s.

- Your computer needs to know whether to interpret those 1s and 0s as ASCII code, binary numbers, or the code for a picture or sound. Most computer files contain a **file header** with information on the code that was used to represent the file data. A file header is stored along with the file and can be read by the computer, but never appears on the screen.

FIGURE D-1: Comparing decimal and binary numbers

▶ The decimal system uses ten symbols to represent numbers: 0, 1, 2, 3, 4, 5, 6, 7, 8, and 9; the binary number system uses only two symbols: 0 and 1

DECIMAL (BASE 10)	BINARY (BASE 2)
0	0
1	1
2	10
3	11
4	100
5	101
6	110
7	111
8	1000
9	1001
10	1010
11	1011
1000	1111101000

FIGURE D-2: A sample of Extended ASCII code

▶ The Extended ASCII code uses a series of eight 1s and 0s to represent 256 characters, including lowercase letters, upper-case letters, symbols, and numerals. The first 63 ASCII characters are not shown in this table because they represent special control sequences that cannot be printed.

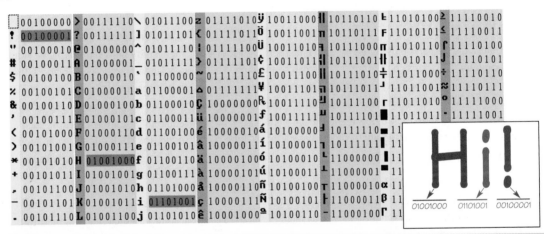

Quantifying bits and bytes

A bit is one binary digit and a byte is eight bits. The word "bit" can be abbreviated as a lowercase "b" and byte can be abbreviated as an uppercase "B."

Bits and bytes are used in different ways. Transmission speeds are usually expressed in bits, whereas storage space is usually expressed in bytes. The speed 56 Kbps means 56 kilobits per second; the capacity 8 GB means 8 gigabytes. "Kilo" is usually a prefix that means 1,000. For example, $50 K means $50,000. However, when it refers to bits or bytes, a "kilo" is 1,024 because computer engineers measure everything in base 2, and 2^{10} in base 2 is 1,024, not 1,000. So a **kilobit** (abbreviated Kb or Kbit) is 1,024 bits and a **kilobyte** (abbreviated KB or Kbyte) is 1,024 bytes. The prefix "mega" refers to a million, or in the context of bits and bytes, precisely 1,048,576 (the equivalent of 2^{20}). Mb or Mbit is the abbreviation for **megabit**. MB or Mbyte is the abbreviation for **megabyte**.

The prefix "giga" refers to a billion, or precisely 1,073,741,824. A **gigabit** (Gb or Gbit) is approximately one billion bits. A **gigabyte** (GB or GByte) is one billion bytes. Gigabytes are typically used to refer to RAM and hard disk capacity. Tera- (trillion), peta- (thousand trillion), and exa- (quintillion) are prefixes

for large amounts of data. Figure D-3 summarizes the commonly used terms to quantify computer data.

FIGURE D-3

Bit	One binary digit
Byte	8 bits
Kilobit	1,024 or 2^{10} bits
Kilobyte	1,024 or 2^{10} bytes
Megabit	1,048,576 or 2^{20} bits
Megabyte	1,048,576 or 2^{20} bytes
Gigabit	2^{30} bits
Gigabyte	2^{30} bytes
Terabyte	2^{40} bytes
Petabyte	2^{50} bytes
Exabyte	2^{60} bytes

Introducing integrated circuits

Computers are electronic devices that use electrical signals and circuits to represent, process, and move data. Bits take the form of electrical pulses that can travel over circuits. An **integrated circuit (IC)** is a super-thin slice of semi-conducting material packed with microscopic circuit elements such as wires, transistors, capacitors, logic gates, and resistors.

DETAILS

- If it weren't for digital electronics, computers would be huge, and the inside of a computer's system unit would contain a jumble of wires and other electronic components. Today's computers contain relatively few parts. A computer's system unit contains circuit boards, storage devices, and a power supply that converts current from an AC wall outlet into the DC current used by computer circuitry. See Figure D-4.

- Integrated circuits can be used for processors, memory, and support circuitry. The terms computer chip, microchip, and chip originated as jargon for integrated circuit. Chips are classified by the number of miniaturized components they contain—from small-scale integration (SSI) of less than 100 components per chip to ultra large-scale integration (ULSI) of more than 1 million components per chip.

- The processor, memory modules, and support circuitry chips are packaged in a protective carrier or "chip package." Chip carriers vary in shape and size including small rectangular **DIPs (dual in-line packages)** with caterpillar-like legs protruding from a black, rectangular body; long, slim **DIMMs (dual in-line memory modules)**; pin-cushion-like **PGAs (pin-grid arrays)**; and cassette-like **SEC (single-edge contact) cartridges**, such as those pictured in Figure D-5. The pins on each chip package provide the electronic connection between the integrated circuit and other computer components.

- **Semiconducting materials** (or "semiconductors"), such as silicon and germanium, are used to make chips. The conductive properties of selective parts of the semiconducting material can be enhanced to create miniature electronic pathways and components, such as transistors.

- The computer's main circuit board, called a **motherboard** or main board, houses all essential chips and provides the connecting circuitry between them. See Figure D-6. Some chips are permanently soldered in place. Other chips are plugged into special sockets and connectors, which allow chips to be removed for repairs or upgrades. When multiple chips are required for a single function, such as generating stereo-quality sound, the chips might be gathered together on a separate small circuit board, such as a sound card, which can be plugged into a special slot-like connector on the motherboard.

- A **processor** (sometimes referred to as a microprocessor) is an integrated circuit designed to process instructions. It is the most important component of a computer, and usually the most expensive single component. Looking inside a computer, you can usually identify the processor because it is the largest chip on the motherboard. Depending on the brand and model, a processor might be housed in a cartridge-like SEC cartridge or in a square PGA. Inside the chip carrier, a processor is a very complex integrated circuit, containing as many as 300 million miniaturized electronic components.

Comparing today's processors

A typical computer ad contains a long list of specifications describing a computer's components and capabilities. Most computer specifications begin with the processor brand, type, and speed. Intel is the world's largest chipmaker and supplies a sizeable percentage of the processors that power PCs. In 1971, Intel introduced the world's first processor, the 4004. The company has continued to produce a steady stream of new processor models based on the 8088 processor.

AMD (Advanced Micro Devices) is Intel's chief rival in the PC chip market. It produces processors that work just like Intel's chips, but at a lower price. AMD's Athlon and Opteron processors are direct competitors to Intel's Pentium and Itanium lines and have a slight performance advantage according to some benchmarks.

Motorola is the main chip supplier for Apple computers. Transmeta Corporation specializes in chips for mobile computing devices, such as tablet computers.

The processors that are marketed with today's computers will handle most business, educational, and entertainment applications. While it is technically possible to upgrade your computer's processor, the cost and technical factors discourage processor upgrades.

FIGURE D-4: Inside a typical desktop computer

Power supply and fan

Processor with built-in fan

Expansion cards

CD-ROM drive

Floppy disk drive

Hard disk drive

Cables that transfer data from storage devices to motherboard

Main circuit board (motherboard)

FIGURE D-5: Integrated circuits

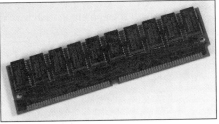

▲ A DIP has two rows of pins that connect the IC circuitry to a circuit board

▲ A DIMM is a small circuit board containing several chips, typically used for memory

▲ A PGA is a square chip package with pins arranged in concentric squares, typically used for processors

▲ An SEC cartridge was pioneered by Intel to house Pentium III processors

FIGURE D-6: The motherboard

▶ A computer motherboard provides sockets for chips, slots for small circuit boards, and the circuitry that connects all these components

Connectors for storage devices

Battery that powers the computer's real-time clock

Expansion slots hold additional expansion cards, such as a modem or sound card

DIMM module containing memory chips

SEC-style processor

Expansion card

DIP holding a ROM chip

Circuitry that transports data from one component to another

Connector for power supply

Exploring processor performance factors

All processors have two main parts: the arithmetic logic unit (ALU) and the control unit. To process data, each of these units performs specific tasks. The performance of a processor is affected by several factors, including clock speed, word size, cache size, instruction set, and processing techniques. This lesson looks at the two main parts of a processor and the factors that affect processor performance.

DETAILS

● The **arithmetic logic unit (ALU)** is the circuitry that performs arithmetic operations, such as addition and subtraction. It also performs logical operations, such as comparing two numbers using the logical operators such as less than (<), greater than (>), or equal to (=). Logical operations also allow for comparing characters and sorting and grouping information. The ALU uses **registers** to hold data that is being processed. Figure D-7 illustrates how the ALU works.

● The processor's **control unit** fetches each instruction, as illustrated in Figure D-8. A processor executes instructions that are provided by a computer program. The list of instructions that a processor can perform is called its **instruction set**. These instructions are hard-wired into the processor's circuitry and include basic arithmetic and logical operations, fetching data, and clearing registers. A computer can perform very complex tasks, but it does so by performing a combination of simple tasks from its instruction set.

● How efficiently the ALU and the control unit work are determined by different performance factors. Processor speed is one of the most important indicators in determining the power of a computer system. The **processor clock** is a timing device that sets the pace (the clock speed) for executing instructions. The clock speed of a processor is specified in **megahertz (MHz)**—millions of cycles per second or **gigahertz (GHz)**—billions of cycles per second. A cycle is the smallest unit of time in a processor's universe. Every action that a processor performs is measured by these cycles. The clock speed is not equal to the number of instructions that a processor can execute in one second. In many computers, some instructions occur within one cycle, but other instructions might require multiple cycles. Some processors can even execute several instructions in a single clock cycle. A specification such as 2.8 GHz means that the processor's clock operates at a speed of 2.8 billion cycles per second.

● **Word size**, another performance factor, refers to the number of bits that a processor can manipulate at one time. Word size is based on the size of the registers in the ALU and the capacity of circuits that lead to those registers. A processor with a 32-bit word size, for example, has 32-bit registers, processes eight bits at a time, and is referred to as a 32-bit processor. Processors with a larger word size can process more data during each processor cycle. Today's personal computers typically contain 32-bit or 64-bit processors.

● **Cache**, sometimes called RAM cache or cache memory, is special high-speed memory that a processor can access more rapidly than memory elsewhere on the motherboard. Cache capacity is usually measured in kilobytes.

● Another performance factor is the type of instruction set a processor uses. As chip designers developed various instruction sets for processors, they tended to add increasingly more complex instructions, each of which required several clock cycles for execution. A processor with such an instruction set uses **CISC (complex instruction set computer)** technology. A processor with a limited set of simple instructions uses **RISC (reduced instruction set computer)** technology. Most processors in today's Macs use RISC technology; most PCs use CISC technology. A processor's ability to handle graphics can be enhanced by adding specialized graphics and multimedia instructions to a processor's instruction set. 3DNow!, MMX, and SSE-2 are instruction set enhancements.

● The processing technique also affects performance. With **serial processing**, the processor must complete all of the steps in the instruction cycle before it begins to execute the next instruction. However, using a technology called **pipelining**, a processor can begin executing an instruction before it completes the previous instruction. Many of today's processors also perform **parallel processing**, in which multiple instructions are executed at the same time. Hyper-Threading refers to a technology that enables processors to execute multiple instructions in parallel.

FIGURE D-7: How the ALU works

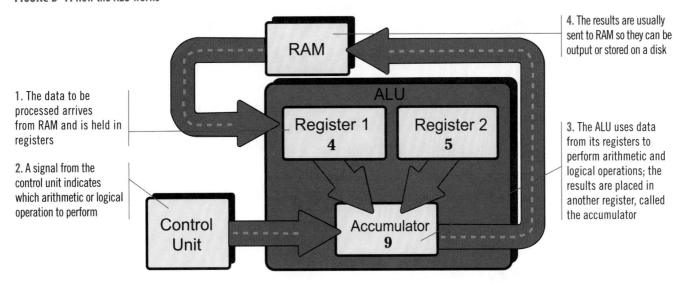

1. The data to be processed arrives from RAM and is held in registers

2. A signal from the control unit indicates which arithmetic or logical operation to perform

4. The results are usually sent to RAM so they can be output or stored on a disk

3. The ALU uses data from its registers to perform arithmetic and logical operations; the results are placed in another register, called the accumulator

FIGURE D-8: How the control unit works

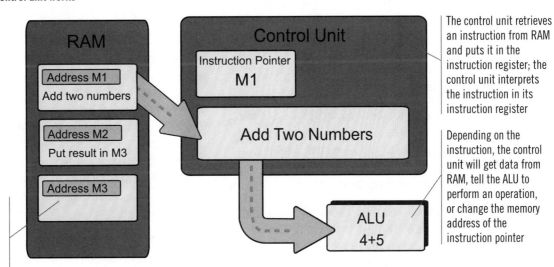

The control unit retrieves an instruction from RAM and puts it in the instruction register; the control unit interprets the instruction in its instruction register

Depending on the instruction, the control unit will get data from RAM, tell the ALU to perform an operation, or change the memory address of the instruction pointer

The RAM address of the instruction is kept in the instruction pointer; when the instruction has been executed, the address in the instruction pointer changes to indicate the RAM address of the next instruction to be executed

Benchmarking

All things being equal, a computer with a 2.8 GHz processor is faster than a computer with a 1.5 GHz processor and a computer with a processor that has a larger word size can process more data during each processor cycle than a computer with a processor that has a smaller word size. Furthermore, all things being equal, a computer with more Level 1 cache (L1), which is built into the processor chip, is faster than a computer with the same amount of Level 2 cache (L2), which is located on a separate chip and takes a little more time to get data to the processor.

But all things aren't equal. So how do you tell the overall performance of a computer and its processor? Various testing laboratories run a series of tests called **benchmarks** to gauge the overall speed of a processor. These results can be used to compare the results to other processors. The results of benchmark tests are usually available on the Web and are published in computer magazine articles.

Understanding computer memory: RAM

Memory is the electronic circuitry linked directly to the processor that holds data and instructions when they are not being transported from one place to another. Computers use four categories of memory: random access memory (RAM), virtual memory, read-only memory (ROM), and CMOS memory. Each type of memory is characterized by the type of data it contains and the technology it uses to hold the data.

DETAILS

● **RAM (random access memory)** is a temporary holding area for data, application program instructions, and the operating system. In a personal computer, RAM is usually several chips or small circuit boards that plug into the motherboard within the computer's system unit. Next to the processor, RAM is one of the most expensive computer components. The amount of RAM in a computer can, therefore, affect the overall price of a computer system. Along with processor speed, RAM capacity is the other most important factor in determining and comparing the power of a computer system.

● RAM is the "waiting room" for the computer's processor. Refer to Figure D-9. It holds raw data that is waiting to be processed and the program instructions for processing that data. In addition, RAM holds the results of processing until they can be stored more permanently on disk or tape.

● RAM also holds operating system instructions that control the basic functions of a computer system. These instructions are loaded into RAM every time you start your computer, and they remain there until you turn off your computer.

● People who are new to computers sometimes confuse RAM and disk storage, perhaps because both of these components hold data. To distinguish between RAM and disk storage, remember that RAM holds data in circuitry, whereas disk storage places data on storage media such as floppy disks, hard disks, or CDs. RAM is temporary storage; disk storage is more permanent. In addition, RAM usually has less storage capacity than disk storage.

● In RAM, microscopic electronic parts called capacitors hold the bits that represent data. You can visualize the capacitors as microscopic lights that can be turned on or off. Refer to Figure D-10. A charged capacitor is "turned on" and represents a "1" bit. A discharged capacitor is "turned off" and represents a "0" bit. You can visualize the capacitors as being arranged in banks of eight. Each bank holds eight bits, or one byte, of data.

● Each RAM location has an address and holds one byte of data. A RAM address on each bank helps the computer locate data as needed for processing.

● In some respects, RAM is similar to a chalkboard. You can use a chalkboard to write mathematical formulas, erase them, and then write an outline for a report. In a similar way, RAM can hold numbers and formulas when you balance your checkbook, then hold the text of your English essay when you use word processing software. The contents of RAM can be changed just by changing the charge of the capacitors. Unlike a chalkboard, however, RAM is volatile, which means that it requires electrical power to hold data. If the computer is turned off, or if the power goes out, all data stored in RAM instantly and permanently disappears.

● The capacity of RAM is usually expressed in megabytes (MB). Today's personal computers typically feature between 128 and 256 MB of RAM. The amount of RAM needed by your computer depends on the software that you use. RAM requirements are routinely specified on the outside of a software package. If it turns out that you need more RAM, you can purchase and install additional memory up to the limit set by the computer manufacturer.

● RAM components vary in speed. RAM speed is often expressed in **nanoseconds**, or billionths of a second. Lower numbers mean faster transmission, processing, and storage of data. For example, 8 ns RAM is faster than 10 ns RAM. RAM speed can also be expressed in MHz (millions of cycles per second). Just the opposite of nanoseconds, higher MHz ratings mean faster speeds. For example, 400 MHz RAM is faster than 133 MHz RAM.

FIGURE D-9: Contents of RAM

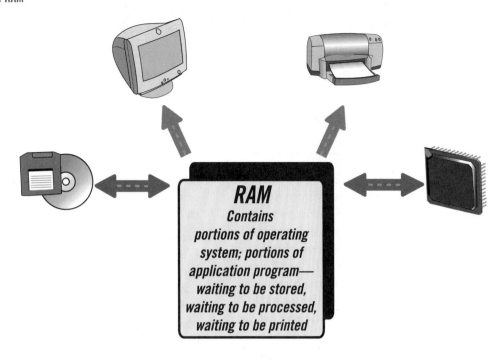

RAM
Contains portions of operating system; portions of application program— waiting to be stored, waiting to be processed, waiting to be printed

FIGURE D-10: How RAM works

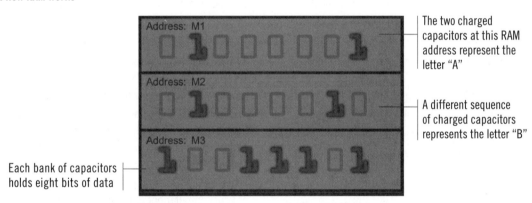

Address: M1 — The two charged capacitors at this RAM address represent the letter "A"

Address: M2 — A different sequence of charged capacitors represents the letter "B"

Address: M3

Each bank of capacitors holds eight bits of data

What is SDRAM?

Most of today's personal computers use SDRAM or RDRAM. **SDRAM (synchronous dynamic RAM)** is fast and relatively inexpensive. **RDRAM (rambus dynamic RAM)** was first developed for the popular Nintendo 64® game system and adapted for use in personal computers in 1999. Although more expensive than SDRAM, RDRAM is usually found in high-performance workstations with processors that run at speeds faster than 1 GHz. RAM is usually configured as a series of DIPs soldered onto a small circuit board, as shown in Figure D-11. SDRAM is the most popular type of RAM in today's computers. It is typically available on a small circuit board called a DIMM (dual inline memory module).

FIGURE D-11

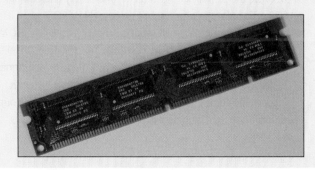

Exploring computer memory

In addition to RAM, a computer uses three other types of memory: virtual memory, ROM, and CMOS. This lesson looks at these types of computer memory and how all computer memory types work together.

DETAILS

● It might seem logical that the more you do with your computer, the more memory it needs. However, if you want to work with several programs and large graphics at the same time, personal computer operating systems are quite adept at allocating RAM space to multiple programs. If a program exceeds the allocated space, the operating system uses an area of the hard disk called **virtual memory** to store parts of a program or data file until they are needed. By selectively exchanging the data in RAM with the data in virtual memory, your computer effectively gains almost unlimited memory capacity.

One disadvantage of virtual memory is reduced performance. Too much dependence on virtual memory can have a negative affect on your computer's performance because getting data from a mechanical device, such as a hard disk, is much slower than getting data from an electronic device, such as RAM. Loading up your computer with as much RAM as possible will help your computer speed through all of its tasks.

● **ROM (read-only memory)** is a type of memory circuitry that holds the computer's startup routine. ROM is housed in a single integrated circuit, usually a fairly large, caterpillar-like DIP package that is plugged into the motherboard.

While RAM is temporary and volatile, ROM is permanent and non-volatile. ROM circuitry holds "hard-wired" instructions that remain in place even when the computer power is turned off. This is a familiar concept to anyone who has used a hand calculator, which includes various "hard-wired" routines for calculating square roots, cosines, and other functions. The instructions in ROM are permanent, and the only way to change them is to replace the ROM chip.

● When you turn on your computer, the processor receives electrical power and is ready to begin executing instructions. But, because the power had been off, RAM is empty and contains no instructions for the processor to execute. Now ROM plays its part. ROM contains a small set of instructions called the **ROM BIOS (basic input/output system)**. These instructions tell the computer how to access the hard disk, find the operating system, and load it into RAM. Once the operating system is loaded, the computer can understand your input, display output, run software, and access your data. While ROM BIOS

instructions are accomplished mainly without user intervention or knowledge, the computer will not function without the ROM chip and the BIOS instructions.

● In order to operate correctly, a computer must have some basic information about storage, memory, and display configurations. For example, your computer needs to know how much memory is available so that it can allocate space for all of the programs that you want to run. RAM goes blank when the computer power is turned off, so configuration information cannot be stored there. ROM would not be a good place for this information either because it holds data on a permanent basis. If, for example, your computer stored memory specification information in ROM, you could never add more memory; or if you were able to add it, you couldn't change the memory specification information in ROM. To store some basic system information, your computer needs a type of memory that's more permanent than RAM but less permanent than ROM.

● **CMOS memory (complementary metal oxide semiconductor)**, pronounced "SEE moss," is a type of memory that requires very little power to hold data. CMOS memory is stored on a chip that can be powered by a small, rechargeable battery integrated into the motherboard. The battery trickles power to the CMOS chip so that it can retain vital data about your computer system configuration even when your computer is turned off. To access the CMOS setup program, press and hold down the F1 key as your computer boots. But be careful! If you make a mistake with these settings, your computer might not be able to start.

When you change the configuration of your computer system by adding RAM, for example, the data in CMOS must be updated. Some operating systems recognize such changes and automatically perform the update; or you can manually change CMOS settings by running the CMOS setup program. See Figure D-12.

● Even though virtual memory, ROM, and CMOS have important roles in the operation of a computer, it is really RAM capacity that makes a difference you can notice. The more data and programs that can fit into RAM, the less time your computer will spend moving data to and from virtual memory. With lots of RAM, you'll find that documents scroll faster, and many graphics operations take less time than with a computer that has less RAM capacity.

FIGURE D-12: CMOS setup program

▶ CMOS holds computer configuration settings, such as the date and time, hard disk capacity, number of floppy disk drives, and RAM capacity

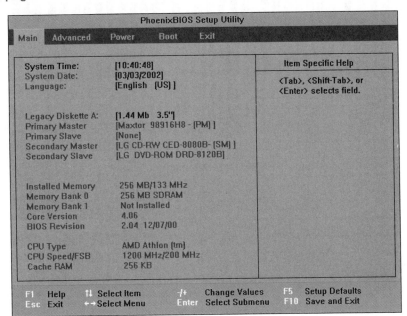

FYI

The difference between memory types: RAM is temporary; virtual memory is disk-based; ROM is permanent; CMOS is battery-powered and more permanent than RAM but less permanent than ROM.

Understanding memory specified in computer ads

Most ads specify RAM capacity, speed, and type. When you see the specification "512 MB 400 MHz SDRAM (max. 2 GB)" in a computer ad similar to the one in Figure D-13, you'll know that the computer's RAM capacity is 512 megabytes (plenty to run most of today's software), that it operates at 400 megahertz (fairly fast), and that it uses SDRAM (a little slower and less expensive than RDRAM). You'll also have important information about the maximum amount of RAM that can be installed in the computer—2 GB, which is more than enough for the typical computer owner who does a bit of word processing, surfs the Web, and plays computer games.

FIGURE D-13: A computer ad typically specifies the amount and type of RAM

> Intel Pentium 4 32-bit processor
> 2.8 GHz with Hyper-Threading
> ■ 512 KB L2 cache
> ■ 512 MB 400 MHz SDRAM (max. 2 GB)
> ■ 80 GB UltraATA-100 HD (5400 rpm)
> ■ 48 X Max DVD+RW/+R/CD-RW combo
> ■ 3.5" 1.44 MB floppy disk drive

Introducing computer file basics

The term "file" was used for filing cabinets and collections of papers long before it became part of the personal computer lexicon. Today, a **computer file** or simply "file" is defined as a named collection of data that exists on a storage medium, such as a hard disk, floppy disk, CD, DVD, or tape. A file can contain a group of records, a document, a photo, music, a video, an e-mail message, or a computer program. This lesson looks at several common characteristics of computer files—type, filename, and format.

Info Web

FILE
FORMATS

DETAILS

- There are several categories of files, such as data files, executable files, configuration files, and drivers. A computer file is classified according to the data it contains, the software that was used to create it, and the way you should use it. See Table D-1.

- Every file has a filename. The filename has two parts—the filename itself and the filename extension.

- A **filename** is a unique set of characters and numbers that identifies a file and should describe its contents. When you save a file, you must provide it with a valid filename that adheres to specific rules, referred to as **file-naming conventions**. Each operating system has a unique set of file-naming conventions. See Figure D-14.

  If an operating system attaches special significance to a symbol, you might not be able to use it in a filename. For example, Windows uses the colon (:) and the backslash (\) to separate the device letter from a filename or folder, as in C:\Music. A filename such as Report:\2004 is not valid because the operating system would become confused about how to interpret the colon and backslash.

  Some operating systems also contain a list of **reserved words** that are used as commands or special identifiers. You cannot use these words alone as a filename. You can, however, use these words as part of a longer filename. For example, under Windows XP, the filename Nul would not be valid, but you could name a file something like Nul Committee Notes.doc.

- A **filename extension** (or file extension) is separated from the main filename by a period, as in Paint.exe. A filename extension further describes the file contents. Generally, the software application you are using automatically assigns the filename extension when you save a file. If you don't see a filename extension

when you use the Save or Save As dialog box to save a file, the option to show filename extensions has been deactivated. When using Windows, you can choose to hide (but not erase) or display the filename extensions through the Folder Options setting in the Control Panel.

  Knowledge of filename extensions comes in handy when you receive a file on a disk or over the Internet but you don't know much about its contents. If you are familiar with filename extensions, you will know the file format and, therefore, which application to use when you want to open the file.

- A filename extension is usually related to the **file format**, which is defined as the arrangement of data in a file and the coding scheme that is used to represent the data. Files that contain graphics are usually stored using a different file format than files containing text. Hundreds of file formats exist, and you'll encounter many of them as you use a variety of software. As you work with a variety of files, you will begin to recognize that some filename extensions, such as .txt (text file) or .jpg (graphics file), indicate a file type and are not specific to application software.

  You will also recognize that other filename extensions, such as .doc (Word), .xls (Excel), and .zip (WinZip), can help you identify which application was used to create the file. These filename extensions indicate the **native file format**, which is the file format used to store files created with that software program. For example, Microsoft Word stores files in doc format, whereas Adobe Illustrator stores graphics files in ai format. When using a software application such as Microsoft Word to open a file, the program displays any files that have the filename extension for its native file format, as shown in Figure D-15.

FIGURE D-14: File-naming conventions

	DOS AND WINDOWS 3.1	WINDOWS 95/98/Me/XP/ NT/2000	MAC OS (CLASSIC)	UNIX/LINUX
Maximum length of filename	8-character filename plus an extension of 3 characters or less	Filename and extension cannot exceed 255 characters	31 characters (no extensions)	14–256 characters (depending on UNIX/Linux version) including an extension of any length
Spaces allowed	No	Yes	Yes	No
Numbers allowed	Yes	Yes	Yes	Yes
Characters not allowed	* / [ ] ; " = \ : , | ?	* \ : < > | " / ?	:	* ! @ # $ % ^ & ( ) { } [ ] " \ ? ; < >
Filenames not allowed	Aux, Com1, Com2, Com3, Com4, Con, Lpt1, Lpt2, Lpt3, Prn, Nul	Aux, Com1, Com2, Com3, Com4, Con, Lpt1, Lpt2, Lpt3, Prn, Nul	Any filename is allowed	Depends on the version of UNIX or Linux
Case sensitive	No	No	No	Yes (use lowercase)

FIGURE D-15: Filename extensions

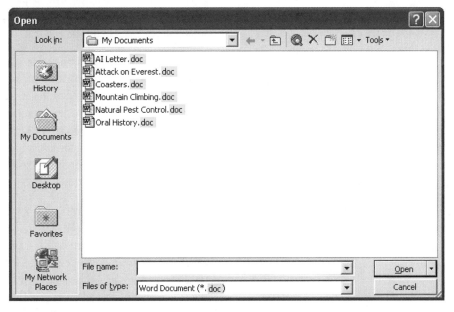

◀ If you don't see any filename extensions, in dialog boxes or in Explorer, the Windows setting that can hide (but not erase) filename extensions is set to hide file extensions. To view filename extensions, open Windows Explorer, click Tools on the menu bar, click Folder Options, then click the Hide file extensions check box to clear the mark.

TABLE D-1: Types of files

TYPE OF FILE	DESCRIPTION	EXTENSION
Configuration file	Information about programs that the computer uses to allocate the resources necessary to run them	.cfg .sys .mif .bin .ini
Help	The information that is displayed by online Help	.hlp
Temporary file	Contains data while a file is open, but that is discarded when you close the file	.tmp
Program files	The main executable files for a computer program	.exe .com
Support files	Program instructions that are executed in conjunction with the main .exe file for a program	.ocx .vbx .vbs .dll
Data files	Documents, images, spreadsheets, databases, music, sound, video, Web page, any file created with a program	.doc .bmp .jpg .gif .html .xls .mdb .mpg

Understanding file locations

Programs and data files have unique names and locations to ensure that the computer can find them. To designate a file's location, you must specify where the file is stored on the storage media. This lesson looks more closely at file locations—how to assign them and the information about each file that is available at the file's location.

DETAILS

● The Windows operating system labels storage devices with letters, such as A: and C:. See Figure D-16. The floppy disk drive is usually assigned device letter A and is referred to as "drive A." A device letter is usually followed by a colon, so drive A could be designated as A: or as 3½" Floppy (A:). The main hard disk drive is usually referred to as "drive C." Additional storage devices can be assigned letters from D through Z. Although most PCs use the standard of drive A for the floppy disk drive and drive C for the hard disk drive, the device letters for CD, Zip, and DVD drives are not standardized. For example, the CD-writer on your computer might be assigned device letter E, whereas the CD-writer on another computer might be assigned device letter R.

● An operating system maintains a list of files called a **directory** for each storage disk, tape, CD, or DVD. The main directory of a disk is referred to as the **root directory**. On a PC, the root directory is typically identified by the device letter followed by a backslash. For example, the root directory of the hard disk drive would be C:\. You should try to avoid storing your data files in the root directory of your hard disk, and instead store them in a subdirectory.

● A root directory is often subdivided into smaller **subdirectories**. When you use Windows, Mac OS, or a Linux graphical file manager, these subdirectories are depicted as **folders** because they work like the folders in a filing cabinet to store an assortment of related items. Each folder has a name, so you can easily create a folder called Documents to hold reports, letters, and so on. You can create another folder called Music to hold your MP3 files. Folders can be created within other folders. You might, for example, create a folder within your Music folder to hold your jazz collection and another to hold your reggae collection.

● A folder name is separated from a drive letter and other folder names by a special symbol. In Microsoft Windows, this symbol is the backslash (\). For example, the folder for your reggae music (within the Music folder on drive C) would be written as C:\Music\Reggae. Imagine how hard it would be to find a specific piece of paper in a filing cabinet that was stuffed with a random assortment of reports, letters, and newspaper clippings. By storing a file in a folder, you assign it a place in an organized hierarchy of folders and files.

● A computer file's location is defined by a **file specification** (sometimes called a **path**), which begins with the drive letter and is followed by the folder(s), filename, and filename extension. Suppose that you have stored an MP3 file called Marley One Love in the Reggae folder on your hard disk drive. Its file specification would be as shown in Figure D-17.

● A file contains data, stored as a group of bits. The more bits, the larger the file. **File size** is usually measured in bytes, kilobytes, or megabytes. Knowing the size of a file can be important especially when you are sending a file as an e-mail attachment. Your computer's operating system keeps track of file sizes.

● Your computer keeps track of the date on which a file was created or last modified. The **file date** is useful if you have created several versions of a file and want to make sure that you know which version is the most recent. It can also come in handy if you have downloaded several updates of player software, such as an MP3 player, and you want to make sure that you install the latest version.

● The operating system keeps track of file locations, filenames, filename extensions, file size, and file dates. See Figure D-18. This information is always available to you through a file management utility, which will be discussed in the next lesson.

FIGURE D-16: Labeling storage devices

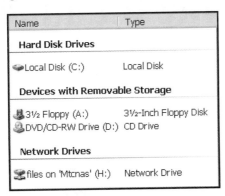

FIGURE D-17: A file specification

C:\Music\Reggae\Marley One Love.mp3

| Drive letter | Primary folder | Secondary folder | Filename | Filename extension |

FIGURE D-18: File sizes and dates

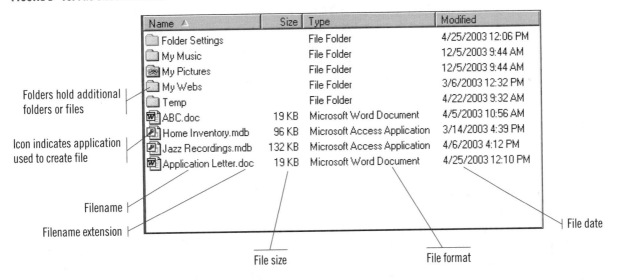

Folders hold additional folders or files

Icon indicates application used to create file

Filename

Filename extension

File size

File format

File date

Deleting files

You may have noticed when using Windows that when you delete a file it is moved to the Recycle Bin. The Windows Recycle Bin and similar utilities in other operating systems are designed to protect you from accidentally deleting hard disk files that you actually need. The operating system moves the file to the Recycle Bin folder. The "deleted" file still takes up space on the disk, but does not appear in the usual directory listing. The file does, however, appear in the directory listing for the Recycle Bin folder, and you can undelete any files in this listing. It is important to remember that only files you delete from your

hard disk drive are sent to the Recycle Bin; files you delete from a floppy disk drive are not sent to the Recycle Bin.

To delete data from a disk in such a way that no one can ever read it, you can use special file shredder software that overwrites "empty" sectors with random 1s and 0s. You might find this software handy if you plan to donate your computer to an organization, and you want to make sure that your personal data no longer remains on the hard disk.

UNIT D

Exploring file management

File management encompasses any procedure that helps you organize your computer-based files so that you can find and use them more efficiently. Depending on your computer's operating system, you may be able to organize and manipulate your files from within an application program, or by using a special file management utility provided by the operating system.

DETAILS

- Applications, such as word processing software or graphics software, typically provide file management capabilities for files created within the application. For example, most applications provide a way to open files and save them in a specific folder on a designated storage device. An application might also provide additional file management capabilities, such as deleting and renaming files.

- Most application software provides access to file management tasks through the Save and Open dialog boxes. These dialog boxes provided by Windows applications allow you to do more than just save a file. You can use them to perform other file management tasks such as rename a file, delete a file, or create a folder, as shown in Figure D-20. At times, however, you might want to work with groups of files, or perform other file operations that are inconvenient to perform within the Save or Open dialog boxes. Most operating systems

provide **file management utilities** that give you the "big picture" of the files you have stored on your disks and help you work with them. For example, Windows provides a file management utility called **Windows Explorer** that can be accessed from the My Computer icon or from the Windows Explorer command on the Start menu. On computers with Mac OS, the file management utility is called **Finder**. These utilities, shown in Figure D-21, help you view a list of files, find files, move files from one place to another, make copies of files, delete files, and rename files.

- File management utilities are designed to help you organize and manipulate the files that are stored on your computer. Most file management operations begin with locating a particular file or folder. A file management utility should make it easy to find what you're looking for by drilling down through your computer's hierarchy of folders and files.

The Save vs. Save As dialog box

Knowing how to save a file is a crucial file management skill. The Save As command is generally an option on the File menu. In addition to the Save As option, the menu also contains a Save option. The difference between the two options is subtle, but useful. The Save As option allows you to select a name and storage device for a file, whereas the Save option simply saves the latest version of a file under its current name and at its current location. When you try to use the Save option for a file that doesn't yet have a name, your application will display the Save As dialog box, even though you selected the Save option. The flow chart in Figure D-19 will help you decide whether to use the Save or the Save As command.

FIGURE D-19: Save or Save As

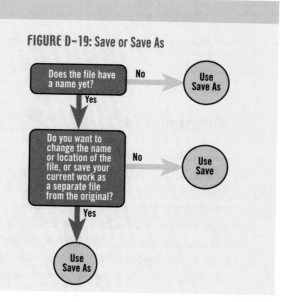

FIGURE D-20: The Save As dialog box

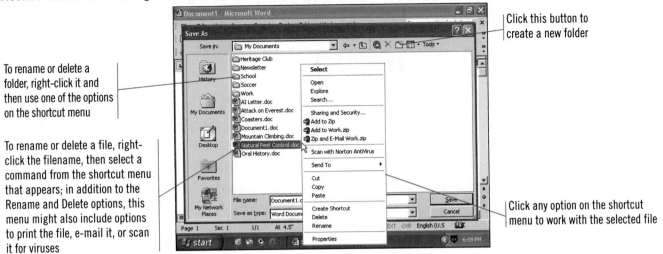

To rename or delete a folder, right-click it and then use one of the options on the shortcut menu

To rename or delete a file, right-click the filename, then select a command from the shortcut menu that appears; in addition to the Rename and Delete options, this menu might also include options to print the file, e-mail it, or scan it for viruses

Click this button to create a new folder

Click any option on the shortcut menu to work with the selected file

FIGURE D-21: Operating system file managers

▶ The Windows file manager utility, Windows Explorer, can be tailored to show files as icons or as a list

▼ Mac OS provides a file management utility called the Finder

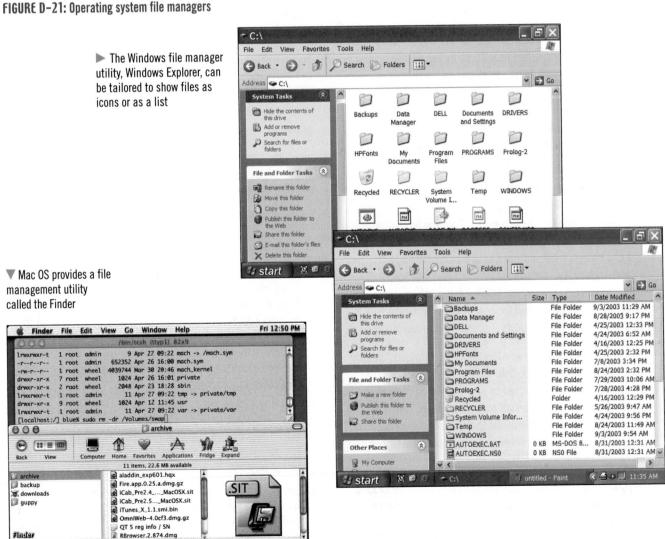

Understanding logical file storage

File management utilities often use some sort of metaphor to help you visualize and mentally organize the files on your disks and other storage devices. These metaphors are sometimes referred to as **logical storage models** because they help you form a mental (logical) picture of the way in which your files are stored. Windows Explorer is based on logical file storage. This lesson looks at logical file storage metaphors and how Windows Explorer implements the models.

DETAILS

● After hearing so much about files and folders, you might have guessed that the filing cabinet is a popular metaphor for computer storage. In this metaphor, each storage device of a computer corresponds to one of the drawers in a filing cabinet. The drawers hold folders and the folders hold files, as illustrated in Figure D-22.

● You might also find it helpful to think of the logical storage model as an outline. In the hierarchy of an outline, the highest or top level is the general level (root directory). As you move down to lower levels in the outline you have greater detail (primary subfolders and then secondary subfolders and so on). When you expand a higher level (a folder), you can see all the subordinate (subfolder) levels for that folder.

● The tree metaphor as shown in Figure D-23 is also helpful. In this metaphor, a tree represents a storage device. The trunk of the tree corresponds to the root directory. The branches of the tree represent folders. These branches can split into small branches representing folders within folders. The leaves at the end of a branch represent the files in a particular folder. For practicality, storage metaphors are translated into screen displays. Figure D-24 shows how Microsoft programmers combined the filing cabinet metaphor with the tree structure metaphor within the Windows Explorer file management utility.

The Windows Explorer window is divided into two "window panes." The pane on the left side of the window lists each of the storage devices connected to your computer, plus several important system objects, such as My Computer, Network Neighborhood, and the Desktop. Each storage device is synonymous with a file drawer in the file cabinet metaphor.

An icon for a storage device or other system object can be "expanded" by clicking its corresponding plus-sign icon. Once an icon is opened, its contents appear in the pane on the right side of the Windows Explorer window. Opening an icon displays the next level of the storage hierarchy, usually a collection of folders. Each folder is synonymous with the folders in the file cabinet metaphor.

Any of these folders can contain files or subfolders. Files are synonymous with papers in the file cabinet metaphor. Subfolders can be further expanded by clicking their plus-sign icons. You continue expanding folders in this manner until you reach the file you need. The minus-sign icon can be used to collapse a device or folder to hide the levels of the hierarchy.

● To work with either a single or a group of files or folders, you must first select them. Windows Explorer displays all of the items that you select by highlighting them. Once a folder or file or a group of folders or files is highlighted, you can use the same copy, move, or delete procedure that you would use for a single item.

● In addition to locating files and folders, Windows Explorer provides a set of file management tools that will help you manipulate files and folders in the following ways:

* Rename. You might want to change the name of a file or folder to better describe its contents. When renaming a file, you should be careful to keep the same filename extension so that you can open it with the correct application software.

* Copy. You can copy a file or folder. For example, you can copy a file from your hard disk to a floppy disk if you want to send it to a friend or colleague. You might also want to make a copy of a document so that you can revise the copy and leave the original intact. When you copy a file, the file remains in the original location and a duplicate file is added to a different location.

* Move. You can move a file from one folder to another, or from one storage device to another. When you move a file, it is erased from its original location, so make sure that you remember the new location of the file. You can also move folders from one storage device to another, or from one folder to another.

* Delete. You can delete a file when you no longer need it. You can also delete a folder. Be careful when you delete a folder because most file management utilities also delete all the files (and subfolders) that a folder contains.

FIGURE D-22: A filing cabinet as a metaphor

The file cabinet represents all of the storage devices connected to a computer

Each drawer represents one storage device

A drawer can contain folders that hold documents and other folders

FIGURE D-23: A tree as a metaphor

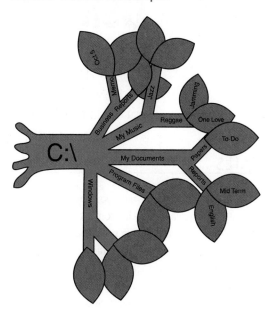

▲ You can visualize the directory of a disk as a tree on its side; the trunk corresponds to the root directory, the branches to folders, and the leaves to files

FIGURE D-24: Windows Explorer

▶ Windows Explorer borrows the folders from the filing cabinet metaphor and the branches on a tree from the tree metaphor and places them in a hierarchical structure, which makes it easy to drill down through the levels of the directory hierarchy to locate a folder or file

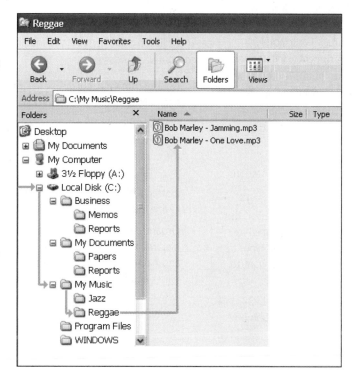

Using files

Creating, opening, saving, renaming, and starting are all actions that you perform on and with files as you work with software. A file management utility provides tools and procedures to help you keep track of your program and data files, but these tools are most useful when you have a logical plan for organizing your files and when you follow some basic file management guidelines.

DETAILS

- Before you can save or use files, you have to format the media to create the equivalent of electronic storage bins. Today, most floppy, Zip, and hard disks are preformatted at the factory; however, computer operating systems provide formatting utilities you can use to reformat some storage devices—typically floppy and hard disks. Formatting utilities are also supplied by the companies that manufacture hard disk drives, writable CD drives, and writable DVD drives. When you use a formatting utility, it erases any files that are on the disk, and then prepares the tracks and sectors necessary to hold data in new files. Refer to Figure D-25 which illustrates how to use Windows to format a floppy disk.

- Applications, such as word processing software or graphics software, typically provide a way to run a program file, open data files, and save data files on a designated storage device. A software application can typically open files that exist in its "native" file format, plus several additional file formats. For example, Microsoft Word opens files in its native document (.doc) format, plus files in formats such as HTML (.htm or .html), Text (.txt), and Rich Text Format (.rtf). Within the Windows environment, you can discover which formats a particular software program can open by looking at the Files of type list in the Open dialog box, as shown in Figure D-26.

- You use many files during a typical Windows application session.

  - Start the program. Typically, you would open your word processing software. When you start the word processor, the necessary files are copied from the hard disk and placed in RAM. You then begin to type the document. As you type, the document is held in RAM. At some point, you'll want to save the document.

  - Save a file. The Save As dialog box, shown in Figure D-27, allows you to specify a name for the file and its location on

  one of your computer's storage devices. To save a file in all Windows applications, click File on the menu bar, and then click Save As to open the Save As dialog box. You click the Look in list arrow to display a list of storage devices. Double-clicking any device displays its folders. You select a storage device and folder to indicate where you want the file to be stored, then type a name for the file in the File name text box. You can change the default file type by clicking the Files of type list arrow, then click the Save button.

  - Retrieve a file. You click File on the menu bar, then click Open to open the Open Dialog box. You locate a file on the storage device by clicking the Look in list arrow, select the file, then click Open.

  - Rename the file. Use the Save As command to save the current file using a new filename. The original file will be intact on the media and the open file will now have a new filename.

- The following tips pertain to managing files on your own computer.

  - Use descriptive names. Give your files and folders descriptive names, and avoid using cryptic abbreviations.

  - Maintain filename extensions. When renaming a file, keep the original file extension so that you can easily open it with the correct application software.

  - Group similar files. Separate files into folders based on subject matter. For example, store your creative writing assignments in one folder and your MP3 music files in another folder.

  - Organize your folders from the top down. When devising a hierarchy of folders, consider how you want to access files and back them up. For example, it is easy to specify one folder and its subfolders for a backup. If your important data is scattered in a variety of folders, however, making backups is more time consuming.

FIGURE D-25: Formatting a floppy disk

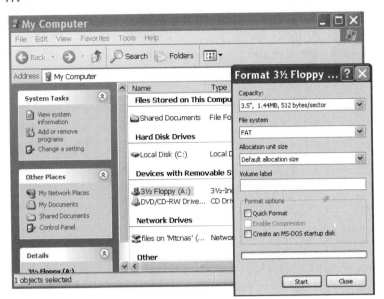

◀ Windows includes a floppy disk formatting utility, which can be accessed from the A: (Floppy disk) icon in the My Computer window or Windows Explorer

FIGURE D-26: Files of type list for an application

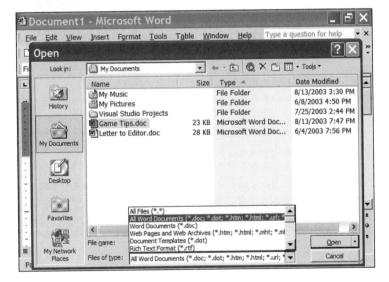

▶ An application's *Files of type* list usually displays the file formats a program can open. You can also look for an Import option on the File menu.

FIGURE D-27: Saving a file

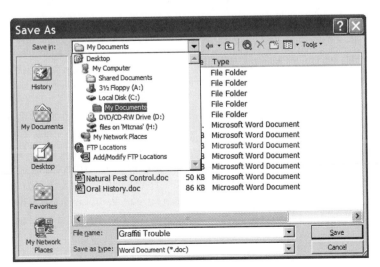

◀ The Save As dialog box is used to name a file and specify its storage location

Understanding physical file storage

So far, you've seen how an operating system like Windows can help you visualize computer storage as files and folders. The structure of files and folders that you see in Windows Explorer is called a "logical" model because it helps you create a mental picture. You have also seen how files are created, saved, and retrieved. What actually happens to a file when you save it is called physical file storage.

DETAILS

- When the storage medium is formatted it is divided into **tracks**, and each track is divided into wedge-shaped **sectors**. See Figure D-28. Tracks and sectors are numbered to provide addresses for each data storage bin. The numbering scheme depends on the storage device and the operating system. On CDs and DVDs, one or more tracks spiral out from the center of the disk; on floppy, Zip, and hard disks, tracks are arranged as concentric circles.

- The operating system uses a **file system** to keep track of the names and locations of files that reside on a storage medium, such as a hard disk. Different operating systems use different file systems. Most versions of Mac OS use the Macintosh Hierarchical File System (HFS). Ext2fs (extended 2 file system) is the native file system for Linux. Windows NT, Windows 2000, and Windows XP use a file system called New Technology File System (NTFS). Windows versions 95, 98, and ME use a file system called FAT32.

- To speed up the process of storing and retrieving data, a disk drive usually works with a group of sectors called a **cluster** or a "block." The number of sectors that form a cluster varies depending on the capacity of the disk and how the operating system works with files. A file system's primary task is to maintain a list of clusters and keep track of which ones are empty and which ones hold data. This information is stored in a special file.

- If your computer uses the FAT32 file system, for example, this special file is called the **File Allocation Table (FAT)**. If your computer uses NTFS, it is called the **Master File Table (MFT)**.

- Each of your disks contains its own index file so that information about its contents is always available when the disk is in use. Unfortunately, storing this crucial file on disk also presents a risk because if the index file is damaged by a hard disk head crash or scratch, you'll generally lose access to all the data stored on the disk. Index files become damaged all too frequently, so it is important to back up your data.

- When you save a file, your PC's operating system looks at the index file to see which clusters are empty. It selects one of these clusters, records the file data there, and then revises the index file to include the filename and its location. A file that does not fit into a single cluster spills over into the next contiguous cluster unless that cluster already contains data. When contiguous clusters are not available, the operating system stores parts of a file in noncontiguous (nonadjacent) clusters. Figure D-29 helps you visualize how an index file, such as the MFT, keeps track of filenames and locations.

- When you want to retrieve a file, the OS looks through the index for the filename and its location. It moves the disk drive's read-write head to the first cluster that contains the file data. Using additional data from the index file, the operating system can move the read-write heads to each of the clusters containing the remaining parts of the file.

- When you click a file's icon and then select the Delete option, the operating system simply changes the status of the file's clusters to "empty" and removes the filename from the index file. The filename no longer appears in a directory listing, but the file's data remains in the clusters until a new file is stored there. You might think that this data is as good as erased, but it is possible to purchase utilities that recover a lot of this "deleted" data—law enforcement agents, for example, use these utilities to gather evidence from "deleted" files on the computer disks of suspected criminals.

- As a computer writes files on a disk, parts of files tend to become scattered all over the disk. These **fragmented files** are stored in noncontiguous clusters. Drive performance generally declines as the read-write heads move back and forth to locate the clusters that contain the parts of a file. To regain peak performance, you can use a **defragmentation utility** to rearrange the files on a disk so that they are stored in contiguous clusters. See Figure D-30.

FIGURE D-28: Tracks and sectors on a disk

▶ Formatting prepares the surface of a disk to hold data

Disks are divided into tracks and wedge-shaped sectors—each side of a floppy disk typically has 80 tracks divided into 18 sectors; each sector holds 512 bytes of data

On a typical CD, a single spiral track is divided into 336,000 sectors; each sector holds 2,048 bytes of data

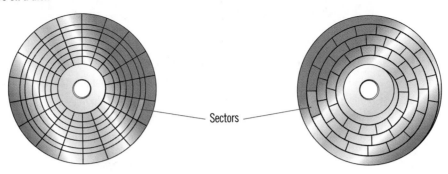

Sectors

FIGURE D-29: How the MFT works

▶ Each colored cluster on the disk contains part of a file. Bio.txt is stored in contiguous clusters. Jordan.wks is stored in noncontiguous clusters

A computer locates and displays the Jordan.wks file by looking for its name in the Master File Table

Master File Table

File	Cluster	Comment
MFT	1	Reserved for MFT files
DISK USE	2	Part of MFT that contains list of empty sectors
Bio.txt	3, 4	Bio.txt file stored in clusters 3 and 4
Jordan.wks	7, 8, 10	Jordan.wks file stored noncontiguously in clusters 7, 8, and 10
Pick.wps	9	Pick.wps file stored in cluster 9

FIGURE D-30: Defragmenting a disk

▶ Defragmenting a disk helps your computer operate more efficiently; consider using a defragmentation utility a couple of times per year to keep your computer running in top form

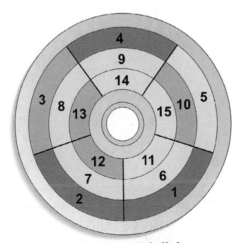

Fragmented disk

▲ On this fragmented disk, the purple, yellow, and blue files are stored in non-contiguous clusters

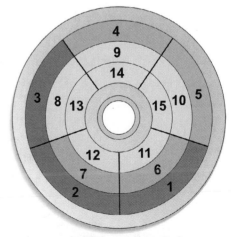

Defragmented disk

▲ When the disk is defragmented, the sectors of data for each file are moved to contiguous clusters

How a Processor Executes Instructions

Remarkable advances in processor technology have produced exponential increases in computer speed and power. In 1965, Gordon Moore, co-founder of chip-production giant Intel Corporation, predicted that the number of transistors on a chip would double every 18 to 24 months. Much to the surprise of engineers and Moore himself, "Moore's law" accurately predicted 30 years of chip development. In 1958, the first integrated circuit contained two transistors. The Pentium III Xeon processor, introduced in 1999, had 9.5 million transistors. The Pentium 4 processor, introduced only a year later, featured 42 million transistors.

What's really fascinating, though, is how these chips perform complex tasks simply by manipulating bits. How can pushing around 1s and 0s result in professional-quality documents, exciting action games, animated graphics, cool music, street maps, and e-commerce Web sites? To satisfy your curiosity about what happens deep in the heart of a processor, you'll need to venture into the realm of instruction sets, fetch cycles, accumulators, and pointers.

A computer accomplishes a complex task by performing a series of very simple steps, referred to as instructions. An instruction tells the computer to perform a specific arithmetic, logical, or control operation. To be executed by a computer, an instruction must be in the form of electrical signals, those now-familiar 1s and 0s that represent "ons" and "offs." In this form, instructions are referred to as machine code. They are, of course, very difficult for people to read, so typically when discussing them, we use more understandable mnemonics, such as JMP, MI, and REG1.

An instruction has two parts: the op code and the operands. An op code, which is short for "operation code," is a command word for an operation such as add, compare, or jump. The operands for an instruction specify the data, or the address of the data, for the operation.

In the instruction JMP M1, the op code is JMP and the operand is M1. The op code JMP means jump or go to a different instruction. The operand M1 stands for the RAM address of the instruction to which the computer is supposed to go. The instruction JMP M1 has only one operand, but some instructions have more than one operand. For example, the instruction ADD REG1 REG2 has two operands: REG1 and REG2.

The list of instructions that a processor is able to execute is known as its instruction set. This instruction set is built into the processor when it is manufactured. Every task that a computer performs is determined by the list of instructions in its instruction set.

FIGURE D-31: The instruction cycle

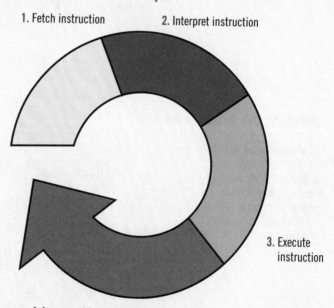

1. Fetch instruction
2. Interpret instruction
3. Execute instruction
4. Increment instruction pointer

The term **instruction cycle** refers to the process in which a computer executes a single instruction. Some parts of the instruction cycle are performed by the processor's control unit; other parts of the cycle are performed by the ALU. The steps in this cycle are summarized in Figure D-31.

Computers and Astronomy

Like most modern scientists, astronomers use Web-based resources and computer-equipped tools to assist in their research. Even before leaving home to view the night sky, astronomers can use their desktop computers to access a special weather-forecasting Web site, which predicts ideal viewing conditions for the late evening. They can check the Web to find out whether any especially interesting objects, such as the international space station, might be viewable from their latitude and longitude that night. Many amateur and professional astronomers use sky map software to plan what they'll look at on a particular night. Based on the date, and coordinates for longitude and latitude, the software displays an image of the night sky and indicates key objects. For example, an astronomer could request the software to "show me the night sky looking south from Marquette, MI at 2 a.m. on May 15, 2005." The software responds with an image of the night sky, highlights constellations, and provides background information and photos for any selected celestial object.

Many astronomers' telescopes have a computerized positioning system, consisting of a handheld controller and a small computer mounted on the side of the telescope. The computer contains a database of thousands of celestial objects—stars, nebulae, planets, and galaxies. When astronomers set up a computerized telescope, they first align the computer by manually pointing the telescope at one or two stars that are easy to see with the naked eye, such as Polaris, the North Star, or Sirius, the Dog Star. After the computer "knows" the location of these stars, an astronomer can use the handheld controller to choose a celestial object from the database. The computerized positioning system finds the coordinates for the object and moves the telescope to point in the correct direction. Most computerized positioning systems also track the object—that is, as the object moves through the sky during the evening, the computer automatically moves the telescope so that the object is always centered in the eyepiece.

Amateur astronomers often carry specialized digital cameras that use CCD technology. A CCD (charge coupled device) is a light-sensitive integrated circuit that performs particularly well in low light, making it well suited for photographing dim objects, such as faraway galaxies and nebulae. Astrophotographers take pictures of celestial objects by mounting a CCD camera on a telescope. The CCD camera can take several pictures over a given time period or be adjusted to use a long exposure time—in some cases, over an hour—for extremely dim objects.

Taking a picture is only the first step in producing a spectacular celestial photograph. After photographing an object (see Figure D-32), astrophotographers upload the image to a desktop or notebook computer. Using graphics software, they can enhance the image by removing artifacts caused by external light sources, such as street lights, by emphasizing or reducing parts of the image, or by combining several images of the same object to create a clearer and brighter image. Many of the celestial images in magazines, on the Internet, and on television have been created by amateurs working in local parks, wilderness areas, or their own backyards.

Astrophotography isn't used only to take pretty pictures, however. With CCD imaging, both professional and amateur astronomers can document and analyze areas of the night sky and identify new celestial objects. "Comet hunters"—a slang term describing astronomers who specialize in finding and identifying new celestial objects—take several pictures of the same area of the sky over the span of many nights. The images are then combined and compared manually or with specialized software. Moving objects, such as comets or asteroids, show up as blurred or dotted lines when the time-lapse images are combined. Using this technique, both amateurs and professionals have discovered new asteroids, comets, exploding super-novae, and other objects.

When starlight passes through the atmosphere, it descends through many layers of different temperatures and densities. These atmospheric changes, called turbulence, distort the light and give stars their distinctive twinkling effect. Twinkling stars might be pretty to look at, but they're not good subjects for observation or research. Large earth-based telescopes, such as the one at the Gemini Observatory in Hawaii, use a computer-controlled technology called "adaptive optics" to manipulate a flexible mirror to negate atmospheric disturbance. Adaptive optics work by measuring the atmospheric distortion and bending a flexible mirror to eliminate these distortions. Light is gathered and sent to a wavefront sensor, which measures the level of atmospheric distortion in a light wave. Wavefront sensors in an adaptive optics system sample light waves entering the telescope many times a second. Data from these samples is routed to a computer attached to a flexible mirror called a "deformable mirror," which is usually a thin disk of quartz coated with a reflective layer of silver. Piston-like actuators attached to the back of the mirror push and pull its surface into the exact arc necessary to view a celestial object without atmospheric distortion.

FIGURE D-32

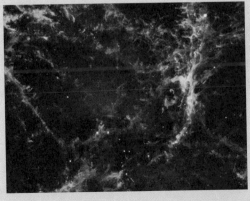

New Chip Technologies

The need for more and more storage and faster and faster processors has teams of scientists in all the major labs around the world working on ways to create new chips. Ever since Robert Noyce and Jack Kilby constructed the first integrated circuits with components connected by aluminum lines on a silicon-oxide surface layer on a plane of silicon in 1959, scientists have been working to create ways of storing and processing data on smaller devices with greater reliability and speed. In 1965, Gordon Moore, head of research and development for Fairchild Semiconductor and co-founder of Intel, predicted that transistor density on integrated circuits would double every 12 months for the next ten years. This prediction, known as Moore's Law, was revised in 1975 to state that the density would double every 18 months. To everyone's amazement, including Moore himself, Moore's Law holds true even today, as scientists have continued to create faster and denser chips using silicon. If Moore's Law is to continue to hold true, then chip features must shrink or the technologies must greatly improve to keep increasing functionality and performance.

The limitations of silicon have been known for years, and the challenge has been to find new materials to take chip development to the next level. Current manufacturing processes use lithography to imprint circuits on semiconductor materials. While lithography has improved dramatically over the last two decades, it is widely believed that lithography is quickly approaching its physical limits. So where do chip developers go next?

The primary performance-enhancing strategy for over 30 years has been based on the scaling theory, which shrinks the dimensions and energy required by a processor's components. The result has been greater transistor density, faster transistors, and higher performance. Some scientists are researching nanotechnology, which is the "field of science whose goal is to control individual atoms and molecules to create computer chips and other devices that are thousands of times smaller than current technologies permit" (Webopedia), as a means of creating smaller, more powerful chips. What are the benefits of smaller and more powerful chips? One benefit is energy consumption. Smaller chips should consume less energy and should produce less heat, which should in turn make chips more environmentally friendly. But what is the best way to make these smaller chips? For more than a decade, Intel has been driving the pace of Moore's Law. Recent developments at Intel include a 90-nanometer processor.

To create this processor, Intel developed a new type of technology in the production of its processors that stretches atoms across the transistor to increase speed and efficiency. According to Intel, the technol-ogy uses "strained silicon," in which atoms in the 90-nanometer chips are spaced farther apart than normal. According to scientists at Intel, a strained silicon chip can function with less energy, which means devices consume less power and work faster. The technique of using strained silicon has been proven on larger transistors, but until the announcement of the 90-nanometer processor, it has remained a question as to whether or not it could work in significantly smaller scales. Intel officials have said that the company will be able to use nearly one-fourth of its existing manufacturing equipment with the new technology.

Are there alternatives to silicon-based chips? Yes, in fact, some of the most promising research involves carbon nanotubes, first discovered by Japanese scientist Sumio Iijima in 1991. A carbon nanotube is a single cylinder-shaped molecule about 10,000 times thinner than a human hair. The electrical properties of carbon nanotubes are similar to the semiconductors used in today's processors. Because carbon nanotubes are so small, they could be used for processors and memory. IBM researchers were able to construct a prototype carbon-nanotube transistor in 2001.

IBM has been working on molecular computing for years as it tries to find an alternative to silicon-based semiconductors. IBM scientists have built the tiniest computer circuit yet using individual molecules, a move they say advances their push toward smaller, faster electronics. IBM researchers at its Almaden Research Center in San Jose, California, have built and operated a computer circuit in which individual molecules of carbon monoxide move like toppling dominoes across a flat copper surface. This computer circuit involves nanotechnology and quantum computing.

Quantum computing is the application of quantum mechanics to computer systems. It has been described as a "bizarre, subatomic world in which two electrons can be two places at the same time." This description is fairly accurate. The subatomic bits used in quantum computing are called qubits. The good news for chip development is that qubits have the potential of representing not just a 1 or a 0, but of representing both a 1 and a 0 at the same time. This definitely means faster and more powerful computing. As research in these areas continues, the goal for chip developers is to translate the work in research labs into chips based on nanotechnology and quantum computing that can be manufactured and then used in products like cell phones and personal computers.

As scientists look at alternative methods for developing chips, some researchers are thinking beyond the physical restrictions of a chip and thinking instead about the computing process. These scientists are finding tremendous potential in a cheap, non-toxic, renewable material found in all living creatures—DNA. DNA (deoxyribonucleic acid) molecules are the material of which our genes are made. In fact, DNA is very similar to a computer hard drive in how it stores permanent information about your genes. DNA computing is the science of using DNA to code mathematical systems. In 1994, Leonard Adleman, a computer scientist at the University of Southern California, introduced the idea of using DNA to solve complex mathematical problems. Adleman is often called the inventor of DNA computers. Unlike conventional computers, DNA computers perform calculations parallel to other calculations. Parallel computing allows DNA to solve complex mathematical problems very quickly; DNA molecules have already been harnessed to perform complex mathematical problems. Whereas conventional computers might take hundreds of years, DNA computers can solve problems in hours. DNA might one day be integrated into a computer chip that will push computers even faster.

What is the future of computer chips? Will Moore's Law continue to hold with advances in computer chip technology? Current research suggests that Moore's Law might not be applicable to new mediums being considered for chips. But current research does suggest new chips will be faster, more energy efficient, and more environmentally friendly.

▼ EXPAND THE IDEAS

1. We may be reaching the limit of Moore's Law as it applies to silicon-based chips. Research Moore's Law. Discover what scientists believe is the upper limit to Moore's Law and when they think we might reach that limit. Write a concluding paragraph indicating what will happen to computing if we reach the limit of Moore's Law and no alternative means for computing has been developed.

2. Advances in processor technology are announced frequently. Log on to the Internet and locate two news stories on recent advances. You can research developments at Intel by going to www.intel.com. What are the new barriers that are being broken? Is Moore's Law still being upheld? Write a short paragraph discussing your findings.

3. The new chips are becoming faster, more energy efficient, and able to solve problems more quickly. Will computers surpass human intelligence? How is human intelligence going to change? Will human and machine intelligence become intertwined? Research the work and writings of Raymond Kurzweil. Begin by looking at http://www.kurzweilai.net. Summarize your findings and write a short paragraph explaining your theory on how far computing "intelligence" can go.

Issue

End of Unit Exercises

▼ KEY TERMS

ALU	Directory	Gigahertz (GHz)	Processor clock
ASCII	EBCDIC	Instruction cycle	RAM
Benchmark	Extended ASCII	Instruction set	RDRAM
Binary number system	File Allocation Table (FAT)	Integrated circuit (IC)	Register
Bit	File date	Kilobit	Reserved word
Byte	File format	Kilobyte	RISC
Cache	File header	Logical storage model	ROM
Character data	File management	Master File Table	ROM BIOS
CISC	File management utility	Megabit	Root directory
Cluster	File-naming conventions	Megabyte	SDRAM
CMOS memory	File size	Megahertz (MHz)	SEC cartridge
Computer file	File specification	Motherboard	Sector
Control unit	File system	Nanosecond	Semiconducting material
Data representation	Filename	Native file format	Serial processing
Defragmentation utility	Filename extension	Numeric data	Subdirectory
Digital device	Finder	Parallel processing	Track
Digital electronics	Folder	Path	Unicode
Digitize	Fragmented file	PGA	Virtual memory
DIMM	Gigabit (Gb)	Pipelining	Windows Explorer
DIP	Gigabyte (GB)	Processor	Word size

▼ UNIT REVIEW

1. Review the bold terms in this unit. Then pick 10 terms that are most unfamiliar to you. Be sure that you can use your own words to define the terms you have selected.

2. Describe how the binary number system and binary coded decimals can use only 1s and 0s to represent numbers.

3. Describe the difference between numeric data, character data, and numerals. Then, list and briefly describe the four codes that computers typically use for character data.

4. Make sure that you understand the meaning of the following measurement terms; indicate what aspects of a computer system they are used to measure: KB, Kb, MB, Mb, GB, Kbps, MHz, GHz, ns.

5. List four types of memory and briefly describe how each one works.

6. Describe how the ALU and the control unit interact to process data.

7. Describe the difference between the Save and the Save As options provided by an application.

8. Explain the kinds of file management tasks that might best be accomplished using a file management utility such as Windows Explorer.

9. In your own words, describe the difference between a logical storage model and a physical storage model.

10. Make sure that you can describe what happens in the MFT when a file is stored or deleted.

▼ FILL IN THE BEST ANSWER

1. The _Binary_ number system represents numeric data as a series of 0s and 1s.

2. ASCII is used primarily to represent _character_ data.

3. Most personal computers use the _EXTENDED ASCII_ code to represent character data.

4. Digital _Electronic_ makes it possible for a computer to manipulate simple "on" and "off" signals to perform complex tasks.

5. An integrated _Circuit_ contains microscopic circuit elements, such as wires, transistors, and capacitors that are packed onto a very small square of semiconducting material.

6. The _ALU_ in the processor performs arithmetic and logical operations.

7. The _Control UNIT_ in the CPU directs and coordinates the operation of the entire computer system.

8. The timing in a computer system is established by the _Processor clock_

9. In RAM, microscopic electronic parts called _capacitors_ hold the electrical signals that represent data.

10. The instructions for the operations your computer performs when it is first turned on are permanently stored in _ROM_ .

11. System configuration information about the hard disk, date, and RAM capacity is stored in battery-powered _____ memory.

12. An operating system's file-naming _conventions_ provide a set of rules for naming files.

13. A file _format_ refers to the arrangement of data in a file and the coding scheme that is used to represent the data.

14. The main directory of a disk is sometimes referred to as the _root_ directory.

15. A file's location is defined by a file _specification_, which includes the drive letter, folder(s), filename, and extension.

16. Windows XP maintains a(n) _finder_ File Table, which contains the name and location of every file on a disk.

17. The _finder_ option on an application's File menu allows you to name a file and specify its storage location.

18. A(n) _Logical_ storage model helps you form a mental picture of how your files are arranged on a disk.

19. On a floppy disk or hard disk, data is stored in concentric circles called _tracks_, which are divided into wedge-shaped _sectors_ .

20. Windows Explorer is an example of a file _MANAGEMENT_ utility.

▼ PRACTICE TESTS

When you use the Interactive CD, you can take Practice Tests that consist of 10 multiple-choice, true/false, and fill-in-the blank questions. The questions are selected at random from a large test bank, so each time you take a test, you'll receive a different set of questions. Your tests are scored immediately, and you can print study guides to determine which questions you answered incorrectly. If you are using a Tracking Disk, insert it in the floppy disk drive to save your test scores.

▼ INDEPENDENT CHALLENGE 1

 The three leading manufacturers of processors are Intel, AMD, and Transmeta. These companies manufacture processors for personal computers as well as other devices.

1. Based on what you read in this unit, list and describe the factors that affect processor performance. Create a table using the performance factors as column heads.

2. Use your favorite search engine on the Internet to research any two companies that produce processors.

3. List their Web sites and any other pertinent contact information for the companies that you chose.

4. List three of the models that each company produces as row labels in the table you created in Step 1. Complete the table to show how these models rate, that is, their specifications for each performance factor.

5. Write a brief statement describing any new research or new products that each company is developing.

▼ INDEPENDENT CHALLENGE 2

 How quickly could you code a sentence using the Extended ASCII code? What is the history of coding and coding schemes? You can find a wealth of information about coding schemes that have been developed throughout the history of computing as well as coding used to transmit information.

1. Log onto the Internet, then use your favorite search engine to research the history of Morse code. Write a brief paragraph outlining your findings.

2. Use the International Morse Code alphabet to write your full name.

3. Research the history of the ASCII code. Write a one-page summary of your findings.

4. Use the extended ASCII code to write your full name.

5. Research the history of the EBCDIC code. Write a one-page summary of your findings.

6. Use the extended EBCDIC code to write your full name.

▼ INDEPENDENT CHALLENGE 3

How will you organize the information that you store on your hard drive? Your hard disk will be your electronic filing cabinet for all your work and papers. You can create many different filing systems. The way you set up your folders will guide your work and help you keep your ideas and projects organized so you can work efficiently with your computer. Take some time to think about the work that you do, the types of documents or files you will be creating, and then decide how you will create files and folders.

1. Read each of the following plans for organizing files and folders on a hard disk and comment on the advantages and disadvantages of each plan.

    a. Create a folder for each file you create.

    b. Store all the files in the root directory.

    c. Store all files in the My Documents folder.

    d. Create a folder for each application you plan to use and store only documents you generate with that application in each folder.

    e. Create folders for broad topics such as memos, letters, budget, art, personal, and then store all related documents and files within those folders.

    f. Create folders based on specific topics such as tax, applications, household, school, then store all related documents and files within those folders.

    g. Create a new folder for each month and store all files or documents created in that month in that appropriate folder.

2. Write up a summary of how you plan to organize your hard disk and explain why you chose the method you did.

▼ INDEPENDENT CHALLENGE 4

You can use Windows Explorer or any file management program on your computer to explore and find specific files and folders on your hard disk.

1. Start Windows Explorer then expand the My Computer icon. List the devices under My Computer.

2. Open the My Documents folder on the Local Disk C: (if not available, find the folder that has your documents). List how many folders are in the My Documents folder on your hard disk.

3. Open one of the folders in the My Documents folder, then display the Details View. Are filename extensions showing? If so, list them and identify which programs would open those files.

4. How many different types of files can you find on your hard disk? List up to 10.

5. Make a list of five filenames that are valid under the file-naming conventions for your operating system. Create a list of five filenames that are not valid and explain the problem with each one.

6. Create five filenames that meet the file-naming conventions for Windows and for MAC OS. Then create five filenames that do not meet the file-naming conventions for Windows or for MAC OS, and explain why these filenames do not meet the file-naming conventions.

7. Pick any five files on the computer that you typically use, and write out the full path for each one. If you can, identify the programs that were used to create each of the files you found.

▼ STUDENT EDITION LABS

Reinforce the concepts you have learned in this unit through the **Understanding the Motherboard, Managing Files and Folders,** and **Binary Numbers** Student Edition Labs, available online at the Illustrated Computer Concepts Web site.

▼ SAM LABS

If you have a SAM user profile, you have access to additional content, features, and functionality. Log in to your SAM account and go to your assignments page to see what your instructor has assigned for this unit.

▼ VISUAL WORKSHOP

Your computer probably came with a specific amount of RAM. What if you wanted to upgrade to more RAM? How would you go about finding RAM to purchase? How much RAM is enough? Is there too much RAM? Figure D-33 shows the Web page for Kingston Technology, a leading distributor and manufacturer of computer memory. You can use the Internet for researching and buying RAM. You will research RAM and determine the best buy for your system.

FIGURE D-33

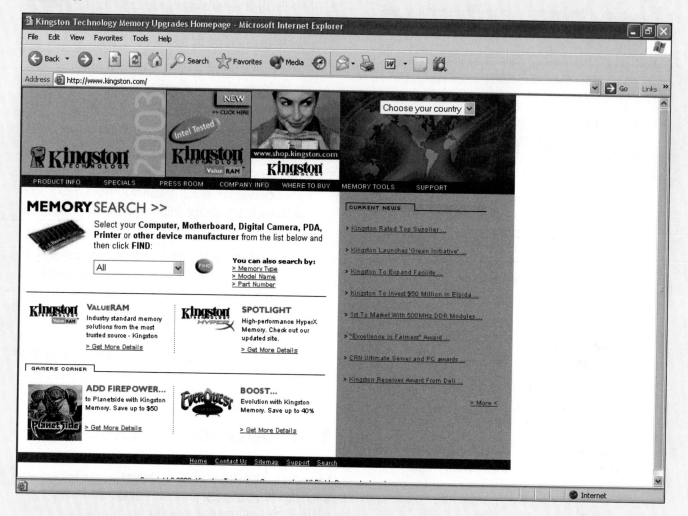

1. Use a search engine to search on RAM. What kinds of Web sites did you find? Did you need to be more specific in your search to find the RAM for your computer?

2. Complete a search on DRAM. Was this more successful in finding Web sites that would sell you chips to update the memory capacity on your computer?

3. Go to www.kingston.com, the page shown in Figure D-33. See if you can find the best memory for upgrading your system.

4. Write a brief summary of your findings.

5. Click the links for different types of memory. Read the pages and write a brief summary of what you read for two of the links.

Glossary

3-D graphics software ▶ Provides a set of tools for creating "wireframes" that represent three-dimensional objects.

Absolute reference ▶ In a worksheet formula, cell references (usually preceded by a $ symbol) that cannot change as a result of a move or copy operation.

Access time ▶ The estimated time for a storage device to locate data on a disk, usually measured in milliseconds.

Accounting and finance software ▶ A category of software that helps you keep a record of monetary transactions and investments.

Accounting software ▶ See Accounting and Finance Software.

Active matrix screen ▶ A type of LCD technology that produces a clear, sharp image because each pixel is controlled by its own transistor.

AGP (accelerated graphics port) ▶ An AGP is a type of interface, or slot, that provides a high-speed pathway for advanced graphics.

ALU (arithmetic logic unit) ▶ The part of the CPU that performs arithmetic and logical operations on the numbers stored in its registers.

Always-on connection ▶ A permanent connection, as opposed to a connection that is established and dropped as needed.

Application software ▶ Computer programs that help you perform a specific task such as word processing. Also called application programs, applications, or programs.

ASCII (American Standard Code for Information Interchange) ▶ A code that represents characters as a series of 1s and 0s. Most computers use ASCII code to represent text, making it possible to transfer data between computers.

Audio editing software ▶ A category of software that includes sound playback as well as recording capabilities. Windows and Mac OS operating system utilities typically supply audio editing software. Menus provide additional digital editing features, such as speed control, volume adjustments, clipping, and mixing of sounds.

Automatic recalculation ▶ A feature found in spreadsheet software that automatically recalculates every formula after a user makes a change to any cell.

Beep code ▶ A series of audible beeps used to announce diagnostic test results during the boot process.

Benchmark ▶ A test used to measure computer hardware or software performance.

Binary digits ▶ Series of 1s and 0s representing data.

Binary number system ▶ A method for representing numbers using only two digits, 0 and 1; contrast this system to the decimal system, which uses ten digits: 0, 1, 2, 3, 4, 5, 6, 7, 8, and 9.

Bit ▶ A bit is the smallest unit of information handled by a computer. A bit can hold one of two values, either a 0 or a 1. Eight bits comprise a byte, which can represent a letter or number.

Bit depth ▶ The number of bits that determines the range of possible colors that can be assigned to each pixel. For example, an 8-bit color depth can create 256 colors. Also called color depth.

Blog ▶ Derived from the phrase "WeB LOG," refers to a personal journal focusing on a single topic or covering a variety of issues posted on the Web for access by the general public.

Bookmark ▶ A link to a Web page; a list of saved URLS in a browser. Click the URL to return to the page. Also called Favorites.

Boot process ▶ The sequence of events that occurs within a computer system between the time the user starts the computer and the time it is ready to process commands.

Bootstrap program ▶ A program stored in ROM that loads and initializes the operating system on a computer.

Browser ▶ A program that communicates with a Web server and displays Web pages.

Byte ▶ An 8-bit unit of information that represents a single character.

Cable ▶ Used to connect a peripheral device to a computer through a port.

Cable modem ▶ A communications device that can be used to connect a computer to the Internet via the cable TV infrastructure.

Cable modem service ▶ Internet access offered to a cable company's customers for an additional monthly charge. The connection usually requires two pieces of equipment: a network card and a cable modem.

Cache ▶ Special high-speed memory that gives the CPU rapid access to data that would otherwise be accessed from disk. Also called RAM cache or cache memory.

CAD software ▶ A special type of 3-D graphics software designed for architects and engineers who use computers to create blueprints and product specifications.

Card reader ▶ A device that transfers data to or from a computer; others plug directly into a computer's system unit.

CD ▶ An optical storage media that can store up to 700 MB of data. There are a wide variety of CDs including CD-ROM, CD-R, and CD-RW.

CD drive ▶ A storage device that uses laser technology to read data from a CD-ROM.

CD-DA (compact disc digital audio) ▶ The format for commercial music CDs. Music is typically recorded on audio CDs by the manufacturer.

CD-R ▶ An acronym for compact disc-recordable. CD-R is a type of optical disk technology that allows the user to create CD-ROMs and audio CDs.

CD-ROM disc ▶ An optical storage media that can store up to 700 MB of data. There are a wide variety of CDs including CD-ROM, CD-R, and CD-RW.

CD-ROM drive ▶ A storage device that uses laser technology to read data from a CD-ROM.

CD-RW ▶ An acronym for compact disc-rewritable. CD-RW is a type of optical disk technology that allows the user to write data onto a CD, then change that data.

CD-writer ▶ A general term for recordable CD technologies such as CD-R and CD-RW.

Cell ▶ In spreadsheet terminology, the intersection of a column and a row. In cellular communications, a limited geographical area surrounding a cellular phone tower.

Cell reference ▶ The column letter and row number that designates the location of a worksheet cell. For example, the cell reference C5 refers to a cell in column C, row 5.

Central processing unit ▶ See CPU.

Character data ▶ Letters, symbols, or numerals that will not be used in arithmetic operations (name, social security number, etc.).

Chat group ▶ A discussion in which a group of people communicates online simultaneously.

CISC (complex instruction set computer) ▶ A general-purpose processor chip designed to handle a wider array of instructions than a RISC chip.

Clip art ▶ Graphics designed to be inserted into documents, Web pages, and worksheets, usually available in CD-ROM or Web-based collections.

Cluster ▶ A group of sectors on a storage medium that, when accessed as a group, speeds up data access.

CMOS (complementary metal oxide semiconductor) memory ▶ A type of battery-powered integrated circuit that holds semi-permanent configuration data.

CMYK color ▶ A printing technology used by most ink jet printers that requires only cyan (blue), magenta (pink), yellow, and black inks to create a printout that appears to have thousands of colors.

Color depth ▶ The number of bits that determines the range of possible colors that can be assigned to each pixel. For example, an 8-bit color depth can create 256 colors. Also called bit depth.

Commercial software ▶ Copyrighted computer applications sold to consumers for profit.

CompactFlash (CF) card ▶ A solid state storage device that is about the size of a matchbook and provides high storage capacities and access speeds; includes a built-in controller that reads and writes data within the solid state grid; are ideal for use on high-end digital cameras that require megabytes of storage for each photo.

Compiler ▶ Software that translates a program written in a high-level language into low-level instructions before the program is executed.

Computer ▶ A device that accepts input, processes data, stores data, and produces output.

Computer file ▶ A single collection of data stored on a storage medium.

Computer language ▶ A set of tools that allows a programmer to write instructions or software that a computer can execute. Also called programming language.

Computer network ▶ A collection of computers and related devices, connected in a way that allows them to share data, hardware, and software.

Computer program ▶ A set of detailed, step-by-step instructions that tells a computer how to solve a problem or carry out a task.

Computer programmer ▶ A person who codes or writes computer programs.

Computer projection device ▶ An output device that produces a large display of the information shown on the computer screen.

Computer system ▶ The hardware, peripheral devices, and software working together to input data, process data, store data, and produce output.

Computer-aided design software (CAD) ▶ A type of 3-D graphics software designed for architects and engineers who use computers to create blueprints and product specifications.

Concurrent-use license ▶ A software license agreement that is priced per copy and allows a specific number of copies to be used at the same time.

Control unit ▶ The part of the ALU that directs and coordinates processing.

Controller ▶ A circuit board in a hard drive that positions the disk and read-write heads to locate data.

Copyright ▶ A form of legal protection that grants certain exclusive rights to the author of a program or the owner of the copyright.

Copyright notice ▶ A line such as "Copyright 2002 ACME Co." that identifies a copyright holder.

CPU (central processing unit) ▶ The main processing unit in a computer, consisting of circuitry that executes instructions to process data.

CRT (cathode ray tube) ▶ A display technology that uses a large vacuum tube similar to that used in television sets.

Cursor ▶ A symbol that marks the user's place on the screen and shows where typing will appear.

Cylinder ▶ A vertical stack of tracks that is the basic storage bin for a hard disk drive.

Data ▶ In the context of computing and data management, the symbols that a computer uses to represent facts and ideas.

Data bus ▶ An electronic pathway or circuit that connects the electronic components (such as the processor and RAM) on a computer's motherboard.

Data file ▶ A file containing words, numbers, or pictures that the user can view, edit, save, send, or print.

Data module ▶ A file linked to a program that provides data necessary for certain functions of the program.

Data representation ▶ The use of electrical signals, marks, or binary digits to represent character, numeric, visual, or audio data.

Data transfer rate ▶ The amount of data that a storage device can move from a storage medium to computer memory in one second.

Database ▶ A collection of information that may be stored in more than one file.

Database software ▶ A category of software designed for tasks associated with maintaining and accessing data stored in data files.

Defragmentation utility ▶ A software tool used to rearrange the files on a disk so that they are stored in contiguous clusters.

Desktop computer ▶ A category of computer small enough to fit on a desk and built around a single processor chip.

Desktop operating system ▶ An operating system such as Windows ME or Mac OS X that is specifically designed for personal computers.

Desktop publishing software ▶ A category of software used to create high-quality output suitable for commercial printing. DTP software provides precise control over layout.

Device driver ▶ The software that provides the computer with the means to control a peripheral device.

Dial-up connection ▶ A connection that uses a phone line to establish a temporary Internet connection.

Digital ▶ Any system that works with discrete data, such as 0s and 1s, in contrast to analog.

Digital camera ▶ An input device that records an image in digital format.

Digital device ▶ A device that works with discrete (distinct or separate) numbers or digits.

Digital electronics ▶ Circuitry that's designed to work with digital signals.

Digitize ▶ The conversion of non-digital information or media to a digital format through the use of a scanner, sampler, or other input device.

DIMM (dual in-line memory module) ▶ A small circuit board that holds RAM chips. A DIMM has a 64-bit path to the memory chips.

DIP (dual in-line package) ▶ A chip configuration characterized by a rectangular body with numerous plugs along its edge.

Directory ▶ A list of files contained on a computer storage device.

Disk density ▶ The closeness of the particles on a disk surface. As density increases, the particles are packed more tightly together and are usually smaller.

Display device ▶ The main output device for a computer; one of two key components of a display system—a monitor or a screen uses one of three technologies: CRT, LCD, and gas plasma.

Distribution disks ▶ One or more floppy disks or CDs that contain programs and data, which can be installed to a hard disk.

DMA (direct memory access) ▶ Technology allows a computer to transfer data directly from a drive into RAM, without intervention from the processor.

Document production software ▶ Computer programs that assist the user in composing, editing, designing, and printing documents.

DOS (disk operating system) ▶ The operating system software shipped with the first IBM PCs and used on millions of computers until the introduction of Microsoft Windows.

Dot matrix printer ▶ A printer that creates characters and graphics by striking an inked ribbon with small wires called "pins," generating a fine pattern of dots.

Dot pitch ▶ The diagonal distance between colored dots on a display screen. Measured in millimeters, dot pitch helps to determine the quality of an image displayed on a monitor.

Downloading ▶ The process of transferring a copy of a file from a remote computer to a local computer's disk drive.

Dpi (dots per inch) ▶ Printer resolution as measured by the number of dots it can print per linear inch.

Drawing software ▶ Provides a set of lines, shapes, and colors that can be assembled into diagrams, corporate logos, and schematics. The drawings created with this type of software tend to have a "flat" cartoon-like quality, but they are very easy to modify and look good at just about any size.

Drive bay ▶ An area within a computer system unit that can accommodate an additional storage device.

DSL (Digital Subscriber Line) ▶ A high-speed Internet connection that uses existing telephone lines, requiring close proximity to a switching station.

DSS (Digital Satellite System) ▶ A type of Internet connection that uses a network of satellites to transmit data.

Duty cycle ▶ Determines how many pages a printer is able to print out; is usually measured in pages per month.

DVD (digital video disc or digital versatile disc) ▶ An optical storage medium similar in appearance and technology to a CD-ROM but with higher storage capacity.

DVD drive ▶ An optical storage device that reads data from CD-ROM and DVD discs.

DVD+R (digital versatile disc recordable) ▶ A DVD disk that stores data using recordable technology similar to a CD-R, but with DVD.

DVD+RW (digital versatile disc rewritable) ▶ A DVD disk that stores data using rewritable technology similar to CD-RW, but with DVD storage.

DVD-ROM (digital versatile disc read-only memory) ▶ A DVD disc that stores data that has been permanently stamped on the disc surface.

DVD-Video (digital versatile disc video) ▶ The format for commercial DVDs that contain feature-length films.

DVD-writer ▶ Device that can be used to create and copy CDs and DVDs.

Dye sublimation printer ▶ An expensive, color-precise printer that heats ribbons containing color to produce consistent, photograph-quality images.

Ear training software ▶ The category of software that targets musicians and music students who want to learn to play by ear, develop tuning skills, recognize notes and keys, and develop other musical skills.

EBCDIC (Extended Binary-Coded Decimal Interchange Code) ▶ A method by which digital computers, usually mainframes, represent character data.

E-commerce (electronic commerce) ▶ Business connected over the Internet, including online shopping, linking businesses to businesses (sometimes called e-business or B2B), online stock trading, and electronic auctions.

Educational software ▶ A category of software that helps you learn and practice new skills.

EIDE (enhanced integrated drive electronics) ▶ A type of drive that features high storage capacity and fast data transfer.

E-mail (electronic mail) ▶ A single electronic message or the entire system of computers and software that handles electronic messages transmitted between computers over a communications network.

E-mail account ▶ A service that provides an e-mail address and mailbox.

E-mail address ▶ The unique address for each mailbox on the Internet, which typically consists of a user ID, an @ symbol, and the name of the computer that maintains the mailbox.

E-mail attachment ▶ A separate file that is transmitted along with an e-mail message.

E-mail client software ▶ The software that is installed on a client computer and has access to e-mail servers on a network. This software is used to compose, send, and read e-mail messages.

E-mail message ▶ A computer file containing a letter or memo that is transmitted electronically via a communications network.

E-mail server ▶ A computer that uses special software to store and send e-mail messages over the Internet.

E-mail system ▶ The collection of computers and software that works together to provide e-mail services.

Executable file ▶ A file, usually with an .exe extension, containing instructions that tell a computer how to perform a specific task. Also called user executable file.

Expansion bus ▶ The segment of the data bus that transports data between RAM and peripheral devices.

Expansion card ▶ A circuit board that is plugged into a slot on a PC motherboard to add extra functions, devices, or ports.

Expansion port ▶ A socket into which the user plugs a cable from a peripheral device, allowing data to pass between the computer and the peripheral device.

Expansion slot ▶ A socket or slot on a PC motherboard designed to hold a circuit board called an expansion card.

Extended ASCII ▶ Similar to ASCII but with 8-bit character representation instead of 7-bit, allowing for an additional 128 characters.

Favorites ▶ A list of URLs for Web sites that you can create for your browser to store so that you can revisit those sites easily.

Field ▶ The smallest meaningful unit of information contained in a data file.

File ▶ A named collection of data (such as a computer program, document, or graphic) that exists on a storage medium, such as a hard disk, floppy disk, or CD-ROM.

File allocation table (FAT) ▶ A special file that is used by the operating system to store the physical location of all the files on a storage medium, such as a hard disk or floppy disk.

File date ▶ Saved as part of the file information, the date on which a file was created or last modified; useful if you have created several versions of a file and want to make sure that you know which version is the most recent.

File format ▶ The method of organization used to encode and store data in a computer. Text formats include DOC and TXT. Graphics formats include BMP, TIFF, GIF, and PCX.

File header ▶ Saved as part of the file, information that can be read by the computer, but never appears on the screen on the about code that was used to represent the file data.

File management software ▶ A category of operating system software that helps the user organize and find files and folders on their hard drive or other storage media.

File management utility ▶ Software, such as Windows Explorer, that helps users locate, rename, move, copy, and delete files.

File size ▶ The physical size of a file on a storage medium, usually measured in kilobytes (KB).

File specification ▶ A combination of the drive letter, subdirectory, filename, and extension that identifies a file (for example, A:\word\ filename.doc). Also called a path.

File system ▶ A system that is used by an operating system to keep files organized.

Filename ▶ A set of letters or numbers that identifies a file.

Filename extension ▶ A set of letters and/or numbers added to the end of a filename that helps to identify the file contents or file type.

File-naming conventions ▶ A set of rules established by the operating system that must be followed to create a valid filename.

Finder ▶ On computers with Mac OS, the file management utility that helps you view a list of files, find files, move files from one place to another, make copies of files, delete files, and rename files.

Floppy disk ▶ A removable magnetic storage medium, typically 3.5" in size, with a capacity of 1.44 MB.

Floppy disk drive ▶ A storage device that writes data on, and reads data from, floppy disks.

Folder ▶ The subdirectory, or subdivision, of a directory that can contain files or other folders.

Font ▶ A typeface or style of lettering, such as Arial, Times New Roman, and Gothic.

Footer ▶ In a document, text that you specify to appear in the bottom margin of every page.

Format ▶ Refers to how all text, pictures, titles, and page numbers appear on the page.

Formula ▶ In spreadsheet terminology, a combination of numbers and symbols that tells the computer how to use the contents of cells in calculations.

Fragmented file ▶ A file stored in scattered, noncontiguous clusters on a disk.

Frame ▶ An outline or boundary frequently defining a box. For document production software, a pre-defined area into which text or graphics may be placed.

Freeware ▶ Copyrighted software that is given away by the author or owner.

Function ▶ In worksheets, a built-in formula for making a calculation. In programming, a section of code that manipulates data but is not included in the main sequential execution path of a program.

Function key ▶ One of the keys numbered F1 through F12 located at the top of the computer keyboard that activates program specific commands.

Giga- ▶ Prefix for a billion.

Gigabit (Gb) ▶ Approximately one billion bits.

Gigabyte (GB) ▶ One billion bytes, typically used to refer to RAM and hard disk capacity.

Gigahertz (GHz) ▶ A measure of frequency equivalent to one billion cycles per second, usually used to measure speed.

Graphical user interface (GUI) ▶ A type of user interface that features on-screen objects, such as menus and icons, manipulated by a mouse. (Abbreviation is pronounced "gooey".)

Graphics ▶ Any pictures, photographs, or images that can be manipulated or viewed on a computer.

Graphics card ▶ A circuit board inserted into a computer to handle the display of text, graphics, animation, and videos. Also called a video card.

Graphics software ▶ Computer programs for creating, editing, and manipulating images.

Graphics tablet ▶ A device that accepts input from a pressure-sensitive stylus and converts strokes into images on the screen.

Groupware ▶ Business software designed to help several people collaborate on a single project using network or Internet connections.

Handheld computer ▶ A small, pocket-sized computer designed to run on its own power supply and provide users with basic applications.

Hard disk ▶ See hard disk drive.

Hard disk drive ▶ A computer storage device that contains a large-capacity hard disk sealed inside the drive case. A hard disk is not the same as a 3.5" floppy disk that has a rigid plastic case.

Hard disk platter ▶ The component of a hard disk drive on which data is stored. It is a flat, rigid disk made of aluminum or glass and coated with a magnetic oxide.

Hardware ▶ The electronic and mechanical devices in a computer system.

Head crash ▶ A collision between the read-write head and the surface of the hard disk platter, resulting in damage to some of the data on the disk.

Header ▶ Text that you specify to appear in the top margin of every page automatically.

High-level language ▶ A computer language that allows a programmer to write instructions using human-like language.

History list ▶ A list that is created by your browser of the sites you visited so that you can display and track your sessions or revisit the site by clicking the URL in the list.

Home page ▶ In a Web site, the document that is the starting, or entry, page. On an individual computer, the Web page that a browser displays each time it is started.

Horizontal market software ▶ Any computer program that can be used by many different kinds of businesses (for example, an accounting program).

HTML (Hypertext Markup Language) ▶ A standardized format used to specify the format for Web page documents.

HTML tag ▶ An instruction, such as ..., inserted into an HTML document to provide formatting and display information to a Web browser.

HTTP (Hypertext Transfer Protocol) ▶ The communications protocol used to transmit Web pages. HTTP:// is an identifier that appears at the beginning of most Web page URLs (for example, http://www.course.com).

Hyperlink ▶ Provides the fundamental tool for navigating Web pages. Click a text or graphic link to jump to a location in the same Web page, open a different Web page, or go to a different Web site. Also called link.

Hypertext ▶ A way of organizing an information database by linking information through the use of text and multimedia.

IMAP (Internet Messaging Access Protocol) ▶ A protocol similar to POP that is used to retrieve e-mail messages from an e-mail server, but offers additional features, such as choosing which e-mails to download from the server.

Information ▶ The words, numbers, and graphics used as the basis for human actions and decisions.

Ink jet printer ▶ A non-impact printer that creates characters or graphics by spraying liquid ink onto paper or other media.

Input ▶ As a noun, "input" means the information that is conveyed to a computer. As a verb, "input" means to enter data into a computer.

Input device ▶ A device, such as a keyboard or mouse, that gathers input and transforms it into a series of electronic signals for the computer.

Insertion point ▶ Appears on the screen as a flashing vertical bar or flashing underline and indicates where the characters you type will appear on the screen. Change the location insertion point using the arrow keys or the mouse pointer. Also called cursor.

Install ▶ The process by which programs and data are copied to the hard disk of a computer system and otherwise prepared for access and use.

Installation agreement ▶ A version of the license agreement that appears on the computer screen when software is being installed and prompts the user to accept or decline.

Instant messaging ▶ A private chat in which users can communicate with each other.

Instruction cycle ▶ The steps followed by a computer to process a single instruction; fetch, interpret, execute, then increment the instruction pointer.

Instruction set ▶ The collection of instructions that a CPU is designed to process.

Integrated circuit (IC) ▶ A thin slice of silicon crystal containing microscopic circuit elements, such as transistors, wires, capacitors, and resistors; also called chips and microchips.

Internet ▶ The worldwide communication infrastructure that links computer networks using TCP/IP protocol.

Internet backbone ▶ The major communications links that form the core of the Internet.

Internet telephony ▶ A set of hardware and software that allows users to make phone-style calls over the Internet, usually without a long-distance charge.

Interpreter ▶ A program that converts high-level instructions in a computer program into machine language instructions, one instruction at a time.

IP address ▶ A unique identifying number assigned to each computer connected to the Internet.

ISA (Industry Standard Architecture) ▶ A standard for moving data on the expansion bus. Can refer to a type of slot, a bus, or a peripheral device. An older technology, it is rapidly being replaced by PCI architecture.

ISDN (Integrated Services Digital Network) ▶ A telephone company service that transports data digitally over dial-up or dedicated lines.

ISP (Internet Service Provider) ▶ A company that provides Internet access to businesses, organizations, and individuals.

Joystick ▶ A pointing input device used as an alternative to a mouse.

Kernel ▶ The core module of an operating system that typically manages memory, processes, tasks, and disks.

Keyboard ▶ An arrangement of letter, number, and special function keys that acts as the primary input device to the computer.

Keyboard shortcut ▶ The use of the [Alt] or the [Ctrl] key in combination with another key on the keyboard to execute a command, such as copy, paste, or cut.

Keyword ▶ A word or term used as the basis for a database or Web-page search.

Kilobit (Kbit or Kb) ▶ 1,024 bits.

Kilobyte (KB) ▶ Approximately 1,000 bytes; exactly 1,024 bytes.

Label ▶ In a worksheet, any text that is used to describe data.

LAN (local area network) ▶ An interconnected group of computers and peripherals located within a relatively limited area, such as a building or campus.

Lands ▶ Non-pitted surface areas on a CD that represents digital data.

Laser printer ▶ A printer that uses laser-based technology, similar to that used by photocopiers, to produce text and graphics.

LCD (liquid crystal display) ▶ A type of flat panel computer screen, typically found on notebook computers.

LCD screen ▶ See LCD.

Link ▶ Provides the fundamental tool for navigating Web pages. Click a text or graphic link to jump to a location in the same Web page, open a different Web page, or go to a different Web site. Also called hyperlink.

Linux ▶ A server operating system that is a derivative of UNIX and available as freeware.

Logical storage model ▶ Any visual aid or metaphor that helps a computer user visualize a file system.

Mac (Macintosh computer) ▶ A personal computer platform designed and manufactured by Apple Computer.

Mac OS ▶ The operating system software designed for use on Apple Macintosh and iMac computers.

Machine code ▶ Program instructions written in binary code that the computer can execute directly.

Machine language ▶ A low-level language written in binary code that the computer can execute directly.

Magnetic storage ▶ The recording of data onto disks or tape by magnetizing particles of an oxide-based surface coating.

Mailing list server ▶ Any computer and software that maintains a list of people who are interested in a topic and that facilitates message exchanges among all members of the list.

Mainframe computer ▶ A large, fast, and expensive computer generally used by businesses or government agencies to provide centralized storage processing and management for large amounts of data.

Master File Table (MFT) ▶ Special files used by the operating system of NTFS computers to keep track of the names and locations of files that reside on a storage medium, such as a hard disk.

Mathematical modeling software ▶ A category of software such as MathCAD and Mathematica, that provides tools for solving a wide range of math, science, and engineering problems.

Megabit (Mb or Mbit) ▶ 1,048,576 bits.

Megabyte (MB) ▶ Approximately 1 million bytes; exactly 1,048,576 bytes.

Megahertz (MHz) ▶ A measure of frequency equivalent to 1 million cycles per second.

Memory ▶ The computer circuitry that holds data waiting to be processed.

Microcomputer ▶ A category of computer that is built around a single processor chip.

Microsoft Windows ▶ An operating system developed by Microsoft Corporation that provides a graphical interface. Versions include Windows 3.1, Windows 95, Windows 98, Windows ME, Windows 2000, Windows XP, and Windows NT.

MIDI sequencing software ▶ A category of software used for creating sound effects and for controlling keyboards and other digital instruments.

Millisecond (ms) ▶ A thousandth of a second.

MIME (Multipurpose Internet Mail Extension) ▶ A conversion process used for formatting non-ASCII messages so that they can be sent over the Internet.

Modem ▶ A device that sends and receives data to and from computers over telephone lines.

Modem card ▶ A device that provides a way to transmit data over phone lines or cable television lines.

Modifier key ▶ The [Ctrl], [Alt], or [Shift] key, used in conjunction with another key to expand the repertoire of available commands.

Monitor ▶ A display device that forms an image by converting electrical signals from the computer into points of colored light on the screen.

Motherboard ▶ The main circuit board in a computer that houses chips and other electronic components.

Mouse ▶ An input device that allows the user to manipulate objects on the screen by moving the mouse on the surface of a desk.

MP3 ▶ A file format that provides highly compressed audio files with very little loss of sound quality.

MP3 player ▶ Software that plays MP3 music files.

MPEG-2 ▶ A special type of data coding for movie files that are much too large to fit on a disk unless they are compressed.

Multifunction device ▶ A hardware device that works both as input and output devices to combine the functions of a printer, scanner, copier, fax, and answering machine.

MultiMedia card (MMC) ▶ Solid state storage that includes a built-in controller in a package about the size of a postage stamp that was initially used in mobile phones and pagers, but now also used in digital cameras and MP3 players.

Multiple-user license ▶ A software license that allows more than one person to use the software; priced per user and allows the allocated number of people to use the software at any time. Also called concurrent-use license.

Multitasking operating system ▶ An operating system that runs two or more programs at the same time.

Multiuser operating system ▶ An operating system that allows two or more users to run programs at the same time and use their own input/output devices.

Nanosecond ▶ A unit of time representing 1 billionth of a second.

Native file format ▶ A file format that is unique to a program or group of programs and has a unique file extension.

Natural language query ▶ A query using language spoken by human beings, as opposed to an artificially constructed language such as machine language.

Navigation keypad ▶ On a keyboard, the keypad with the Home, End, and arrow keys, which you can use to efficiently move the screen-based insertion point or cursor.

Netiquette ▶ Internet etiquette or a set of guidelines for posting messages and e-mails in a civil, concise way.

Network card ▶ An expansion board mounted inside a computer to allow access to a local area network.

Network operating system ▶ Programs designed to control the flow of data, maintain security, and keep track of accounts on a network.

Newsgroup ▶ An online discussion group that centers around a specific topic.

Notation software ▶ A category of software used to help musicians compose, edit, and print musical scores.

Notebook computer ▶ Small, lightweight, portable computer that usually runs on batteries. Sometimes called laptop.

Numeric data ▶ Numbers that represent quantities and can be used in arithmetic operations.

Numeric keypad ▶ Calculator-style input devices for numbers located towards the right side of a keyboard.

Object code ▶ The low-level instructions that result from compiling source code.

Online ▶ Refers to being connected to the Internet.

Open source software ▶ A category of software, such as Linux, that includes its uncompiled source code, which can be modified and distributed by programmers.

Operating system (OS) ▶ Software that controls the computer's use of its hardware resources, such as memory and disk storage space.

Optical storage ▶ A means of recording data as light and dark spots on a CD, DVD, or other optical media.

Output ▶ The results produced by a computer (for example, reports, graphs, and music).

Output device ▶ A device, such as a monitor or printer, that displays, prints, or transmits the results of processing from the computer memory.

Packet ▶ A small unit of data transmitted over a network or the Internet.

Page layout ▶ The physical positions of elements on a document page, such as headers, footers, page numbers, and graphics.

Paint software ▶ A category of software that provides a set of electronic pens, brushes, and paints for painting images on the screen. Graphic artists, Web page designers, photographers, and illustrators use paint software as their primary computer-based graphics tool. Also called image editing software.

Palm OS ▶ One of the two dominant operating systems of handheld computers.

Parallel processing ▶ A technique by which two or more processors in a computer perform processing tasks simultaneously.

Password ▶ A special set of symbols used to restrict access to a computer or network.

Path ▶ A file's location in a file structure. See File specification.

Payroll software ▶ Horizontal market software used by business to maintain payroll records, collect data and make calculations in order to produce payroll checks and W2 forms.

PC ▶ A microcomputer that uses Windows software and contains an Intel-compatible processor.

PCI (Peripheral Component Interconnect) ▶ A method for transporting data on the expansion bus. Can refer to type of data bus, expansion slot, or transport method used by a peripheral device.

PCMCIA (personal computer memory card international association) slot ▶ A special type of external slot found on most notebook computers that can hold more than one PC card such as memory expansion cards, modems, sound cards, and network cards, and devices such as hard disk drives. Also called PCMCIA expansion card.

PDA (Personal Digital Assistant) ▶ A computer that is smaller and more portable than a notebook computer. Also called a palm-top computer.

Peer-to-Peer (P2P) ▶ A file sharing technology that makes it possible to access files stored on another Internet user's hard disk—with permission; is the basis for popular music and file exchange Web sites.

Peripheral device ▶ A component or equipment, such as a printer or scanner, that expands a computer's input, output, or storage capabilities.

Personal computer (PC) ▶ A microcomputer designed for use by an individual user for applications such as Internet browsing and word processing.

Personal finance software ▶ A category of software designed to help manage individual finances.

PGA (pin-grid array) ▶ A common chip design used for processors.

Photo editing software ▶ A category of software that provides tools and wizards that simplify common photo editing tasks; includes features specially designed to fix poor-quality photos by modifying contrast and brightness, cropping out unwanted objects, and removing red eye.

Physical storage model ▶ The way data is stored on a storage media.

Pipelining ▶ A technology that allows a processor to begin executing an instruction before completing the previous instruction.

Pits ▶ Dark spots that are burned onto the surface of a CD to represent digital data.

Pixel (picture element) ▶ The smallest unit in a graphic image. Computer display devices use a matrix of pixels to display text and graphics.

Plasma screen technology ▶ Display device technology that is used in gas plasma screens to create an on-screen image by illuminating miniature colored fluorescent lights arrayed in a panel-like screen. The name "plasma" comes from the type of gas that fills fluorescent lights and gives them their luminescence. Plasma screens are compact, lightweight, and more expensive than CRT monitors.

Platform ▶ A family or category of computers based on the same underlying software and hardware.

Plug and Play (PnP) ▶ The ability of a computer to recognize and adjust the system configuration for a newly added device automatically.

Pointing stick ▶ Pointing device typically used with notebook computers as an alternative to a mouse that looks like the tip of an eraser and is embedded in the keyboard of a notebook computer. Push up, down, or sideways to move the on-screen pointer. Also called TrackPoint.

POP (Post Office Protocol) ▶ A protocol that is used to retrieve e-mail messages from an e-mail server.

POP server ▶ A computer that receives and stores e-mail data until retrieved by the e-mail account holder.

PostScript ▶ A printer language developed by Adobe Systems that uses a special set of commands to control page layout, fonts, and graphics.

Power-on self-test (POST) ▶ A diagnostic process that runs during startup to check components of the computer, such as the graphics card, RAM, keyboard, and disk drives.

Presentation software ▶ A category of software that provides tools to combine text, graphics, graphs, animation, and sound into a series of electronic slides that can be output on a projector, or as overhead transparencies, paper copies, or 35-millimeter slides.

Printer ▶ A peripheral device used to create hard copy output.

Printer Control Language (PCL) ▶ A standard language used to send page formatting instructions from a computer to a laser or ink jet printer.

Processing ▶ The manipulation of data using a systematic series of actions.

Processor ▶ An integrated circuit that contains the circuitry for processing data. It is a single-chip version of the central processing unit (CPU) found in all computers.

Processor clock ▶ A device on the motherboard of a computer responsible for setting the pace of executing instructions.

Programming language ▶ Provides the tools that a programmer uses to create software. Also called computer language.

Project management software ▶ A category of software specifically designed as a tool for planning, scheduling, and tracking projects and their costs.

Public domain software ▶ Any software that is available for use by the public without restriction, except that it cannot be copyrighted.

Query ▶ A search specification that prompts the computer to look for particular records in a file.

Query by example (QBE) ▶ A type of database interface in which users fill in a field with an example of the type of information that they are seeking.

Query language ▶ A set of command words that can be used to direct the computer to create databases, locate information, sort records, and change the data in those records.

RAM (random access memory) ▶ A type of computer memory circuit that holds data, program instructions, and the operating system while the computer is on.

Random access ▶ The ability of a storage device (such as a disk drive) to go directly to a specific storage location without having to search sequentially from a beginning location.

RDRAM (Rambus dynamic RAM) ▶ A fast (up to 600 MHz) type of memory used in newer personal computers.

Read-write head ▶ The mechanism in a disk drive that magnetizes particles on the storage disk surface to write data, or senses the bits that are present to read data.

Record ▶ In the context of database management, a record is the set of fields of data that pertain to a single entity in a database.

Recordable technology ▶ Optical storage technology used to create CDs and DVDs.

Reference software ▶ A category of software that provides you with a collection of information and a way to access that information; spans a wide range of applications.

Register ▶ A scratch pad area of the ALU and control unit where data or instructions are moved so that they can be processed.

Relational database ▶ A database structure incorporating the use of tables that can establish relationships with other similar tables.

Relative reference ▶ In a worksheet, cell references that can change if cells change position as a result of a move or copy operation.

Reserved word ▶ Special words used as commands in some operating systems that may not be used in filenames.

Resolution ▶ The density of the grid used to display or print text and graphics; the greater the horizontal and vertical density, the higher the resolution.

Resource ▶ In the context of a computer system, refers to any component that is required to perform work such as the processor, RAM, storage space, and peripherals.

Revolutions per minute (rpm) ▶ A unit of measure that specifies how many times a platter spins each minute: used for the speed of a hard disk drive and classify the access time for a hard disk.

Rewritable technology (RW) ▶ An optical storage technology that uses "phase change" technology to alter a crystal structure on the disc surface to create patterns of light and dark spots. RW makes it possible for stored data to be recorded and erased or modified multiple times much like on a hard disk. Examples of CDs and DVDs using rewritable optical technology are CD-RW (compact disc rewritable) discs and DVD+RW (digital versatile disc rewritable) discs.

RIMM (Rambus in-line memory module) ▶ A memory module using RDRAM.

RISC (reduced instruction set computer) ▶ A processor chip designed for rapid and efficient processing of a small set of simple instructions.

ROM (read-only memory) ▶ One or more integrated circuits that contain permanent instructions that the computer uses during the boot process.

ROM BIOS (basic input/output system) ▶ A small set of basic input/output system instructions stored in ROM that causes the computer system to load critical operating files when the user turns on the computer.

Root directory ▶ The main directory of a disk.

Router ▶ A device found at each intersection on the Internet backbone that examines the IP address of incoming data and forwards the data towards its destination. Also used by LANs.

Safe Mode ▶ A menu option that appears when Windows is unable to complete the boot sequence. By entering Safe Mode, a user can gracefully shut down the computer then try to reboot it.

Scanner ▶ An input device that converts a printed page of text or images into a digital format.

Screen size ▶ On a display device, the measurement in inches from one corner of the screen diagonally across to the opposite corner.

SCSI (small computer system interface) ▶ An interface standard used for attaching peripheral devices, such as disk drives. Pronounced "scuzzy."

SDRAM (synchronous dynamic RAM) ▶ A type of RAM that synchronizes itself with the CPU, thus enabling it to run at much higher clock speeds than conventional RAM.

Search engine ▶ Program that uses keywords to find information on the Internet and return a list of relevant documents.

SEC (single edge contact) cartridge ▶ A common, cassette-like chip design for processors.

Sector ▶ Subdivision of the tracks on a storage medium that provide a storage area for data.

SecureDigital (SD) card ▶ Solid state storage device popular for MP3 storage featuring fast data transfer rates and cryptographic security protection for copyrighted data and music.

Semiconducting material ▶ Materials such as silicon and germanium that are used to make chips. The conductive properties create miniature electronic pathways and components, such as transistors. Also called semiconductors.

Sequential access ▶ A form of data storage, usually on computer tape, that requires a device to read or write data one record after another, starting at the beginning of the medium.

Serial processing ▶ Processing of data that completes one instruction before beginning another.

Server ▶ A computer or software on a network that supplies the network with data and storage.

Server operating system ▶ Provides communications and routing services that allow computers to share data, programs, and peripheral devices by routing data and programs to each user's local computer, where the actual processing takes place. Also called network operating system.

Server software ▶ The software used by servers to locate and distribute data requested by Internet users.

Setup program ▶ A program module supplied with a software package for the purpose of installing the software.

Shareware ▶ Copyrighted software marketed under a license that allows users to use the software for a trial period and then send in a registration fee if they wish to continue to use it.

Shrink-wrap license ▶ A software license usually sealed in an envelope, plastic box, or shrink wrapping that goes into effect as soon as you open the packaging.

Single-user license ▶ A license that limits use of the software to only one person at a time.

Single-user operating system ▶ Operating system designed for one user at a time with one set of input and output devices; operating systems for handheld computers and many personal computers fit into this category.

Site license ▶ A software license generally priced at a flat rate and allows software to be used on all computers at a specific location.

Slides ▶ Presentation software combines text, graphics, graphs, animations, and sound into a series of electronic slides for display on a monitor for a one-on-one presentation or on a computer projection device for group presentations.

Small business accounting software ▶ A category of software that is geared towards small businesses to help invoice customers, keep track of what they owe, store customer data, such as contact information and purchasing history. Inventory functions keep track of the products. Payroll capabilities automatically calculate wages and deduct federal, state, and local taxes.

SmartMedia card ▶ The least durable of the solid state storage media, was originally called "solid state floppy disk card" because it looks like a miniature floppy disk, it does not include a built-in controller, so it requires a SmartMedia reader to manage the read/write process.

SMTP (Simple Mail Transfer Protocol) server ▶ A computer used to send e-mail across a network or the Internet.

Software ▶ The instructions that prepare a computer to do a task, indicate how to interact with a user, and specify how to process data.

Software license ▶ A legal contract that defines the ways in which you may use a computer program. For personal computer software, the license is on the outside of the package, on a separate card inside the package, on the CD packaging, or in one of the program files. Also called license agreement.

Software suite ▶ A collection of application software sold as a single package.

Solid ink printer ▶ A printer that creates images on pages by melting sticks of crayon-like ink and then spraying the liquefied ink through the print head's tiny nozzles. The ink solidifies before the paper can absorb it, and a pair of rollers finishes fusing the ink onto the paper. A solid ink printer produces vibrant colors on most types of paper and is used for professional graphics applications.

Solid state storage ▶ A variety of compact storage cards, pens, and sticks that stores data in a non-volatile, erasable, low-power chip in a microscopic grid of cells.

SO-RIMM (small outline Rambus in-line memory module) ▶ A small memory module that contains RDRAM, used primarily in notebook computers.

Sound card ▶ A circuit board that gives the computer the ability to accept audio input from a microphone, play sound files stored on disks and CD-ROMs, and produce audio output through speakers or headphones.

Source code ▶ Computer instructions written in a high-level language.

Speakers ▶ Output devices that receive signals for the computer's sound card to play music, narration, or sound effects.

Spreadsheet ▶ A numerical model or representation of a real situation, presented in the form of a table.

Spreadsheet software ▶ The software for creating electronic worksheets that hold data in cells and perform calculations based on that data.

SQL (Structured Query Language) ▶ A popular query language used by mainframes and microcomputers.

Statistical software ▶ A category of software that helps you analyze large sets of data to discover relationships and patterns, summarize survey results, test scores, experiment results, or population data. Most statistical software includes graphing capability.

Store-and-forward technology ▶ A technology used by communications networks in which an e-mail message is temporarily held in storage on a server until it is requested by a client computer.

Storage ▶ The area in a computer where data is retained on a permanent basis.

Storage capacity ▶ The amount of data that can be stored on a storage media.

Storage device ▶ A mechanical apparatus that records data to and retrieves data from a storage medium.

Storage medium ▶ The physical material used to store computer data, such as a floppy disk, a hard disk, or a CD-ROM.

Storage technology ▶ Defines the data storage systems used by computers to store data and program files. Each data storage system has two main components: a storage medium and a storage device.

Stored program ▶ A set of instructions that resides on a storage device, such as a hard drive, and can be loaded into memory and executed.

Subdirectory ▶ A directory found under the root directory.

Supercomputer ▶ The fastest and most expensive type of computer, capable of processing more than 1 trillion instructions per second.

SuperDisk ▶ A storage technology manufactured by Imation. Disks have a capacity of 120 MB or 240 MB and require special disk drives; a standard floppy disk drive will not read them. They are backward-compatible with standard floppy disk technology, which means you can use a SuperDisk drive to read and write to standard floppy disks.

Support program ▶ A file that can be called by the main executable program to provide auxiliary instructions or routines.

System requirements ▶ Specifications for the operating system and hardware configuration necessary for a software product to work correctly. The criteria that must be met for a new computer system or software product to be a success.

System software ▶ Computer programs that help the computer carry out essential operating tasks.

System unit ▶ The case or box that contains the computer's power supply, storage devices, main circuit board, processor, and memory.

Table ▶ An arrangement of data in a grid of rows and columns. In a relational database, a collection of record types with their data.

Tablet computer ▶ A portable computing device featuring a touch-sensitive screen that can be used as a writing or drawing pad.

Tape ▶ A sequential magnetic storage technology that consists of a tape for the storage medium and a tape drive for the storage device. Data is arranged as a long sequence of bits that begins at one end of the tape and stretches to the other end.

Tape backup ▶ A copy of data from a computer's hard disk, stored on magnetic tape and used to restore lost data.

Tape cartridge ▶ A removable magnetic tape module similar to a cassette tape.

Tax preparation software ▶ A specialized type of personal finance software designed to help you gather your annual income and expense data, identify deductions, and calculate your tax payment.

TCP/IP (Transmission Control Protocol/Internet Protocol) ▶ A standard set of communication rules used by every computer that connects to the Internet.

Tera- ▶ Prefix for a trillion.

Thermal transfer printer ▶ An expensive, color-precise printer that uses wax containing color to produce numerous dots of color on plain paper.

Toggle key ▶ A key that switches back and forth between two modes, such as Caps Lock on or Caps Lock off.

Touchpad ▶ An alternative input device often found on notebook computers.

Tracks ▶ A series of concentric or spiral storage areas created on a storage medium during the formatting process.

Trackball ▶ Pointing input device used as an alternative to a mouse.

Trackpad ▶ An alternative input device often found on notebook computers.

TrackPoint ▶ An alternative input device often found on notebook computers.

Typing keypad ▶ The basic keys on a computer keyboard that includes the keys or buttons with letters and numbers as well as several keys with characters and special words to control computer-specific tasks. You use the keys to input commands, respond to prompts, and type the text of documents.

UDMA (Ultra DMA) ▶ A faster version of DMA technology.

Ultra ATA ▶ A disk drive technology that is an enhanced version of EIDE. Also referred to as Ultra DMA or Ultra IDE.

Unicode ▶ A 16-bit character representation code that can represent more than 65,000 characters.

Uninstall routine ▶ A program that removes software files, references, and Windows Registry entries from a computer's hard disk.

UNIX ▶ A multi-user, multitasking server operating system developed by AT&T's Bell Laboratories in 1969.

Unzipped ▶ Refers to files that have been uncompressed.

Uploading ▶ The process of sending a copy of a file from a local computer to a remote computer.

URL (Uniform Resource Locator) ▶ The address of a Web page.

USB flash drive ▶ A portable storage device featuring a built-in connector that plugs directly into a computer's USB port.

Usenet ▶ A worldwide Internet bulletin board system of newsgroups that share common topics.

User ID ▶ A combination of letters and numbers that serves as a user's identification. Also referred to as a user name.

User interface ▶ The software and hardware that enable people to interact with computers.

User-executable file ▶ At least one of the files included in a software package designed to be launched, or started, by

users. On PCs, these programs are stored in files that typically have .exe filename extensions. Also called executable file.

Utility ▶ A subcategory of system software designed to augment the operating system by providing ways for a computer user to control the allocation and use of hardware resources. Also called Utilities.

Value ▶ A number used in a calculation.

Vertical market software ▶ Computer programs designed to meet the needs of a specific market segment or industry, such as medical record-keeping software.

Video editing software ▶ Category of software that provides a set of tools for transferring video footage from a camcorder to a computer, clipping out unwanted footage, assembling video segments in any sequence, adding special visual effects, and adding a sound track.

Videogame console ▶ A computer specifically designed for playing games using a television screen and game controllers.

Viewable image size (vis) ▶ A measurement of the maximum image size that can be displayed on a monitor screen.

Viewing angle width ▶ Measurement of a monitor or display device that indicates how far to the side you can still clearly see the screen image.

Virtual memory ▶ A computer's use of hard disk storage to simulate RAM.

Voice band modem ▶ The type of modem that would typically be used to connect a computer to a telephone line. See Modem.

Volatile ▶ Data that can exist only with a constant power supply.

Web (World Wide Web) ▶ An Internet service that links documents and information from computers distributed all over the world using the HTTP protocol.

Web authoring software ▶ Category of software that provides easy-to-use tools for composing the text for a Web page, assembling graphical elements, and automatically generating HTML to develop Web pages that you can publish electronically on the Internet.

Web-based e-mail ▶ An e-mail account that stores, sends, and receives e-mail on a Web site rather than a user's computer.

Web cam ▶ An input device used to capture live video and transmit it over the Internet.

Web page ▶ A document on the World Wide Web that consists of a specially coded HTML file with associated text, audio, video, and graphics files. A Web page often contains links to other Web pages.

Web server ▶ A computer and software that stores and transmits Web pages to computers the Internet.

Web site ▶ Location on the World Wide Web that contains information relating to specific topics.

Windows Explorer ▶ A file management utility included with most Windows operating systems that helps users manage their files.

Windows Mobil OS ▶ A version of the Windows operating system designed for portable or mobile computers.

Windows Registry ▶ A crucial data file maintained by the Windows operating system that contains the settings needed by a computer to correctly use any hardware and software that has been installed on the system. Also called the Registry.

Windows XP tablet edition ▶ A version of the Windows operating system designed for tablet computers.

Word processing software ▶ A category of software that assists the user in producing documents, such as reports, letters, papers, and manuscripts.

Word size ▶ The number of bits a CPU can manipulate at one time, which is dependent on the size of the registers in the CPU and the number of data lines in the bus.

Worksheet ▶ A computerized, or electronic, spreadsheet.

Workstation ▶ (1) A computer connected to a local area network. (2) A powerful desktop computer designed for specific tasks.

Write-protect window ▶ A small hole and sliding cover on a floppy disk that restricts writing to the disk.

Zip disk ▶ Floppy disk technology manufactured by Iomega available in 100 MB, 250 MB, and 750 MB versions.

Zipped ▶ Refers to files that have been compressed.

Index